The Economic and Legal Impact of Covid-19

In response to the outbreak of the COVID-19 pandemic, governments and international institutions took steps to contain the harmful consequences on citizens' lives and health, as well as the economy. In the short term, the goal was to limit the spread of the virus and the effects of the restrictions on the economy and, in the longer run, to prevent the appearance of new cases, facilitate the end of social restrictions, reboot the economy, and return to a path of sustainable growth and development.

This is an economic and legal exploration of the impact of the pandemic, in the Polish context, examining Polish society and the economy as well as the response of the Polish authorities to the pandemic. The choice of Poland as the subject of the research is justified by its specificity. On the one hand, Poland is a country undergoing systemic transformation with access to European and transatlantic institutions. On the other hand, in recent years, it has evolved towards a hybrid democracy and is currently diverging away from the EU project. The book presents Poland's legal and institutional response to the pandemic, analysed through the prism of common European values and Poland's international commitments. It signposts the financial solutions adopted by the EU in the aftermath of the outbreak to assess how they will be used in combatting the short and longer-term consequences of the pandemic in Poland. The information presented in the book is up to date as on the date of its publication, i.e., September/October 2020.

The book is an introduction to original research, shaped by the novelty of the subject matter, and as such, will be essential reading for students and researchers of economics, law, and international relations.

Jerzy Menkes is a Full Professor at SGH Warsaw School of Economics and President of the Polish Branch of the International Law Association (ILA), Warsaw, Poland.

Magdalena Suska is an Assistant Professor of political science at SGH Warsaw School of Economics, Poland.

Routledge Studies in the European Economy

The Political Economy of Independence in Europe
Hana Lipovská

The European Monetary Union After the Crisis
From a Fiscal Union to a Fiscal Capacity
Nazaré da Costa Cabral

Empirical Macroeconomics and Statistical Uncertainty
Spatial and Temporal Disaggregation of Regional Economic Indicators
Mateusz Pipień and Sylwia Roszkowska

Economic Transformation in Poland and Ukraine
National and Regional Perspectives
Edited by Rafał Wisła and Andrzej Nowosad

Competitiveness and Economic Development in Europe
Prospects and Challenges
Edited by Slawomir I. Bukowski, Alina Hyz and Marzanna B. Lament

Brexit and the Political Economy of Ireland
Creating a New Economic Settlement
Paul Teague

The Economic and Legal Impact of Covid-19
The Case of Poland
Edited by Jerzy Menkes and Magdalena Suska

Brexit and the Future of the European Union
Firm-Level Perspectives
Edited by Marian Gorynia, Barbara Jankowska and Katarzyna Mroczek-Dąbrowska

For more information about this series, please visit www.routledge.com/series/SE0431

The Economic and Legal Impact of Covid-19

The Case of Poland

Edited by
Jerzy Menkes and Magdalena Suska

Routledge
Taylor & Francis Group
LONDON AND NEW YORK

First published 2022
by Routledge
2 Park Square, Milton Park, Abingdon, Oxon OX14 4RN

and by Routledge
605 Third Avenue, New York, NY 10158

Routledge is an imprint of the Taylor & Francis Group, an informa business

British Library Cataloguing-in-Publication Data
A catalogue record for this book is available from the British Library

Library of Congress Cataloging-in-Publication Data
A catalog record has been requested for this book

ISBN: 978-0-367-70064-5 (hbk)
ISBN: 978-0-367-70065-2 (pbk)
ISBN: 978-1-003-14443-4 (ebk)

DOI: 10.4324/9781003144434

Typeset in Bembo
by Taylor & Francis Books

Contents

Illustrations

Figures

Tables

Contributors

Adam A. Ambroziak, Ph.D. in economics, is an Associate Professor at SGH Warsaw School of Economics, specialising in EU internal market policy, state aid policy, cohesion policy, common commercial policy, industrial policy, and the use of EU funds. He is also an expert in decision-making processes in the European Union and EU lobbying, as well as Head of the Postgraduate Programme in Public Aid, Head of the Postgraduate Programme in Administration and Management. He is the author of more than 150 scientific publications, including monographs, chapters, and research papers published by prominent international publishers, such as Springer, Routledge, Taylor & Francis Group, as well as analyses drafted for the Polish administration and international organisations on EU economic policy, state aid policy, and the EU internal market. He was also actively involved in Poland's EU association and accession, and membership (for more, see: www.adamambroziak.eu).

Email:adam.a.ambroziak@sgh.waw.pl

Marzenna Błaszczuk-Zawiła, Ph.D. in economics, is an Assistant Professor at SGH Warsaw School of Economics. Before SGH, she worked at the Foreign Trade Research Institute, the Institute for Market, Consumption and Business Cycles Research, and the Polish Economic Institute. Her research interests include economic integration and the international trade system, economic relations between Poland and the European Union with Central, Eastern and Southeastern European countries, as well as the economic development of post-Soviet states. She is the author or co-author of scientific publications on international economic relations, as well as analyses on trade-related issues for the Polish administration (Ministry of Economy, Ministry of Regional Development, Ministry of Foreign Affairs, Ministry of Agriculture and Rural Development) and foreign institutions (JETRO, Government of the Republic of Azerbaijan).

Email: mblaszcz@sgh.waw.pl

Łukasz Dawid Dąbrowski, Ph.D. in law, is an Assistant Professor at SGH Warsaw School of Economics and lecturer in the Department of Human

Rights Protection and International Humanitarian Law at University Cardinal Stefan Wyszyński in Warsaw. He is also an attorney-at-law, as well as a member of the Legislative Commission of the Polish Bar Council, member of the International Law Association Polish branch and of the European Society of International Law. He provides legal services to telecommunications companies and represents legal entities in administrative and civil procedures in all types of courts. He is the author of scientific publications in the field of international criminal law, international protection of human rights law and telecommunications law published by prominent national and international publishers, including Brill and Routledge.

Email: ldabro@sgh.waw.pl

Andrzej Janik, Ph.D. in law (1979), professor emeritus at SGH Warsaw School of Economics—World Economy Faculty (since 1995), legal counsel (admitted 1982), active as lecturer of International Private Law and Banking Law and tutor of seminars leading to master and licensee degree, author of several monographs on business law and civil litigation issues; as legal counsel partner in the international legal firm and author of numerous legal opinions for Polish and foreign firms in the area of the law of contract, company law, financial instruments, real estate and merger control; served as member of the bank's supervisory board and arbitrator in several substantial international litigations.

Email: ajanik1@sgh.waw.pl

Elżbieta Kawecka-Wyrzykowska, Ph.D. in economics, has been a Full Professor since 1992. She was Head of the Jean Monnet Chair of European Integration at SGH Warsaw School of Economics in 1997–2020 and has been the Jean Monnet Professor ad Personam since 2007. In 2008–2013, she was Vice Rector of the Warsaw School of Economics in charge of Foreign Cooperation; in 2002–2005, she was a member of the team of advisors to the President of the Republic of Poland. She was also a visiting Fellow at universities in the USA (1983 and 1997), Italy (1998), and Japan (1990), a consultant to the Economic Commission for Europe (1994) and OECD (1995), as well as a coordinator and participant in several national and international research projects. Her research interests include economics and the policies of European integration, Poland's position in the EU, preferential trade agreements, international trade, and trade policy. She is the author of more than 120 research papers and the author or co-author of more than 100 books on Poland's integration into the European Union, on the EU and GATT as well as WTO, published in Poland and abroad (among others by Springer Publishing, Cambridge Scholars Publishing, Greenwood Press, Duncker and Humboldt, Institute for EastWest Studies). She also has prepared a number of expert opinions for, among others, the Polish Senate, Office of the Committee for European Integration, and ministries. She has extensive teaching experience at universities in Poland and abroad (for more, see: kawecka.eu).

Email: ekawec@sgh.waw.pl

Jerzy Menkes, Ph.D. in law, is a Full Professor at SGH Warsaw School of Economics and President of the Polish Branch of the International Law Association (ILA). He is also a Member of the Polish-Russian Group for Difficult Matters–Ministry of Foreign Affairs, Poland, and Professor at the Academy of Diplomacy–Ministry of Foreign Affairs, Poland, as well as former Senior Counsellor to the Minister of Foreign Affairs (1993–2002) and Professor, Chief of Law Experts Division, Polish Institute of International Affairs, Warsaw (1989–1993). He is the author of textbooks, monographs, research studies, and papers on international law, international institutional law, human rights, European institutional law, and international economic law published, among others, by Brill-Nijhoff, C.H. Beck, CESifo (Center for Economic Studies LMU Munich), LexisNexis, Peter Lang, and Wolters Kluwer. He is also the author of opinions for the President of Poland, the Polish Sejm and Senate, the Polish ministers of Foreign Affairs, National Defence, and Economy, and the Office of the Committee for European Integration.

Email: jmenke@sgh.waw.pl

Magdalena Suska, Ph.D. in political science, is an Assistant Professor at SGH Warsaw School of Economics. She also has MAs in International Economic and Political Relations from SGH Warsaw School of Economics and MAs in English Philology from Warsaw University. She lectures in the field of Global Business, including Multinational Corporations, Economics and Management of Innovation, Institutional Determinants of Business, and Multilateral Business Cooperation. She has been engaged in the education of doctoral candidates and implementing international doctoral candidate programmes. Her research interests include international economics and political relations, including unrecognised states in international economic, multinational corporations in international economics, as well as corporate social responsibility (CSR) and sustainable development. She is the author of scientific publications in the field of human rights, economics, and management.

Email: msuska@sgh.waw.pl

Alina Dorota Szypulewska-Porczyńska, Ph.D. in economics, is an Associate Professor at SGH Warsaw School of Economics. She has MAs from the International Trade Faculty at Université Paris XII Val-de-Marne and Foreign Trade Faculty at SGH Warsaw School of Economics, as well as a French diploma of the third cycle in Banking and Financial Markets from Université Paris Dauphine. She is currently Head of Ph.D. Programmes at the Collegium of World Economy, SGH. Her teaching and research fields are international economics. She lectures on European Integration, Global and European Economic Governance, Regional Trading Arrangements, and Services in the Global Economy. She specialises in European economic integration, especially on the EU internal market for services and Poland's participation in it, the European Banking Union, and the Economic and Monetary Union of the EU. She is the author or co-author of scientific publications in the field of international economics in Poland and abroad.

Email: aszypu@sgh.waw.pl

Introduction

The COVID-19 pandemic poses a threat to people's health and life, but also to the functioning of societies, states, and international cooperation, and has constricted the economies of particular states and the global economy. The response to the challenge of the pandemic requires a modification of the way of life of individuals and societies, a different exercise of the functions and competences of international organisations (universal via the UN system and regional, such as the EU). It also requires a different way of thinking when mere modifications of the previous status quo is not sufficient. These challenges also bring new opportunities.

In response to the pandemic outbreak, states and international organisations (including the EU) have acted to contain the harmful disease and its consequences on people's life and health, as well as on the economy. One can observe many economic crises in the 19th and 20th centuries, however the present recession derives entirely from different reasons, and its social and economic dimensions vary from the earlier crises. Apart from the huge negative consequences, the present situation also has created new opportunities for some sectors of economies, primarily the acceleration of the digital transformation. What is more, this change is occurring in a quite different time than earlier crises, one with a much more developed legal framework, both domestically and internationally. As a result, the expectations towards international institutions and individual states are much higher.

It is worth noting that although the COVID-19 pandemic is one thing, its course and consequences are varied. These differences are noticeable when comparing countries or groups of countries (regions and regional institutions). The differences in the wealth of countries determine access to therapy. Economic and institutional differences influence the capacity of the state to mitigate the socio-economic consequences of the pandemic.

To offset the negative economic and social effects of lockdowns, states have implemented various measures, including ones focused on increasing financial liquidity for businesses and income support for workers and the unemployed. The first actions undertaken by the EU Member States were decisively unilateral, with extremely limited coordination at the European Union level. That situation harmed the EU as an institution but, at the

DOI: 10.4324/9781003144434-1

universal level, the individual actions by states sometimes exacerbated difficulties for other Member States (e.g., bans on the export of medical devices, including personal protective equipment; in turn, the rapid closure of national borders significantly delayed the delivery of goods that were already on their way and inhibited the movement of workers in border regions). Despite this, in a relatively short time the EU started to coordinate anti-pandemic responses across the Member States and offered different types of support to national economies, especially regulatory facilitation. Moreover, the pandemic affected the approach to the negotiations on the Multiannual Financial Framework (MFF) for 2021–2027 and resulted in the creation of new funds and mechanisms of financial support, both at the micro- and macro-economic levels. Despite the immense economic and social costs of the pandemic, the EU has not abandoned its earlier, comprehensive programme to achieve climate neutrality of the economy by 2050, the European Green Deal. In addition, fiscal and public aid rules, vital for the protection of competition on the EU market, were adjusted to allow Member States to make more financial intervention in the market while laws on public procurement were enhanced to make purchases of protective and medical equipment by Member States easier.

Beyond the EU, international institutions and organisations also introduced some measures towards good neighbourly cooperation. Due to international commitments and the need for cooperation resulting from mutual dependence, states started to work together to protect the health and lives of their inhabitants. Moreover, the international institutions and organisations deployed information exchange and humanitarian cooperation and attempted to coordinate the initiatives of their members or participating states, as well as to construct the appropriate capacity to respond to COVID-19. They also initiated, basically at the very beginning of the pandemic, a plan of action and indispensable steps to be undertaken after the pandemic. These steps have been directed at both the prevention or limitation of the harmful effects of future similar events, and at the management of follow-on social and economic crises.

Due to the comprehensive character of this international cooperation, the differentiated and interrelated implications and countries' uneven capacity to deal with this pandemic, the instruments implemented by individual states and international organisations, including the EU, must be subject to multidisciplinary research. Knowledge and evaluation of the response measures deployed by all actors will allow a strengthening of their capacity to prevent and limit the effects of similar events (disasters or catastrophes) in the future. An important component of expanding this knowledge is domestic case studies placed in the international context. With COVID-19 presenting not only economic and social effects but also legal ones, it is very interesting to verify the ability to follow up on goals and observe the roles of international organisations, in particular in states with relatively young market economies, still in the process of building civil society, and to see the impact on their still-unconsolidated political systems, painstakingly constructed over the last 30 years. In states like these, both citizens' reactions and the response of the economy and public institutions to extraordinary situations with deep consequences like COVID-19 decisively differ from the response in states with a longstanding tradition of democracy and a stable free-market economy.

To this end, the choice of Poland as the object of such research is based on strong substantive arguments (it is also essential that the research was conducted in Poland). On one hand, enactment of democracy, rule of law, and protection of human rights and freedoms enabled Poland to accede to the Council of Europe, NATO, and the European Union. On the other one, in the last 4–5 years, Poland has evolved towards a hybrid democracy. Indicators of this evolution include the fallout with the institutions of the Council of Europe and EU over political system values. From the economic point of view, Poland is an average country, but one which, after 1989, built its market economy up sufficiently to function on the competitive European market. As far as the pace of its economic growth before the pandemic is concerned, Poland was among the EU's leaders. A factor that has undoubtedly contributed to these achievements has been significant funds from the EU budget. The differences in social and economic development between Poland and the "old" members of the EU have been progressively levelled (although the process has been uneven among regions and social groups within Poland). At the same time, despite a number of positive effects of its EU membership, Poland's participation in deepened integration of the EU, including the eurozone, has been rather limited and postponed. Given all this, Poland's response to COVID-19—the nation-wide lockdown and the state's attempts to limit the economic recession—becomes particularly interesting.

Taking into account these elements of the discussion, the first goal of the study was to examine the compliance of the actions undertaken by Poland in the face of COVID-19 with the goals and rules of the international organisations of which it is a member, and to draw conclusions from these experiences for the prevention of possible future disasters and extraordinary circumstances of the kind and to mitigate their effects. The second goal was to assess Poland's actions based on EU regulatory changes (in particular relating to state aid and public procurement) introduced due to the COVID-19 outbreak, and the likely importance of financial support for Poland (within the long-term EU budget for 2021–2027 and extraordinary recovery programme Next Generation EU) directed at mitigating the negative implications of the pandemic and fostering recovery from the recession. The third goal was to evaluate the impact of the pandemic on the implementation of the European Green Deal in Poland.

In the juristic research, the following methods were applied: legal-dogmatic and legal-comparative; in the economic part of the research, the descriptive method was used (critical analysis of Polish and EU documents), as well as selected statistical methods.

The book consists of eight chapters covering the legal and economic aspects of Poland's response to the COVID-19 outbreak. **Chapter I: International *Disaster Response Law* (IDRL) in Poland**, by *Jerzy Menkes* and *Magdalena*

Suska, examines Poland's participation in the creation of IDRL, as well in the international institutions responsible for implementing it amid the international cooperation taken up in response to natural disasters or catastrophes. The goal of this study was to identify IDRL norms and to answer the question whether and how these standards were incorporated into the Polish legal order, asking has Poland fulfilled its international obligations? The relationship between the norms of Polish law and IDRL was also analysed through the prism of the represented value system. Based on this, the will and legal and institutional capacity of Poland to co-create IDRL and implement IDRL standards in international cooperation was assessed.

The aim of **Chapter II: Legal Aspect of the Introduction of the Lockdown in Poland**, by *Jerzy Menkes* was to catalogue and evaluate the norms produced and applied in Poland in response to COVID-19 and compare them with international legal commitments. The object of the analysis was the axiology and expediency of legal orders of states of emergency in Poland in a comparative perspective. Included in the research were Poland's institutional and normative preparedness for the introduction of the state of emergency, as well as legal regulations and their observance. The lockdown-related restrictions were confronted with Poland's commitments deriving from European and international law.

Chapter III: Poland in International Cooperation in the Face of the COVID-19 Challenge, by *Magdalena Suska*, identifies a "patchwork" of international institutions that cooperate in case of a natural disaster or catastrophe of supranational reach. Individual institutions were assigned a weighted number in accordance with their role and significance in a regional and universal sense. Poland's actions within international forums in which it is a member were catalogued—those undertaken individually or within the EU or NATO. Also, the importance attached by Poland to international cooperation in the COVID-19 context was examined. In the study, the elements of this "patchwork" of institutions and actions in matters of international cooperation that included Poland were identified.

In **Chapter IV: Poland and EU Cooperation—Mechanism of Joint Public Procurement (COVID-19)**, by *Łukasz Dawid Dąbrowski*, the object of the study was the actions taken by the Polish government regarding joint public procurement of preventive medical equipment and parallel actions supplemented or complemented by the mechanism. The aim of the study was to answer the question whether the changes in Polish public procurement law, as well as in policy regarding cooperation on acquiring protective and medical equipment, from individual cases to actions within the framework of multilateral cooperation, is appropriate and efficient from a legal standpoint.

Chapter V: EU Funds for Addressing the Consequences of the COVID-19 Pandemic: Implications for Poland, by *Elżbieta Kawecka-Wyrzykowska*, presents the issue of financing of disaster response and recovery. In July 2020, EU leaders agreed on a record-high EUR 1.82 trillion financial package. It combines the standard seven-year budget for 2021–2027 (Multiannual Financial Framework) and an emergency recovery programme, Next Generation EU. Both programmes are intended to foster recovery from the recession following the COVID-19 pandemic while maintaining the EU goals of the ecological (European Green Deal) and digital transformations. The objective of this chapter was to identify how the pandemic has affected the reorientation of EU budget spending as well as to assess EU budgetary proposals from the point of view of the interests of Poland's economy, and to identify factors that determine the role of EU assistance in the Polish economy.

Chapter VI: Financial Measures Adopted in Poland in the Light of COVID-19 State Aid EU Framework, by *Adam A. Ambroziak*, is aimed at identifying changes in principles regarding public aid in the EU in relation to COVID-19, as well as assessing state aid measures offered by Poland from the perspective of their potential impact on competition within the single market. To this end, an analysis was carried out of the changes in EU legislation and the aid schemes introduced in Poland compared to instruments available in other Member States. This chapter is based on analyses of the committed budgets of state aid schemes of Member States approved by the European Commission and data concerning financial intervention within the COVID-19 state aid rules in Poland in the first six months of the COVID-19 pandemic.

Chapter VII: Poland and the European Green Deal amidst the Pandemic, by *Marzenna Błaszczuk-Zawiła*, evaluates the conditions for implementing the European Green Deal in Poland, especially after the outbreak of COVID-19. The main goal of the European Green Deal, announced in December 2019, then becoming the main pillar of the economic recovery, is the ecological transformation of the EU economy, including the achievement of climate neutrality by 2050. Although supported by all Member States, only Poland chose not to adopt the goal of climate neutrality as a national one. As a result of the COVID-19 pandemic and the necessity to resurrect the EU economy, the debate about the feasibility of the ecological transformation as a priority has been revived (including in Poland, Czechia, and Romania). Therefore, selected factors that hindered Poland's adoption of the objective of achieving climate neutrality by 2050, as well as the position of the Polish government and enterprises towards the European Greed Deal are discussed in the chapter.

Chapter VIII: The Emergency Measures Underpinning Poland's Convergence Programme 2020: The Case of the Trade Credit Reinsurance Scheme, by *Alina Dorota Szypulewska-Porczyńska,* puts particular emphasis on the case of a trade credit reinsurance scheme and allows for a closer look at the way Poland has used the room to manoeuvre created by temporarily loosened EU procedures. The activation of the general escape clause in the Stability and Growth Pact in the EU in March 2020 allowing a temporary departure from budgetary requirements brought flexibility sought by EU Member States to cushion the direct economic consequences of COVID-19. This paper analyses the Polish COVID-19 response which envisages incentivising suppliers of trade credit insurance services to accommodate business liquidity needs. Three factors determining the effectiveness of this measure are identified and used to evaluate the Polish response: magnitude of the measure, pace of introduction, and consistency with Polish companies' needs.

Chapter IX: Polish Banking Sector in the Face of COVID-19, by *Andrzej Janik*, deals with the Polish banking sector during the COVID-19 pandemic, especially the knock-on effects on the economy. These effects are in the sphere of monetary policy, in particular the official reduction of interest rates. The second area in focus is concentrated measures by banks providing relief to borrowers, the so-called credit holidays. These measures and others were undertaken as government incentives to maintain or boost the economy. The information presented in the book is up to date as on the date of its publication, i.e., September/October 2020.

1 International Disaster Response Law (IDRL) in Poland

Jerzy Menkes and Magdalena Suska

Introduction

This chapter explores Poland's participation in the creation of *International Disaster Response Law* (IDRL) and in international institutions responsible for implementing it, as well as the international cooperation taken up in response to natural disasters or catastrophes. The goal of this study was to identify the-norms covered by IDRL and present them within the Polish legal order in the context of legal and international requirements. The object of the analysis was the comparison of relations between the norms of Polish law and IDRL norms from the perspective of the represented value system and the complexity of the rules. Based on this, the will and legal-institutional capacity of Poland to act upon the IDRL regime were evaluated. In the study, we mainly applied dogmatic legal and comparative-legal methods.

1 IDRL—why?

In response to the increasing threats derivative of catastrophes and natural disasters, as well as the level of social demands addressed to states to more effectively prevent and perform rescue operations in such crises, states (individually and collectively) have acted to create IDRL norms and institutions for their implementation.

Among the factors leading to this increase in threats of catastrophes and natural disasters is globalisation. In the case of infectious diseases (a natural disaster), globalisation facilitates and accelerates the cross-border movement of pathogens. The increasing risk of catastrophes is connected, among others, with the move of industries to developing countries. In those countries, the lack of or restrictions on infrastructure (and pursuit of cost efficiencies) in conjunction with weak laws enable placing industrial installations (including dangerous ones) in the centres of large populations but where the cities or states are also unprepared to respond adequately to a catastrophic event. The Bhopal disaster was one such case (see: Mandavilli, 2018).

Simultaneously, globalisation has raised expectations of these same states to achieve a desired standard for preventing and responding to catastrophes and natural disasters. The "CNN effect" is the idea that information about crises

DOI: 10.4324/9781003144434-2

immediately reaches people in different parts of the world (see: Robinson, 1999; Mooney and Evans, 2007, pp. 27–28). The recipients of that information then demand a proportional response to the scale of the humanitarian challenge. The manifestations of globalisation indicate duplication of ties, from production to social relations.

The capability of particular states to prevent catastrophes and perform rescue operations in the case of such events or natural disasters is, however, restricted by the availability of resources (Bruntland, 2003). Even in the case of the wealthiest states where their material resources potentially allow them to stand ready to perform a rescue operation, it is justified and necessary to ask the question about the rationality of keeping up with the increasing costs of maximal readiness with regard to risk considered to be low (see: Bostrom and Cirković, 2008, pp. 1–29; Avin et al., 2018). States have recognised that a rational response to the globalisation of challenges is universal cooperation (US Ambassador Richard Holbrooke on 10 January 2000 pushed for the first discussion of HIV and AIDS in the UN Security Council; see McInnes and Rushton, 2010). States have established international cooperation both in direct relations and through international institutions. Cooperation in the field of international disaster response is an element of the implementation of the obligation directly contained in Article 1 of the UN Charter "The Purposes of the United Nations are: … 3. To achieve international co-operation in solving international problems of … humanitarian character, and in promoting and encouraging respect for human rights and for fundamental freedoms for all" (United Nations, 1945).

A condition of such cooperation was (and is) the necessity to create the needed legal and institutional norms, thus there exists a loophole (lack of laws). The evidence of the existence of this loophole in the sphere of regulation of IDRL are works on the protection of persons in the event of disasters by the International Law Commission, which resulted in the adoption of draft articles in 2016 (United Nations, 2016). These works also indicate the capability of states to meet the challenge of the loophole. Particularly effective is the cooperation of states and other international actors in international forums, such as IGOs and NGOs. The IGOs in this case are specialised UN agencies, while for NGOs, a special role has been played by the International Federation of Red Cross and Red Crescent Societies (IFRC). The result of international cooperation is IDRL and its implementation.

2 IDRL—term and norms

IDRL "is a descriptive term for the various legal and other instruments applicable to the international disaster response" (International Federation of Red Cross and Red Crescent Societies, 2003). The catalogue of IDRL norms co-create both the norms of international law as well as the *soft law* norms, binding and non-binding norms. It comprises multi-, pluri- and bilateral treaties, resolutions and declarations of the IGOs and NGOs, operational guidelines, and codes of conduct. IDRL norms regulate the access, facilitation, coordination, quality, and accountability of international disaster response activities in times of non-conflict related disasters, which includes preparedness for imminent disaster and the performance of rescue and humanitarian assistance activities. IDRL norms create both regulation that is substantively closed as well as that which is part of broader regulations (De Guttry, 2012, p. 6).

Treaties are the cornerstone of contemporary IDRL: the 1986 Convention on Assistance in the Case of a Nuclear Accident or Radiological Emergency (International Atomic Energy Agency, 1986) and the 1998 Tampere Convention on the Provision of Telecommunications Resources for Disaster Mitigation and Relief Operations (United Nations, 1998). However, the patterns of the cooperation are rooted in nineteenth-century international sanitary conferences to negotiate agreements to combat the cross-border spread of diseases. At the turn of the nineteenth to the twentieth century, in multilateral telegraph and telecommunications treaties, which were adopted with specific provisions about emergency communications and maritime agreements, codifying customary norms on rescue and assistance to vessels in distress were reached. These regulations were of a fragmentary or episodic character, but they indicated the direction of the creation and implementation of IDRL.

The Convention of 1986 was developed in response to the Chernobyl disaster, as it seems the trauma of that event propelled the Convention to enter into force already by 10 March 1987 (about 6 months after its signature). Poland signed it on 26 September 1986 and ratified it on 24 March 1988 as the last state of the Eastern Bloc to do so. Poland, like others in the bloc, raised reservations with regard to Article 13.2, i.e., the jurisdiction of the ICJ. It took longer to await the entry into force of the Tampere Convention, which came on 8 January 2005. In the case of the Tampere Convention, it was also signed by fewer states (60) and fewer states are parties (49) than in the case of the Convention from 1986 (121 states-parties). Poland signed the Tampere Convention on 18 June 1998, but it has not ratified it even today. Poland is not an exception among the EU and NATO members, with those still remaining "outside the Convention" including the US, Germany, and Italy.

The process of creating the network of bilateral and plurilateral agreements has proceeded substantially faster and more intensively compared to multilateral ones. In the 1990s, a practice of concluding agreements in Europe was developed that included the provision and/or facilitation of assistance in times of natural or technological disaster. The matter of IDRL was also regulated with respect to Europe through agreements concluded under the auspices of the EU, NATO, and UN Economic Commission for Europe. The model of European bilateral agreements was gradually created. The treaty regulations in Europe originated from the agreements of the 1950s drawn up in response to specific needs. The next stage comprised treaties between neighbouring countries, an example of which is the Convention on mutual assistance between French and Spanish fire and emergency services (14 July 1959; United Nations, 1959).

The practice of concluding bilateral treaties accelerated in the 1970s. Western European states concluded agreements on disaster response, including the

Convention on Mutual Assistance in the Event of Disasters or Serious Accidents (3 February 1977, France–Germany; United Nations, 1977).

Agreements concluded after 1989 by Poland and the states of Central and Eastern Europe are, in this area, next-generation agreements; in contemporary agreements between the states of this region, IDRL was not subject to regulation. Simultaneously, agreements concluded in Central and Eastern Europe were followed neither by *traités-contrats* nor the institutionalisation of cooperation. Additionally, a characteristic of these agreements is the differentiation of norms. With regard to norms, they differ not only between the states, but the practice within each state in the region is different. Such agreements-norms do not create a model, and specific regulations seem accidental, not model-like.

Poland has regulated cooperation in relation to catastrophes and natural disasters in numerous bilateral agreements (mainly with its neighbours). An example of such regulation is Article 17 of the Polish–German Treaty on Good Neighbourliness and Friendly Cooperation of 1991: "The Contracting Parties shall co-operate to grant each other mutual assistance in the event of disasters and serious accidents." (Treaty Between the Republic of Poland and the Federal Republic of Germany on Good Neighbourliness and Friendly Cooperation, 1992). Similar content is seen in Articles 17.1 of the Treaty Between the Republic of Poland and Ukraine on Good Neighbourliness, Friendly Relations and Cooperation (1993), 11.2 with Russia (Treaty Between the Republic of Poland and Russian Federation on Friendly and Good Neighbourly Cooperation, 1993), 12.1 with the Czech and Slovak federative republics (Agreement Between the Republic of Poland and the Czech and Slovak Federative Republic on Good Neighbourliness, Solidarity and Friendly Cooperation, 1992), 22 with Lithuania (Treaty Between the Republic of Poland and the Republic of Lithuania on Friendly Relations and Good Neighbourly Cooperation, 1995) and 10.4 with Estonia (Treaty Between the Republic of Poland and the Republic of Estonia on Friendly Cooperation and Baltic Neighbourliness, 1993). Poland is party to agreements on cooperation on protection against "technological and natural disasters" with, e.g., Croatia, Czechia, France, Germany, Hungary, Lithuania, Russia, Slovakia, and Ukraine. Poland also developed cross-border cooperation with German *Länders*: Brandenburg, Mecklenburg, Free State of Saxony.

The most far-reaching regulations are included in the Polish–Belarusian Treaty (Articles 21, 23; Treaty Between the Republic of Poland and the Republic of Belarus on Good Neighbourliness and Friendly Cooperation, 1993) and the Polish–Belarusian Declaration of 1991; directly referring to the Chernobyl disaster, they encouraged the creation and implementation of IDRL at bilateral, regional, and global levels. The norms in the treaty and declaration with Belarus indicated the desired direction of the development of IDRL. What prevented it and the creation, on their basis, of a model of regulation in Central and Eastern Europe (and even potential proliferation outside the region) were, it seems, issues of a political nature.

Western European bilateral and plurilateral cooperation was reinforced due to moving it at the regional level; in 1987, the European Council resolved to set up a multilateral Cooperation Group for the prevention of and protection against disasters.

The cooperation of NATO member states is enhanced. The adoption of procedures through "NATO Cooperation for Disaster Assistance in Peacetime (1953)" began setting the norms and institutionalising the cooperation.[1] In 1998, NATO adopted the policy "Enhanced Practical Cooperation in the Field of International Disaster Relief" and established the Euro-Atlantic Disaster Response Coordination Centre. Poland participates in these areas with its EU and NATO partners.

IDRL cooperation is not limited to Europe. However, the regulation of cooperation via norms and their implementation differs substantially by region. In response to the Indian Ocean earthquake and tsunami (2004), the ASEAN states in 2004 adopted the Declaration on Action to Strengthen Emergency Relief, Rehabilitation, Reconstruction and Prevention in the Aftermath of Earthquake and Tsunami Disaster (Association of Southeast Asian Nations, 2005a) and in 2005, they concluded the Agreement on Disaster Management and Emergency Response (Association of Southeast Asian Nations, 2005b). The institutionalisation of ASEAN cooperation in terms of the creation and implementation of IDRL is significantly more advanced than cooperation in many other fields. The cooperation between ASEAN states in response to the COVID-19 pandemic is evidence of this (Association of Southeast Asian Nations, 2020).

States in different regions are using international institutions to establish this cooperation. An example is the Agreement Among the Governments of the Participating States of the Black Sea Economic Cooperation on Collaboration in Emergency Assistance and Emergency Response to Natural and Manmade Disasters (Black Sea Economic Cooperation, 2020) establishing structured cooperation.

States have gone further in developing IDRL through IGOs and ICRC. In the case of one of the most important, UN GA Resolution 46/182 of 19 December 1991 on Strengthening of the Coordination of Humanitarian Emergency Assistance of the United Nations, adopted in response to the Gulf War (United Nations, 1991), the resolution was adopted—along with Poland—by consensus. Resolution 46/182 includes, among others, 12 guiding principles for humanitarian aid and created mechanisms of cooperation by appointing the Inter-Agency Standing Committee, the Central Emergency Revolving Fund (which in 2005 became the Central Emergency Response Fund), and the Consolidated Appeal Process. Poland sponsored UN GA Resolution 57/150 of 16 December 2002 on Strengthening the Effectiveness and Coordination of International Urban Search and Rescue Assistance (United Nations, 2003).

The pioneering role in terms of the creation and implementation of IDRL was, however, played by The International Red Cross and Red Crescent Movement. The International Conference of the Red Cross (ICRC) in 1869 had adopted a resolution calling on National Societies to provide relief "in case of public calamity which, like war, demands immediate and organised assistance". This became the basis of the practice confirmed in subsequent Statutes of the Movement. Since the 1970s, the Movement has set the direction and pace of creating IRDL. The importance of subsequent regulations cannot be overestimated (e.g., Principles and Rules for Red Cross and Red Crescent Disaster Relief of 1969 (International Federation of Red Cross and Red Crescent Societies, 1969a)), Declaration of Principles for International Humanitarian Relief to the Civilian Population in Disaster Situations of 1969 (International Federation of Red Cross and Red Crescent Societies, 1969b). The ICRC not only creates IRDL regulations but also initiates and manages the international cooperation, which resulted in the Measures to Expedite Emergency Relief (adopted together with the UN General Assembly) and the Code of Conduct for the Red Cross and Red Crescent Movement and Non-Governmental Organisations in Disaster Relief (1994).

The universal forum of cooperation is the International Civil Defence Organisation (ICDO), within which the Framework Convention on Civil Defence Assistance was elaborated. Poland, like other members of the EU and NATO, is not a member of the ICDO.

3 Obligation to safeguard security—axiology

It is commonly and traditionally recognised that one of the fundamental obligations-functions of a state is safeguarding the security of the state's citizens. The traditional reflection on security was subject to self-limitation: one focused on the external security of a state in a military dimension and the internal one through the prism of the stability and effectiveness of the state. The content of the obligation to safeguard security continues to evolve (see: Buzan, 2016). The subjective and objective scope of what falls within state security matters has been extended. The catalogue of threats also includes "health", and first among the catalogue of six major threats, there is "infectious diseases".[2]

The subjective scope of persons entitled to benefit from security is being expanded. The obligation of a state to safeguard security is not limited to citizens, but everybody on the territory of the state. It is recognised that a state/states, as a consequence of natural cohesion, has/have the obligation to safeguard security in the interest of persons/states outside the borders who, in the case of a security vacuum, may be exposed to disastrous consequences. Everyone has the right to security (Mahler, 1981). This obligation falls within the area of the internal competences of a state. However, its execution is ever more often realised in a formula of international cooperation. Such cooperation can be both not institutionalised and institutionalised (McInnes, 2008). Ensuring security serves the interests of the community.

In the case of Poland, this obligation was formulated in the Constitution, Article 5 "The Republic of Poland shall safeguard … the security of the citizens" (Constitution of the Republic of Poland, 1997). This provision is complemented, with regard to health, by Article 68.1, "Everyone shall have the right to have his health protected". The authority appointed to realise this obligation is the executive acting in the formula of the Council of Ministers and the government administration, which derives from Article 146.4.7 of the Constitution, "To the extent and in accordance with the principles specified by the Constitution and statutes, the Council of Ministers, in particular, shall: … 7) ensure the internal security of the State and public order". The Constitution has set the President as the guardian of this obligation ("The President of the Republic shall … safeguard the … security of the State").

These provisions are in accordance with the European constitutional tradition; however, they do not have direct equivalents in the French, German, Spanish, or Swedish constitutions. Paradoxically, from the perspective of perceiving sovereignty in national debates, the regulations that are the closest to the Polish ones are included in the Treaty of the Functioning of the European Union (TFEU).[3]

Pursuant to Article 4.2. (h) The Union shall share competence with the Member States and to principal areas, in which these competences are shared belong to "common safety concerns in public health matters, for the aspects defined in this Treaty". Additionally, "(i)n the areas of development cooperation and humanitarian aid, the Union shall have competence to carry out activities and conduct a common policy".

The obligations of the EU with regard to "health" reinforces Article 114 Para 2, indicating that in these spheres what is possible and desired is the approximation of laws:

> The Commission, in its proposals envisaged in paragraph 1 concerning health, safety, environmental protection and consumer protection, will take as a base a high level of protection, taking account in particular of any new development based on scientific facts. Within their respective powers, the European Parliament and the Council will also seek to achieve this objective.

The key and unambiguous importance both from the perspective of recalling the obligations of a state-member, as well as "in the definition and implementation of all Union policies and activities" and the role of the EU as an institution facilitating the cooperation of the Member States have the norms Title XIV TFEU "Public health" (see: Gestri, 2012).

In Poland, according to the Constitution, in case of a "natural disaster" a "state of natural disaster" can be introduced (Act on the State of Natural Disaster, 2017). However, the Act indicates only the legal instrument; it does not indicate the axiological basis. The gap relating to the lack of axiology and aim of the regulation was to be filled by the Civil Protection Act. However, the work on that has been in progress for many years and the end of it is slipping away. Projects have been postponed, modified, or withdrawn[4]; the delay is not officially justified. However, already as of 31 August 2009 within the project, it was envisaged that the aim of the actions within the civil protection act will be "the protection of life and health of persons remaining on the territory of the Republic of Poland (Article 2.1)" as well as "supporting the undertakings to protect persons remaining outside the national borders within the framework of humanitarian, rescue, technical and expert assistance, on the terms and in the manner deriving from the international law and concluded agreements (Article 2.2)". In the project "humanitarian aid", included is "providing assistance to people affected by the effects of natural disasters, crisis situations, armed conflicts, consequences of forced migration based on the principles of impartiality, neutrality and independence as well as adequacy and rapid response". The entry into force of the act will make the Poland–EU dispute in response to the migration crisis irrelevant (2015). The subsequent project of 2016 maintained the indicated norms; however, it envisaged the instruments of implementation. It was also not adopted. Rumour had it that group interests were the obstacle to the adoption of the act; the assumed establishment of National Training Centre for Civil Protection and the Central storage base (it was proposed to establish three logistic centres) infringed the interests of existing structures. It also seems that establishing the Central storage base could reveal irregularities concerning the storage of devices and equipment. However, already in the subsequent project (29 December 2017) the catalogue of situations in which humanitarian or rescue aid is provided was restricted to "natural or man-made threats", thus "forced migrations" were deleted.

In the newest project,[5] the purpose of the humanitarian aid is to "save lives and alleviate the suffering of people affected by the consequences of natural disasters, crisis situations, armed conflicts and other man-made threats". The response to "forced migration", or the principles of providing humanitarian aid, were removed from the wording.

The retrograde step in the concept of work on the act also concerned the catalogue of persons entitled to "civil protection"—the aim is exclusively to safeguard the security of the citizens, and not everyone remaining on Poland's territory. Despite these efforts, the works are still hibernated, e.g., since July 2019 the Minister of Defence has not made any comments concerning the project. There is no doubt that after several well-publicised scandals connected with the procurement and storage of devices and equipment for the needs of rescue operations, each step could trigger a political avalanche.

It can be stated that the 2009 project was put into a time machine and taken back to the past. Consequently, the Polish legal state and the project differ from the created international pattern. According to the *Draft articles*, the obligation of state to safeguard security is a formula of the implementation of human rights "Persons affected by disasters are entitled to the respect for and protection of their human rights in accordance with international law" (Article 5). By eliminating the principles of providing humanitarian aid from the Polish project, Poland is not implementing international law (Article 6).

4 Poland as a provider and recipient of assistance

Poland both provides and benefits from international assistance. In 2015–2018, the country provided assistance in accordance with the European Consensus on Humanitarian Aid.

Poland provides assistance in cooperation with NGOs. The national expenditure on humanitarian aid is growing from about EUR 4 million in 2015 to EUR 34 million in 2017. Substantial food and medical aid was delivered in Syria, South Sudan, Jordan, and Uganda.[6]

The country also benefits from such assistance. During the floods of 1997, to Poland's rescue came units from Germany, Switzerland, Lithuania, Ukraine, Sweden, Hungary, Denmark, and Austria. The United States European Command offered 250,000 food rations from IFOR supplies. Food transport was arranged by the Hungarian government. Individual states also provided material assistance: funds, medical supplies, food, tents, clothes, and water treatment products. Groups of specialists, such as doctors and flood damage restoration technicians, were also sent. In the period from May to June 2010, Poland, affected by the flood, benefited from heavy duty pumps that were dispatched from the Czech Republic (on the basis of a bilateral agreement), and then activated the EU Community Civil Protection Mechanism and requested assistance from EU countries in the form of Civil Protection modules groups. In Poland, international groups from EU Member States and from Ukraine arrived (the agreement concluded between the Polish government and the Cabinet of Ministers of Ukraine on cooperation and mutual assistance in preventing catastrophes, calamities and other emergency situations, and on eliminating their consequences). Poland was provided with in-kind aid by the US and Russia.

There is very little social awareness in Poland of how the country provides and benefits from international assistance. Public media does not enhance it, rather it seems they are guided by narrow, momentary political interest. Simultaneously, the "new" NGOs (e.g., Polish Humanitarian Action), conducting humanitarian aid operations (outside Poland) in the case of "natural and man-made disasters" are popular and well supported. There has been regress in the activity of the "old" NGOs, the Polish Red Cross has been most affected by the crisis, which is connected to numerous irregularities in the operations of this organisation.

Conclusions

Catastrophes and natural disasters know no boundaries. This statement has multiple dimensions:

- empathy, the willingness to provide assistance, and the demand to be provided with it do not stop at national borders. Irrespective of the nationality of the victims and the location of the event, people all over the world are motivated by humanitarianism and want to provide assistance to victims of an event and demand effective actions from governments and international institutions;

- the consequences of catastrophes and natural disasters may have cross-border effects. The necessary condition to counteract cross-border threats is international cooperation. These are factors that determined the creation and implementation of IDRL.

Poland has participated to a varying extent in the creation and provision of international cooperation in terms of the implementation of IDRL. In 1945–1989, Poland, on the one hand, adopted international regulations but, on the other, neither regulated through treaties bilateral cooperation with its neighbours with regard to catastrophes and natural disasters, nor received or provided assistance. The reasons for such behaviour were also varied. In the case of catastrophes and natural disasters in Poland, information about disasters was considered a state secret, and thus one could not benefit from assistance after an event that officially had not "occurred", whereas the capability to respond to natural disasters was the *raison d'être* of the state in real socialism. Responding to a natural disaster was the domain of power ministries; the image of these ministries depended on them being seen as capable of counteracting "each" threat, and this formed the base, to a considerable extent, of the power of the communist party. Therefore, it was unacceptable to seek humanitarian and rescue assistance from abroad because it portrayed the state's weakness. The obstacle to providing assistance, besides the state's lack of real resources under its planned economy was how it understood state security. Officers of power ministries (military, police, fire service) were subject to extreme restrictions in terms of foreign travel as the keepers of "confidential information", and therefore they were not allowed to participate in rescue operations abroad, which was additionally reinforced by the fear of defections during or after the operation.

After 1989, Poland began to conclude bilateral IDRL agreements and cooperation in this area as an element of membership in the EU and NATO. Engaging in humanitarian aid and rescue operations was to be evidence of the internalisation of transatlantic values as well as a demonstration of the capabilities to cooperate with the services of NATO states. This process has been disrupted in recent years, with the impetus being the rejection of European cooperation in response to the mass refugee crisis. Poland's refusal to cooperate emanated from the populist-driven aversion to foreigners in "state doctrine". It also turned to be an important political instrument for winning elections. As a consequence, Poland has frozen IDRL cooperation with states (both in Europe and globally) and does not undertake new initiatives (e.g., participating in deepening EU cooperation). National legislation was also frozen. The analysis indicated the existence of systemic instrumentation compatible with European standards, but also the loophole. This has had a negative impact on Poland's ability to respond to and cooperate in the case of catastrophes and natural disasters.

Beyond the analysis, there is also the issue of unused capacities. The activity of states in international forums has provided good legislative practices, among others, which Poland does not use, e.g., the Model Act on Disaster Relief. Poland did not use the Model Act, developed by the International Federation of Red Cross and Red Crescent Societies, and the UN Office for Humanitarian Affairs and Inter-Parliamentary Union (International Federation of Red Cross and Red Crescent Societies, 2013).

Based on the study, the following conclusions were drawn: IDRL is not a system *per se* and IDRL values are not internalised in Poland. The country co-creates IDRL and follows its norms but only to a limited extent. Polish instruments in response to natural disasters and catastrophes are harmonised with IDRL but not to a substantial degree.

Notes

1 https://teimun.org/wp-content/uploads/2013/11/Topic-1-NATO-and-Natural-Disasters-Final.pdf.
2 See the Report of the Secretary-General's High-level Panel on Threats, Challenges and Change of 2004 (points 47–51), https://documents-dds-ny.un.org/doc/UNDOC/GEN/N04/602/31/PDF/N0460231.pdf?OpenElement.
3 https://eur-lex.europa.eu/legal-content/EN/TXT/?uri=celex%3A12012E%2FTXT.
4 https://www.ock.gov.pl/prawo/projekty_aktow_prawnych.
5 https://legislacja.rcl.gov.pl/docs//2/12322353/12604997/12604998/dokument403945.pdf.
6 See https://pcpm.org.pl/category/aktualnosci.

Bibliography

Act on the State of Natural Disaster of 15 September 2017 (2017) *Dziennik Ustaw*, item 1897.

Agreement Between the Republic of Poland and the Czech and Slovak Federative Republic on Good Neighbourliness, Solidarity and Friendly Cooperation of 6 October 1991 (1992) *Dziennik Ustaw*, No. 59, item 296.

Association of Southeast Asian Nations (2005a) Declaration on Action to Strengthen Emergency Relief, Rehabilitation, Reconstruction and Prevention in the Aftermath of Earthquake and Tsunami Disaster, Jakarta, 6 January. Available at https://asean.org/?static_post=special-asean-leaders-meeting-on-aftermath-of-earthquake-and-tsunami-jakarta-6-january-2005 (accessed: 24. 11. 20).

Association of Southeast Asian Nations (2005b) Agreement on Disaster Management and Emergency Response, 26 July. Available at https://asean.org/?static_post=asean-agreement-on-disaster-management-and-emergency-response-vientiane-26-july-2005-2 (accessed: 24. 11. 20).

Association of Southeast Asian Nations (2020) ASEAN Health Sector Efforts in the Prevention, Detection and Response to Coronavirus Disease 2019 (COVID-19). Available at https://asean.org/?static_post=updates-asean-health-sector-efforts-combat-novel-coronavirus-covid-19 (accessed: 24. 11. 20).

Avin, S., Wintle, B. C., Weitzdörfer, J., Seán, S., hÉigeartaigh, Ó., Sutherland, J. and Rees, M. J. (2018) Classifying Global Catastrophic Risks, *Futures*, 102, pp. 20–26.

Black Sea Economic Cooperation (2020) Agreement Among the Governments of the Participating States of the Black Sea Economic Cooperation on Collaboration in Emergency Assistance and Emergency Response to Natural and Manmade Disasters. Available at http://www.bsec-organization.org/UploadedDocuments/StatutoryDocumentsAgreements/Emergencyagreement071116.pdf (accessed: 24. 11. 20).

Bostrom, N. and Cirković, M. M. (2008) *Global Catastrophic Risk*. Oxford: Oxford University Press.

Bruntland, G. H. (2003) Global Health and International Security, *Global Governance*, 9 (4), pp. 417–423.

Buzan, B. (2016) *People, States and Fear: An Agenda for the International Security Studies in the Post-cold War Era*. (2nd edition). Colchester: ECPR Press.

Constitution of the Republic of Poland of 2 April 1997 (1997) *Dziennik Ustaw*, No. 78, item 483.

De Guttry, A. (2012) Positioning International Disaster Response Law within Existing International Law, in De Guttry, A., Gestri, M., Venturini, G. (eds) *International Disaster Response Law*. The Hague: T.M.C. Asser Press.

Gestri, M. (2012) EU Disaster Response Law: Principles and Instruments, in De Guttry, A., Gestri, M. and Venturini, G. (eds) *International Disaster Response Law*. The Hague: T.M.C. Asser Press, pp. 105–128. https://documents-dds-ny.un.org/doc/UNDOC/GEN/N04/602/31/PDF/N0460231.pdf?OpenElement (accessed: 24. 11. 20). https://eur-lex.europa.eu/legal-content/EN/TXT/?uri=celex%3A12012E%2FTXT (accessed: 24. 11. 20). https://legislacja.rcl.gov.pl/docs//2/12322353/12604997/12604998/dokument403945.pdf (accessed: 24. 11. 20). https://pcpm.org.pl/category/aktualnosci (accessed: 24.11.20). https://teimun.org/wp-content/uploads/2013/11/Topic-1-NATO-and-Natural-Disasters-Final.pdf (accessed: 24. 11. 20).

International Atomic Energy Agency (1986) Convention on Assistance in the Case of a Nuclear Accident or Radiological Emergency, 18 November. Available at https://www.iaea.org/sites/default/files/infcirc336.pdf (accessed: 24. 11. 20).

International Federation of Red Cross and Red Crescent Societies (1969a) Principles and Rules for Red Cross and Red Crescent Disaster Relief of 1969. Available at https://www.ifrc.org/docs/idrl/I280EN.pdf (accessed: 24. 11. 20).

International Federation of Red Cross and Red Crescent Societies (1969b) Declaration of Principles for International Humanitarian Relief to the Civilian Population in Disaster Situations, September. Available at https://www.ifrc.org/docs/idrl/I49EN.pdf (accessed: 24. 11. 20).

International Federation of Red Cross and Red Crescent Societies (2003) *International Disaster Response Laws (IDRL) Project Report 2002–2003*, 28th ICRC International Conference, Geneva, 2–6 December. Available at https://www.icrc.org/en/doc/assets/files/other/idrl_report_final_ang.pdf (accessed: 24. 11. 20).

International Federation of Red Cross and Red Crescent Societies (2013) Model Act for the Facilitation and Regulation of International Disaster Relief and Initial Recovery Assistance, March. Available at https://www.ifrc.org/PageFiles/125656/MODEL%20ACT%20INGLES.pdf (accessed: 24. 11. 20).

Mahler, H. (1981) The Meaning of "Health for All" by the Year 2000, *World Health Forum*, 2 (1), pp. 5–82.

Mandavilli, A. (2018) The World's Worst Industrial Disaster is still Unfolding, *The Atlantic*, 10 July. Available at https://www.theatlantic.com/science/archive/2018/07/the-worlds-worst-industrial-disaster-is-still-unfolding/560726/ (accessed: 10. 03. 2021).

McInnes, C. (2008) Health, in Williams, P. D., McDonald, M. (eds) *Security Studies: An Introduction*. London: Routledge, pp. 274–287.

McInnes, C. and Rushton, S. (2010) HIV, AIDS and Security: Where Are We Now? *International Affairs*, 86 (1), pp. 225–245.

Mooney, A. and Evans, B. (eds) (2007) *Globalization. The Key Concepts*. London: Routledge.

Robinson, P. (1999) The CNN Effect: Can the News Media Drive Foreign Policy, *Review of International Studies*, 25 (2), pp. 301–309.

Treaty Between the Republic of Poland and the Federal Republic of Germany on Good Neighbourliness and Friendly Cooperation, 17 June 1991 (1992) *Dziennik Ustaw*, No. 14, item 56.

Treaty Between the Republic of Poland and Ukraine on Good Neighbourliness, Friendly Relations and Cooperation, 18 May 1992 (1993) *Dziennik Ustaw*, No. 125, item 573.

Treaty Between the Republic of Poland and Russian Federation on Friendly and Good Neighbourly Cooperation, 22 May 1992 (1993) *Dziennik Ustaw*, No. 61, item 291.

Treaty Between the Republic of Poland and the Republic of Belarus on Good Neighbourliness and Friendly Cooperation, 23 June 1992 (1993) *Dziennik Ustaw*, No. 118 item 527.

Treaty Between the Republic of Poland and the Republic of Estonia on Friendly Cooperation and Baltic Neighbourliness, 2 July 1992 (1993) *Dziennik Ustaw*, No. 121, item 536.

Treaty Between the Republic of Poland and the Republic of Lithuania on Friendly Relations and Good Neighbourly Cooperation, 26 April 1994 (1995) *Dziennik Ustaw*, No. 15, item 71.

United Nations (1945) Charter of the United Nations and Statue of the International Court of Justice, San Francisco. Available at https://treaties.un.org/doc/publication/ctc/uncharter.pdf (accessed: 24. 11. 20).

United Nations (1959) Convention on Mutual Assistance Between French and Spanish Fire and Emergency Services, of 14 July 1959, Treaty Series No. 13576. Available at http://disasterlaw.sssup.it/wp-content/uploads/2014/10/1973-France-and-Spain-Convention-on-mutual-assistance-between-French-and-Spanish-fire-and-emergency-services.pdf (accessed: 24. 11. 20).

United Nations (1977) Convention on Mutual Assistance in the Event of Disasters or Serious Accidents, of 3 February 1977, France–Germany Treaty Series, vol. 1214, No. 19561.

United Nations (1991) UN GA Resolutions 46/182 of 19 December 1991 on Strengthening of the Coordination of Humanitarian Emergency Assistance of the United Nations. Available at http://www.oas.org/dil/Res_46-182_UN_eng.pdf (accessed: 24. 11. 20).

United Nations (1998) Tampere Convention on the Provision of Telecommunications Resources for Disaster Mitigation and Relief Operations, Tampere, 8 June. Available at https://treaties.un.org/doc/Treaties/1998/06/19980618%2006-14%20PM/Ch_XXV_04p.pdf (accessed: 24. 11. 20).

United Nations (2003) UN GA Resolution 57/150 of 16 December 2002 on Strengthening the Effectiveness and Coordination of International Urban Search and Rescue Assistance, 27 February. Available at https://www.insarag.org/images/stories/GA_Res_57-150_English.pdf (accessed: 24. 11. 20).

United Nations (2016) Draft Articles on the Protection of Persons in the Event of Disasters. Available at https://legal.un.org/ilc/texts/instruments/english/draft_articles/6_3_2016.pdf (accessed: 24. 11. 20).

2 The legal aspects of the introduction of a lockdown in Poland

Jerzy Menkes

Introduction

The aim of this chapter is to show and critically analyse the provisions establishing a lockdown in Poland. The analysis was conducted with the use of a legal-dogmatic and legal-comparative method. The reference point of the legal-comparative analysis comprised provisions in the Constitution and Polish acts, standards of European law and international law binding on Poland, constitutional traditions common to the (EU) Member States (Art. 6 para. 3 of the Treaty on European Union), as well as state practice in the transatlantic area.

The lockdown in Poland (provisions of the law were created and amended many times; one legal regime did not function) was introduced before the actual coronavirus outbreak in Poland. It occurred after the WTO declared the outbreak a pandemic (January 2020). The introduction was not preceded by logistical preparation for COVID-19. The Chief Sanitary Inspector, declaring in February 2020 a lack of funds to prevent the spread of the pandemic, the aim to reduce its spread, as well as the need to treat COVID-19 patients, suggested that the opposition should "put ice in their pants".[1] Introducing the lockdown before the spread of the virus in Poland did not actually differ from the practice of many other states. What made the Polish decision-making process different from the *modus operandi* of other democratic countries (e.g., Germany, Sweden, France, the UK, the US) was the exclusion from participation in decision-making of any bodies other than the executive. In Poland, the government did not inform the parliament or citizens about the factual basis (expert recommendations) of the decisions made. The government did not indicate people or bodies analogous to the Robert Koch Institute (Germany), Anders Tegneli (State Epidemiologist of Sweden), Neil Ferguson (UK), Anthony S. Fauci (National Institute of Allergy and Infectious Diseases, US), or Jean-François Delfraissy (France). The face of the struggle with COVID-19 in Poland was Minister of Health Łukasz Szumowski (cardiologist) and Prime Minister Mateusz Morawiecki, as well as other government members. One could suppose that the government-ruling party assumed that the spread of the pandemic would be prevented in Poland and the success will be attributed to the authorities and did not want to share it with experts. Perhaps, also experts—having limited

DOI: 10.4324/9781003144434-3

trust in the authorities—did not want to institutionalise the cooperation by signing a blank bill of exchange. As a consequence, however, the substantive reasons for the decisions were not provided.

1 Poland's "Anti-COVID-19 law"

The statutory legal instrument to "prevent as well as combat the infection of the SARS-CoV-2 virus and the spread of infectious diseases" is the Act of 2 March 2020 on special solutions related to preventing, counteracting, and combating COVID-19, other infectious diseases, and the resulting crisis (Act of 2 March, 2020). The draft Act was a government document, nevertheless, it did not include an "impact assessment of the regulations", that is, an assessment of the economic effects of the Act. The legislator clearly stated that in order to counteract COVID-19, there would be introduced "a state of epidemic emergency, a state of epidemic or a state of natural disaster". However, the "state of natural disaster" was not introduced. Additionally, on 9 March the government—the first in Europe—introduced health checks at Polish borders, and then on 15 March, the government closed the borders to foreigners arriving as passengers.

To prevent the spread of the coronavirus, on 13 March 2020 the health minister introduced a "state of epidemic emergency" as a regulation on the territory of Poland (Regulation of the Minister of Health, 13 March 2020). As the factual basis, he indicated "infection with the SARS-CoV-2 virus", and as the legal basis, Art. 46 paras. 2 and 4 of the Act of 5 December 2008 on the prevention and control of infections and infectious diseases in humans (Notice of the Marshall of Sejm, 2019; Act of 31 June, 2019; Act of 23 January, 2020a; Act of 23 January, 2020b). The regulation closed Polish borders (for an unlimited duration) to rail passenger traffic. It allowed for the entry of people permanently residing in Poland, together with the simultaneous obligation to be subject to a 14-day quarantine; people working in neighbouring countries and drivers in road transport were exempted from this obligation. The export of selected devices as well as medical and health products was prohibited. Restaurants, cinemas, theatres, museums, libraries, gyms, swimming pools, etc. were closed. Shops were closed—except for grocery stores and pharmacies—if they were larger than 2,000 m^2. As of 16 April, the obligation to cover the mouth and nose outside the home was imposed. The number of participants in mass (churches) and public assemblies was reduced to 50 persons. After 7 days—on the same factual and legal basis—the state of epidemic was introduced (Regulation of the Minister of Health, 20 March 2020). The regulation maintained the prohibitions and restrictions, introduced new ones, and tightened penalties connected with any failure to comply with the restrictions. A significant novum was reducing the healthcare service to "teleconsultations". The regulations introduced a state of epidemic emergency and a state of epidemic with an unlimited duration. On 1 April, parks, boulevards and beaches were closed and persons under 18 were not allowed to be outside their home without an adult guardian. The prohibitions were sanctionable by legal and criminal liability.

The legal measures suspended the implementation of the rights enshrined in the European Convention on Human Rights (ECHR).[2] This is illustrated by the example of the quarantine; it was itself a permissible deprivation of freedom to prevent the spread of the infectious disease (Article 5.1e ECHR); however, in practice it was arbitrarily commanded, without any control. The freedom of assembly was drastically restricted, which was particularly essential during the presidential elections. The freedom of movement (Article 2.1 ECHR and Protocol 4) and the right to leave the country were suspended. It does not seem that these measures were unfounded or excessive; however, the expectation that the government would implement the derogation of specified rights enshrined pursuant to Article 15 ECHR was justified. Poland, however, failed to fulfil the obligation of the derogation in the regime of the ECHR and similarly failed to fulfil the obligation of the derogation under Article 4 of the International Covenant on Civil and Political Rights. The Polish practice in terms of the failure to fulfil the obligation under Article 15 ECHR deviated from the practice of many states. Derogation, in accordance with Article 15 of the ECHR, was made by, e.g., Albania, Armenia, Estonia, Georgia, Latvia, North Macedonia, Moldova, Romania, San Marino, and Serbia (Council of Europe, 2020a). The rights enshrined were temporarily suspended for the duration of the public danger, in most cases it was necessary and proportionate; nevertheless, absurd restrictions took place, e.g., "the closing" of parks and forests or prohibiting the use the bicycles (e.g., to get to work). At the root of the lack of the derogations can exclusively be found political reasons, particularly the unwillingness to introduce a "state of natural disaster", together with its legal effects. The practice of the Polish authorities can be recognised as an abuse of rights. Such a practice, in the case of Hungary, was explicitly criticised by the Secretary General of the Council of Europe, Marija Pejčinovič Burič. Recognising the justification of "(t) he COVID-19 pandemic legitimately prompted the Council of Europe member states to take drastic measures to protect public health", specific regulations introduced due to the pandemic,

> (t)hese measures are restricting a number of individual rights and liberties enshrined in constitutions and in the European Convention on Human Rights. Whereas the applicable national and international human rights norms allow for such restrictions, their severity may require the implementation of a derogatory regime in the form of a state of emergency, as provided for by the national constitutional order.

She indicated the regulatory framework of such restrictions:

> I should like to underline that the measures which member states take in the present exceptional circumstances of the pandemic must comply with both national constitutions and international standards, and observe the

> very essence of democratic principles. An indefinite and uncontrolled state of emergency cannot guarantee that the basic principles of democracy will be observed and that the emergency measures restricting fundamental human rights are strictly proportionate to the threat which they are supposed to counter.

The practice of Poland (and Hungary) was met with sharp criticism by 14 Member States of the EU (Runcinam, 2018). In the declaration of 2 April concerning COVID-19, there was explicitly expressed concern/criticism of the infringement of rights and values

> In this unprecedented situation, it is legitimate that Member States adopt extraordinary measures to protect their citizens and overcome the crisis. We are however deeply concerned about the risk of violations of the principles of rule of law, democracy and fundamental rights arising from the adoption of certain emergency measures. Emergency measures should be limited to what is strictly necessary, should be proportionate and temporary in nature, subject to regular scrutiny, and respect the aforementioned principles and international law obligations. They should not restrict the freedom of expression or the freedom of the press. We need to jointly overcome this crisis and to jointly uphold our European principles and values on this path.[3]

To conclude, the assessment of the Polish regulations introduced in response to the COVID-19 pandemic (as a matter of fact, anticipating it) through the prism of Polish law is explicitly negative; the regulations were introduced with a blatant infringement of law. Such an assessment may be a derivative of the decision/assessment of the situation: either the pandemic demanded such a lockdown (as was introduced), or the "state of epidemic" was enough. If such a lockdown was justified, and this presumption can be supported by the assessment and decisions taken by other states, e.g., other EU Members, it should be established in the constitutional formula of a "state of natural disaster", together with all legal requirements and restrictions accompanying this formula. From 13 March, the level of restrictions in Poland shifted on the "COVID-19: Containment and Health Index" for Europe, increasing from 31.25 on 13 March to 71.53 in the period 16 April–24 May (max. level), and after 7 July, it fell below 50.[4] However, the lockdown was introduced without a suitable legal basis; hence, the "state of epidemic" was not such a basis. However, if the "state of epidemic" was an adequate response to the pandemic, the regulations introduced within its framework drastically infringed the law because the "state of epidemic" does not allow the introduction of such regulations. Such an assessment was formulated by confronting the Polish law on lockdown and the way of its introduction with a scheme included in "Respecting democracy, rule of law and human rights in the framework of the COVID-19 sanitary crisis A toolkit for member states" (Council of Europe, 2020b).

In establishing the lockdown, the Polish authorities allowed constitutional delicts and offences, among others, by circumventing the law. The introduced regulations were the same as the "emergency measure", such a state is—according to the jurisprudence of the Constitutional Tribunal (K 9/11)—the actual state of emergency, and the act on the state of emergency is each act introducing and regulating such a state. The act on the state of epidemic introduced "legal rigours characteristic of emergency measures, including the state of natural disaster" (Supreme Court of Poland, 2020a). Formally, not introducing one of the emergency measures included in the Constitution does not alter the reality: introducing a "state of epidemic" together with its rigours, the failure to introduce a "state of natural disaster" was circumvention of the law. What is essential is not the content of the measures, although they were invasive, but the way of introducing them.

A pandemic like COVID-19 is, according to Polish law, a "natural disaster (an event connected with natural processes, massive outbreaks of infectious diseases)". The Constitution foresees, to prevent the effects of such a catastrophe, introducing a state of natural disaster regulated by the Act on the State of Natural Disaster (2017). A state of natural disaster should be imposed by the Council of Ministers with the regulation; its non-imposition given the need to—as confirmed by the actions taken by the authorities—is a delict. The Act allows for, but also defines, the limits of restrictions of rights and freedoms of a person and citizen. The introduced rules of law establishing the lockdown were—in this respect—consistent with the rules of Chapter 3 of the Act. However, they were not introduced in a lawful manner, and there were also sanctions for their violation without a legal basis. Nor were they introduced by the sole authorised body, namely the Council of Ministers. Courts, when considering cases, have consistently ruled that lockdown-style limitations (whether a ban on assemblies that can only be imposed under a declared emergency or an obligation to wear "masks" on the face that can only be imposed on patients under an epidemic condition) have been introduced without a legal basis. The government *ex post* admits to acting without a legal basis. This is proved by the Motion to the Constitutional Tribunal on the examination of the constitutionality of Article 417 of the Civil Code.[5] The purpose of the motion is to block proceedings for compensation. The Constitutional Tribunal will either formally block the process of pursuing claims or freeze proceedings without resolving the case (this is the "regular" practice). The European Parliament has argued that it

> is concerned about the very restrictive ban on public assemblies which was in force during the COVID-19 pandemic without the introduction of a state of natural disaster as laid down in Article 232 of the Polish Constitution and insists on the need to apply the principle of proportionality when restricting the right to assembly
>
> (European Parliament, 2020).

Poland implemented ordinary urgent legislative measures instead of specific emergency constitutional mechanisms. The umbrella under which partially the practices (*propter legem* and *contra legem*) of the Polish authorities can be hidden are a similar *modus operandi* of some states of the "old union", among others, Germany and France. In the case of Germany, it was, it seems, motivated by memory. Simultaneously, *Bundesländer* formally declared emergency measures (e.g., Bavaria, the Bavarian Catastrophe Protection Act). In the case of France, there was willingness to avoid excessive repression (maybe remembering the recent *le mouvement des Gilets jaunes*—the Yellow Vests movement). However, such circumstances did not create a standard because not all states have, in their constitutions, regulations on emergency measures (e.g., Belgium or Italy do not have them); the states of the "old union" also used constitutional emergency measures, e.g., Spain (European Parliamentary Research Service, 2020).

2 Emergency measures in Poland—roots, types

An "emergency measure" is a specific legal regime extended to the territory of the whole country or its part, established by entitled bodies in the manner provided by the law in order to remove a threat of a specific character (it is recognised that its removal in an "ordinary measure" will be impossible or more expensive). The executive, due to the suspension of, among others, the selected legal safeguard, is to act more effectively (Levitsky and Ziblatt, 2018). The suspension of the implementation of special fundamental human rights and freedoms is also to serve the collective interest and the interest of an individual.

In Poland after 1998, there was relatively rapid introduction (compared to democratic states) of complex regulations of emergency measures in the Constitution and executive acts, pursuant to Article 228 of the Constitution, which states that: "In situations of particular danger, if ordinary constitutional measures are inadequate, any of the following extraordinary measures may be introduced: martial law, a state of emergency or a state of natural disaster".

Poland, in creating the pandemic response regulations, could have chosen one of two models: French or German. The French model is a republican one (post-revolutionary), *l'état de siege*. In its framework, there are found fundamental institutions and solutions of emergency measures, among others, in the form of suspending constitutionally enshrined fundamental human rights and freedoms. While the emergency measures had their roots in the constitution, the content and range of regulations were determined by the acts. The German model is a monarchist model (*Notrecht*), to which the introduction of measures is reserved to the executive.

However, in practice the choice was limited: the German model acquired the character of a standard and was most frequently copied. The nature of the standard of the German model is proven by the fact that even the Fifth French Republic incorporated it. The full formula of the German monarchist model was expressed in Article 48 of the Weimar Constitution[6] and repeated—in a softer form—in Article 16 of the Constitution of the Fifth Republic.[7] Poland followed the same path.

The emergency measures defined and differentiated in the Polish legislation as "martial law", "state of emergency", and "state of natural disaster" are known in the legislation of states whose systems are based on the absolute obligation of respecting the rule of democracy, the rule of law, as well as fundamental human rights and freedoms (Menkes and Kociołek-Pęksa, 2016). Hence, the practice of the conduct of the Polish authorities concerning COVID-19 should be critically assessed.

A comparison of the Polish constitutional emergency measures with the lockdown leads to the following clear conclusions.

Purposes of the emergency measure regulation:

a catastrophes and natural disasters. A time-limited event, usually of short duration. The purpose of the emergency measure is limiting the direct consequences of the catastrophe/disaster, facilitating the conduct—limiting the difficulties of rescue operation, managing the event—accelerating aid and reconstruction. The event is visible.

b armed attack, conflict with use of force. The aim of the emergency measure is making the attack more difficult—facilitating defence, minimising the effects of the attack(s), accelerating aid and reconstruction. A visible event, but the enemy is not always visible.

Common features: threats/events known to societies and individuals; the emergency measure (action of the state) has operational and psychological functions (demonstration of state power as a counterweight to the force of terror); predictability of the end of the event.

Purpose of regulation in response to COVID-19:

a reducing or slowing the rate of contagion proliferation;

b using the time gained to build up (enlarge) medical infrastructure (capacity) to assist those in need. The number of needy people (in a given time) is significantly higher than the capacity available.

c striving for a dynamic balance between the positive (slowing down the spread of the pandemic) and negative effects of the introduced restrictions (socio-economic lockdown effects).

Features of the event: invisible event; duration unpredictable; an event (on a comparable scale) forgotten in the Euro-Atlantic area; lack of urgency/immediateness of the event limits the terror effect.

Response components: restriction of individual rights and freedoms with regard to personal (mainly) and political rights.

In the area of:

a personal rights and freedoms—the rights that are restricted include humanitarian treatment and respect for human dignity, freedom and personal security, justice, prohibition of arbitrary arrest or detention, protection of private and family life, protection of personal data, freedom of movement, right to asylum;

b political rights—there are restrictions on rights to vote, freedom of assembly, participation in public life and management of public affairs;

c solidarity rights—the exercise of the right to democracy has been restricted.

3 Free but not fair—presidential election à la polonaise

In democratic states, the lawfully designated-in-advance and constitutional date of elections and provisions of electoral law are known. What is unknown is the winner of the elections. In Poland, in a state of hybrid democracy, what was unknown, or altered *contra legem*, was the date of the presidential elections; also unknown—altered *contra legem*—were the provisions of electoral law (both the substantive-legal provisions and the procedural ones); however, the winner was predictable. It makes, in this subject matter, a difference whether it is a democracy or hybrid democracy; simultaneously, it makes hybrid democracy resemble an illiberal democracy or an undemocratic state (Gessen, 2020). What differentiated the elections in Poland in 2020 from the elections in non-democracies was the lack of massive fraud when voting, including when counting the votes (Krastev and Holmes, 2020). No election irregularities influencing the outcome were confirmed by the Supreme Court of Poland (SCP).

Due to the end of the term of office of the president on 6 August 2020, Marshal of the Sejm Elżbieta Witek ordered that the elections be held on 10 May 2020 (Resolution of the Marshal of the Sejm, 5 February 2020). This date fulfilled the requirements of Article 128 of the Polish Constitution, which stipulates that the elections must be held on a non-working day falling between 75 and 100 days after the end of the term of office of the incumbent president. This date was set before the COVID-19 pandemic. However, after the order of the Marshal of the Sejm, there were *de facto* declared emergency measures: on 13 March, a state of epidemic emergency, and on 20 March, a state of epidemic. Both regulations were issued under Article 46 paras. 2 and 4 of the Act of 5 December 2008 on the prevention and control of infections and infectious diseases in humans (*Dziennik Ustaw* 2019, items 1239 and 1495; *Dziennik Ustaw* 2020, items 284, 322 and 374). In this situation, requests were made to postpone the elections. The authors stated that holding the elections within the constitutionally required period would endanger the health and life of citizens and democracy (Polish Ombudsman, 2020). These voices were disregarded, and instead the Sejm on 6 April passed—with the votes of the governing coalition—a draft act on postal voting submitted on the same day. The draft act was explicitly criticised by, among others, the Supreme Court of Poland (see on the subject of the Act of 6 April 2020 on special rules for conducting the general election of the president of the Republic of Poland ordered in 2020, Supreme Court of Poland, 2020b) and the Office for Democratic Institutions and Human Rights and the Organization for Security and Cooperation in Europe (on the draft Act on special rules for conducting the general election of the president of the Republic of Poland ordered in 2020; Organization for Security and Cooperation in Europe, 2020b). The draft was vetoed by the Senate. However, on 6 May the governing coalition decided to reject the veto of the Senate and postpone the elections to a later date.

On 7 May, the Sejm ultimately adopted the Act amending acts on elections, and on 8 May the president signed the Act on special rules for conducting the general election of the president of the Republic of Poland ordered in 2020 (Act of 6 April, 2020). The Act allowed for—as one of two possible options—postal voting. Pursuant to Article 1 of the Act, the elections were to be held (and were held) in accordance with the "special rules" resulting from the "state of epidemic". The Act amended the Electoral Code (Act of 5 January, 2011). Paradoxically, the Act itself in accordance with the relevant instruction of Article 1 indicates the contradiction between the Act and the elections held on its basis, and the Constitution. Pursuant to Article 228 para. 6 of the Constitution,

> During a period of introduction of extraordinary measures, the following shall not be subject to change: the Constitution, the Acts of Elections to the Sejm, the Senate and organs of local self-governments, the Act on Elections to the Presidency, as well as statuses on extraordinary measures.

Obviously, also in this circumstance one can defend their position that the constitutional catalogue of extraordinary measures (Article 228 para. 1) includes only: "martial law, a state of emergency or a state of natural disaster"; however, the mentioned Article 1 of the Act recognises the extraordinariness of the situation of the "state of epidemic" and introducing the incidental regulation, it confirms its unconstitutionality. On 7 May, the National Electoral Commission (2020a) informed that voting would not take place because it had lost its organisational competences to hold it (in the form of setting the template and ordering the printing of voting cards). Next, the National Electoral Commission (2020b) stated that there was no possibility of voting, which meant that there were no candidates. On 3 June, the Marshal of the Sejm ordered new elections with voting (in the first round) for 28 June (Resolution of the Marshall of Sejm, 3 June 2020).

Before adopting the Act on special principles of organising universal elections, acting without a legal basis and only with the draft act (Draft Act, 2020) according to which the elections were to be held only in the manner of postal voting, voting packages were printed, including, among others, voting cards, whereas the Polish Postal Service proceeded to organise the elections. The decision to order voting packages was taken by the Minister of State Assets. About EUR 15 million was spent without a legal basis; the prepared electoral packages proved to be unsuitable. The Polish Postal Service demanded from village heads, mayors, and presidents of cities data from electoral registers; this demand also did not have a legal basis and was not signed in person. The assessment that the government acted without a legal basis was confirmed by the Provincial Administrative Court in Warsaw in its judgment of 15 September 2020 (VII SA/Wa 1012/20) (Tarka, 2020).

The elections were held in two rounds (28 June and 12 July) and each voter could vote "at polling places" or by post. The second round of voting preceded by sending *à rebours* a text message alert to voters by means of the Governing Centre for Security (GCS): "The second round of the presidential elections is on Sunday, 12 July. People over 60, pregnant women and people with disabilities will vote in polling stations without queuing" (the text in Polish contained spelling mistakes).

According to law, the alert from GCS can be sent in extraordinary situations of a threat to life or health on a substantial territory of Poland[8] and its aim is to warn people. The *de facto* aim of the *à rebours* alert informing about no threat of the pandemic was to convince mainly older voters—recognised as among the electorate of Andrzej Duda—to vote. This breach of the law did not encounter any reactions.

Changes to electoral law were introduced during the pre-election "legislative blackout". In this period, in a state of emergency, modifications of electoral law are prohibited. This norm of the character of a constitutional principle is a common norm for all democratic states; there are only differences of approaches concerning its duration. In the view of the Polish Constitutional Tribunal, it is a 6-month period, in the view of the Venice Commission (European Commission for Democracy through Law), 12 months; however, in each case the time limit begins before the first day of the electoral calendar, which means that in Poland, the period expired before 5 February and all changes to electoral laws introduced after this date infringed the constitutional principles. The principle of the "legislative blackout" was confirmed by the Constitutional Tribunal (2006, 2011) many times—in the judgement of 20 July 2011 (K 9/11, OTK-A 2011 no. 6, item 61); in the judgement of 3 November 2006 (K 31/06, OTK ZU no. 10/A/2006, item 147).

The Constitutional Tribunal recognises that the "legislative blackout" directly results from Article 2 of the Constitution. A similar position was taken by the Venice Commission (2018), which in the Code of Good Practice in Electoral Matters (no. 190/2002) stated:

> 63. Stability of the law is crucial to credibility of the electoral process, which is itself vital to consolidating democracy. Rules which change frequently—and especially rules which are complicated—may confuse voters. Above all, voters may conclude, rightly or wrongly, that electoral law is simply a tool in the hands of the powerful, and that their own votes have little weight in deciding the results of elections. (…) 65. It is not so much changing voting systems which is a bad thing – they can always be changed for the better – as changing them frequently or just before (within one year of) elections. Even when no manipulation is intended, changes will seem to be dictated by the immediate party's political interests. According

> to this constitutional principle, all changes to electoral law (both substantive and procedural ones) should be introduced well in advance of the elections so that all essential rules of electoral law are known. This constitutional principle is one of the principles counted by the Venice Commission to the principles of Europe's electoral heritage.

The hybrid rule of voting was repealed in two municipalities where only postal voting was allowed (due to the pandemic[9]), whereas the rights of Polish citizens abroad were *de facto* restricted. The Supreme Court of Poland (SCP) with the Resolution of 3 August 2020 confirmed the validity of the elections (Supreme Court of Poland, 2020a) and on 6 August, Andrzej Duda was sworn in as president. The SCP confirmed the validity of the elections, stating that "in 93 cases, the allegations of protests are well founded"; simultaneously, it expressed the view that "the detected infringements did not have an impact on the outcome of the elections". Nevertheless, the SCP did not clarify that. The SCP confirmed the view of the Constitutional Tribunal on the significance of the stability of electoral law and prohibition of its modification in the period directly preceding the elections; however, it recognised that the change in electoral law at a time when it cannot be changed resulted from a "specific situation". The Extraordinary Control and Public Affairs Chamber of the SCP confirmed the validity of the elections. The Chamber deciding about the validity of the elections consists of, mainly, judges appointed by the "new National Council of the Judiciary (newNCJ)". This chamber—in the view of the Court of Justice of the EU—may not fulfil the requirements of an independent court (Commission Recommendation, 2017, p. 19, point 135). The Commission based the recommendations, among others, on the analysis and assessment of the Venice Commission (2017), explicitly criticising "politicisation", the "newNCJ", as well as the manner and composition of the new Chamber of the SCP (No. 904/2017). Hence, the Chamber of the SCP not fulfilling the requirement of independence stated that the elections, during which irregularities were identified—confirmed even by the Chamber itself—led to choosing the president in a lawful manner. The Court of Justice of the EU in the case C-216/18 PPU - *Minister for Justice and Equality v LM*, stated that in order to recognise a court as independent, there should be given guarantees and principles concerning, among others, the appointment of its members. These guarantees and principles, as well as many other elements of recognising a court (as independent), the Chamber of the SCP, in the assessment of the Court of Justice, failed to address. The "new NCJ" has been suspended—since 17 September 2018—from the exercise of the rights of a member of the European Network of Councils for the Judiciary because it is not a body independent from the executive.[10] The breaches of judicial independence in Poland and tripartition of power was also confirmed by the United Nations Special Rapporteur on the independence of judges and lawyers, Mr. Diego García-Sayán, in the Report of 5 April 2018 (Human Rights Council, 2018). The conclusions of the Rapporteur were clear; he stated that:

> After having successfully 'neutered' the Constitutional Tribunal, the Government has undertaken a far-reaching reform of the judicial system. Between May and December 2017, the ruling majority has adopted three acts that introduce broad changes to the composition and functioning of ordinary courts, the Supreme Court of Poland (SCP) and the National Council of the Judiciary. Each of these acts presents a number of concerns as to its compliance with international legal standards but, taken together, their cumulative effect is to place the judiciary under the control of the executive and legislative branches.

During the whole electoral campaign, the public TV broadcaster conducted unlawful pre-election agitation, both in favour of Duda, who was standing for re-election, and against his challengers (protest of the electoral committee of Rafał Trzaskowski of 16 July 2020[11]). The actions taken by public media co-created electoral fraud. This assessment of the actions of the public media was confirmed by the OSCE ODIHR Special Election Assessment Mission. The Assessment Mission stated that:

> The governance and funding of the public broadcaster TVP does not ensure editorial independence and enables the government to exert pressure on TVP content. During this campaign, (...) TVP failed in its legal duty to provide balanced and impartial coverage. Instead, it acted as a campaign vehicle for the incumbent and frequently portrayed his main challenger as a threat to Polish values and national interests. Some of the reporting was charged with xenophobic and anti-Semitic undertones. TVP provided the legally mandated free airtime to all candidates and organised the only joint televised debate. The debate format in which one-minute-long statements were made in response to identical questions, did not allow meaningful engagement which would enable voters to judge policy proposals on a competitive basis. After the debate, the incumbent was afforded the opportunity to respond in a lengthy live interview, while only short pre-recorded soundbites by other candidates were aired. According to the National Broadcasting Council (NBC), the electronic media regulator in charge of ensuring plurality in media, of 39 complaints received in the run-up to the election 36 directly concerned TVP's coverage of the election. Despite having the mandate to do so, the NBC did not independently monitor the campaign. Editorial bias across the media landscape, combined with the lack of an effective oversight, reduced voters' ability to access comprehensive information that helps to inform their choices.
>
> (Organization for Security and Cooperation in Europe, 2020a)

With regard to the actions taken by the public media, the SCP concerning the equality of rights stated: "Elections … are universal, equal, direct and secret" (Constitution of the Republic of Poland, 1997, Article 127 para. 1). Each voter is entitled to one vote of equal strength, and each candidate has equal rights in the same situation. Candidates' unequal access to mass media does not affect the validity of the elections as long as unrestricted media pluralism (legal and factual) is ensured. The SCP notes that a neutral approach of the public authorities towards the election campaign should be good practice with regard to the electoral process. The electoral campaign should be reported in all media, especially public ones, in a fair manner (see Pappas, 2019). However, breaches of these standards, as reported in the public domain and electoral protests, did not take a form that would restrict free choice. In the view of the SCP, it is not clear, when breaching the standards of diligence would restrict the possibility of a free choice (Keane, 2020).

Conclusions

The aim of this study was to catalogue and evaluate the norms produced and applied in Poland in response to COVID-19 and in relation to international legal commitments. The object of the analysis was the axiology and expediency of legal orders of emergency measures in Poland in a comparative perspective. Included in the research was the assessment of Poland's institutional and normative preparedness for the introduction of the state of emergency (civil emergency), as well as legal regulations and their observance. The lockdown restriction was confronted with Poland's commitments deriving from European and international law. The following conclusions were drawn: the lockdown was characterised by both internal and systemic incoherence (within the system of Polish law); neither the instruments nor their use acknowledges European or international commitments; the hybrid character of democracy in Poland is increasing, so Polish political system norms, and common European norms are systematically breached.

The conclusions drawn from the analysis gave grounds to formulate postulates *de lege ferenda.* It is essential to: rebuild the rules of law and democracy (especially, tripartition of power), restore the judiciary independency. The case of the response of the Polish authorities to the COVID-19 pandemic indicates the systematic and systemic evolution of the Poland's system from democracy to hybrid democracy (Zakaria, 1997) and incapability of the existing institutions to halt this process. Pathologies, which occurred during the pandemic (e.g., spending approximately EUR 15 million without a legal basis), confirm that in hybrid democracy, for *propter* and *contra legem* actions, the sky is the limit.

Notes

1 See the interview with Jarosław Pinkas, https://serwisy.gazetaprawna.pl/zdrowie/artykuly/1456186,jaroslaw-pinkas-koronawirus-maseczki-nie-sa-przeznaczone-dla-osob-zdrowych.html.
2 https://www.echr.coe.int/Documents/Convention_ENG.pdf.
3 https://www.diplomatie.gouv.fr/en/coming-to-france/coronavirus-advice-for-foreign-nationals-in-france/coronavirus-statements/article/joint-statement-on-the-principles-of-the-rule-of-law-in-times-of-covid-19-02.

4 https://ourworldindata.org/grapher/covid-containment-and-health-index?tab=chart&time=earliest..latest&country=~POL.
5 For an examination of the conformity of regulations in relation to the lockdown with the Constitution see https://ipo.trybunal.gov.pl/ipo/view/sprawa.xhtml?&pokaz=dokumenty&sygnatura=K%2018/20.
6 http://germanhistorydocs.ghi-dc.org/pdf/eng/ghi_wr_weimarconstitution_Eng.pdf.
7 https://mjp.univ-perp.fr/france/co1958-0.htm.
8 https://rcb.gov.pl/alertrcb/.
9 https://wiadomosci.wp.pl/wybory-prezydenckie-2020-marklowice-i-baranow-w-tych-gminach-tylko-glosowanie-korespondencyjne-6526020855150209a.
10 https://www.encj.eu/node/495.
11 https://oko.press/publikujemy-protest-wyborczy-komitetu-ommaskowskiego/.

Bibliography

Act of 5 January 2011 (2011) *Dziennik Ustaw*, item 112.

Act of 31 June 2019 (2019) *Dziennik Ustaw*, item 1495.

Act of 23 January 2020 (2020a) *Dziennik Ustaw*, item 284.

Act of 23 January 2020 (2020b) *Dziennik Ustaw*, item 322.

Act of 2 March 2020 (2020) *Dziennik Ustaw*, item 374.

Act of 6 April 2020 (2020) *Dziennik Ustaw*, item 827.

Act on the State of Natural Disaster of 18 April 2002 (2017) *Dziennik Ustaw*, item 1897.

Commission Recommendation (EU) 2017/1520 of 26 July 2017 regarding the rule of law in Poland complementary to Recommendations (EU) 2016/1374 and (EU) 2017/146 (2017) *Official Journal of the European Union*, 02. 09. 2017, L 228.

Constitution of the Republic of Poland of 2 April 1997 (1997) *Dziennik Ustaw*, No. 78, item 483.

Constitutional Tribunal (2006) Judgement of 3 November 2006, K 31/06, OTK ZU no. 10/A/2006, item 147.

Constitutional Tribunal (2011) Judgement of 20 June 2011, K 9/11, OTK-A 2011 no. 6, item 61.

Council of Europe (2020a) Reservations and Declarations for Treaty No.005 - Convention for the Protection of Human Rights and Fundamental Freedoms, 18. 11. 2020. Available at https://www.coe.int/en/web/conventions/full-list/-/conventions/treaty/005/declarations?p_auth=ICgde7oD (accessed: 24. 11. 20).

Council of Europe (2020b) Respecting democracy, rule of law and human rights in the framework of the COVID-19 sanitary crisis. A toolkit for member states, 17 April 2020, SG/Inf(2020)1.

Draft Act on special rules for conducting the general election of the President of the Republic of Poland ordered in 2020 (2020) Print No. 328 of 6 April. Available at http://orka.sejm.gov.pl/Druki9ka.nsf/0/F6895C4E66E2A7CBC12585420054B013/%24File/328.pdf (accessed: 24. 11. 20).

European Parliament (2020) Resolution of 17 September 2020 on the proposal for a council decision on the determination of a clear risk of a serious breach by Poland of the rule of law, Brussels, 20. 12. 2017, COM(2017)0835–2017/0360R(NLE).

European Parliamentary Research Service (2020) States of emergency in response to the coronavirus crisis: Situation in certain Member states, June. Available at https://www.europarl.europa.eu/RegData/etudes/BRIE/2020/649408/EPRS_BRI(2020)649408_EN.pdf (accessed: 24. 11. 20).

Gessen, M. (2020) *Surviving Autocracy*. New York: Riverhead Books.

http://germanhistorydocs.ghi-dc.org/pdf/eng/ghi_wr_weimarconstitution_Eng.pdf (accessed: 24.11.20).

https://ipo.trybunal.gov.pl/ipo/view/sprawa.xhtml?&pokaz=dokumenty&sygnatura=K% 2018/20 (accessed: 24.11.20).

https://mjp.univ-perp.fr/france/co1958-0.html (accessed: 24.11.20).

https://oko.press/publikujemy-protest-wyborczy-komitetu-ommaskowskiego/ (accessed: 24.11.20).

https://ourworldindata.org/grapher/covid-containment- and-health-index?tab=chart&time=earliest..latest&country=~POL (accessed: 24.11.20).

https://rcb.gov.pl/alertrcb/ (accessed: 24.11.20).

https://serwisy.gazetaprawna.pl/zdrowie/artykuly/1456186,jaroslaw-pinkas-koronawirus-maseczki-nie-sa-przeznaczone-dla- osob-zdrowych.html (accessed: 24.11.20).

https://wiadomosci.wp.pl/wybory-prezydenckie-2020-marklowice-i-baranow-w-tych-gminach-tylko-glosowanie-korespondencyjne-6526020855150209a (accessed: 24.11.20).

https://www.diplomatie.gouv.fr/en/coming-to-france/coronavirus-advice-for-foreign-nationals-in-france/coronavirus-statements/article/joint-statement-on-the-principles-of-the-rule-of-law-in-times-of-covid-19-02 (accessed: 24.11.20).

https://www.echr.coe.int/Documents/Convention_ENG.pdf (accessed: 24.11.20).

https://www.encj.eu/node/495 (accessed: 24.11.20).

Human Rights Council (2018) Report of the Special Rapporter on the independence of judges and lawyers on his mission in Poland, 5 April 2018, A/HRC/38/38/Add1.

Keane, J. (2020) *The New Despotism*. Cambridge, MA: Harvard University Press.

Krastev, S. and Holmes, S. (2020) *The Light That Failed: Why The West is Losing the Fight for Democracy*. New York: Penguin Books.

Levitsky, S. and Ziblatt, D. (2018) *How Democracies Die*. New York: Broadway Books.

Menkes, J. and Kociołek-Pęksa, A. (2016) Polish legal regulations and the legal doctrine with regard to states of emergency in a comparative perspective, *Hungarian Journal of Legal Studies*, 57 (2), pp. 217–238.

National Electoral Commission (2020a) Communication from the National Electoral Commission of 7 May 2020. Available at https://pkw.gov.pl/aktualnosci/wyjasnienia-stanowiska-komunikaty/komunikat-panstwowej-komisji-wyborczej-z-dnia-7-maja-2020-roku (accessed: 24. 11. 20).

National Electoral Commission (2020b) Resolution No 129/2020 of the National Electoral Commission of 10 May 2020. Available at https://pkw.gov.pl/uploaded_files/1589173994_uchwala-nr-129.pdf (accessed: 24. 11. 20).

Notice of the Marshall of Sejm of 6 June 2019 (2019) *Dziennik Ustaw*, item 1239.

Organization for Security and Cooperation in Europe (2020a) ODIHR special Election Assessment Mission, Republic of Poland – Presidential Election, 28 June 2020. Available at https://www.osce.org/files/f/documents/4/9/455728.pdf (accessed: 24. 11. 20).

Organization for Security and Cooperation in Europe (2020b) Opinion on the draft Act on special rules for conducting the general election of the President of the Republic of Poland ordered in 2020, Senate Paper No. 99, 27. 04. 2020. Available at https://www.osce.org/odihr/elections/poland/450856 (accessed: 24. 11. 20).

Pappas, T.S. (2019) *Populism and Liberal Democracy. A Comparative and Theoretical Analysis*. Oxford: Oxford University Press.

Polish Ombudsman (2020) Koronawirus. RPo: nie można organizować wyborów 10 maja, 24. 03. 2020. Available at https://www.rpo.gov.pl/pl/content/rpo-wybory-10-maja-2020.

Regulation of the Minister of Health, 13 March 2020 (Dz.U. 2020, item 433).
Regulation of the Minister of Health, 20 March 2020 (Dz.U. 2020, item 491).
Resolution of the Marshal of the Sejm, 5 February 2020 (Dz.U. 2020, item 184).
Resolution of the Marshall of Sejm, 3 June 2020(Dz.U. 2020, item 988).
Runcinam, D. (2018) *How Democracy Ends*. London: Profile Books.
Supreme Court of Poland (2020a) Resolution of 3 August 2020. Available at http://www.sn.pl/aktualnosci/SiteAssets/Lists/Komunikaty_o_sprawach/AllItems/Uzasadnienie%20uchwały%20Sądu%20Najwyższego%20z%20dnia%203%20sierpnia%202020%20r.%20-%20wersja%20ang.pdf (accessed: 24. 11. 20).
Supreme Court of Poland (2020b) Opinion on the subject of the Act of 6 April 2020 on special rules for conducting the general election of the president of the Republic of Poland ordered in 2020, Senate Paper No. 99, 27. 04. 2020. Available at http://www.sn.pl/aktualnosci/SiteAssets/Lists/Wydarzenia/AllItems/2020.04.27%20-%20PP%20I-0131-1416-20%20%20%20Uwagi%20SN%20do%20specustawy%20wyborczej%20-%20druk%20senacki%20nr%2099.pdf (accessed: 24. 11. 20).
Tarka, A. (2020) Wyrok WSA: bezprawne wybory kopertowe 10 maja 2020 roku [Judgement of the Provincial Administrative Court: Unlawful envelope elections of 10 May 2020], *Rzeczpospolita*, 16. 09. 2020. Available at https://www.rp.pl/Ustroj-i-kompetencje/309159924-Wyrok-WSA-bezprawne-wybory-kopertowe-10-maja-2020-roku.html (accessed: 24. 11. 20).
Venice Commission (2017) Opinion on the Draft Act Amending The Act on The National Council of the Judiciary, on the Draft Act Amending The Act on The Supreme Court, Proposed By The President Of Poland, and on The Act on The Organisation of Ordinary Courts Adopted by the Venice Commission at its 113th Plenary Session (8–9 December 2017). Opinion No. 904/2017, Strasbourg, 11 December.
Venice Commission (2018) Code of Good Practice in Electoral Matters, Guidelines and Explanatory Report adopted by the Venice Commission at its 52nd Session (Venice, 18–19 October 2002). Opinion No. 190/2002.
Zakaria, F. (1997) The Rise of Illiberal Democracy, *Foreign Affairs*, 76(6), pp. 22–43.

3 Poland in international cooperation in the face of the COVID-19 challenge

Magdalena Suska

Introduction

Over the last decades, major natural and technological disasters[1] bringing not only death and destruction but also disproportionately affecting the poor and marginalised, have focused world attention on the importance of suitable national legal frameworks and implementation mechanisms for disaster prevention and response. Legislation (and institutionalised implementation) plays a key role in promoting and supporting Disaster Risk Reduction as well as in ensuring the speed and effectiveness of disaster response.

Despite the near omnipresence of disasters and their severe consequences, the international legal framework addressing natural disasters and catastrophes is believed to manage this issue "in a confused and uncoordinated manner" (De Guttry, 2012, p. 4) by means of "an ad hoc incoherence of legal and institutional response" (Caron, 2014, p. xx). The outcome of such treatment is "a rather scattered and heterogenous collection of instruments" (Fisher, 2007, p. 353). It is clear that the absence of a universal and general treaty in the field of disaster prevention and response constitutes an anomaly in comparison to other areas of law (e.g., international humanitarian law in times of armed conflict).

Consequently, the legal framework for International Disaster Response Law (IDRL) is composed of a *potpourri* of binding and nonbinding instruments exerting a different impact on the sphere of regulation and parties involved, especially in the face of large-scale disasters. For example, the Inter-American Convention to Facilitate Disaster Assistance, elaborated by the Organization of American States (OAS) in 1991 which entered into force on 16 October 1996 (Organization of American States, 1991), has only six states-parties. Indeed, in the past few decades several universal treaties addressing specific types of disasters have been developed (usually technological, e.g., the Convention on Assistance in the Case of a Nuclear Accident or Radiological Emergency, 1457 UNTS 134, 26 September 1986; entered into force 26 February 1987) or forms of assistance (the Tampere Convention on the Provision of Telecommunication Resources for Disaster Mitigation and Relief Operations, 2296 UNTS 5, 18 June 1998, entered into force 8 January 2005) as well as a couple of binding documents

DOI: 10.4324/9781003144434-4

accompanied by the creation of institutional mechanisms of coordination and cooperation in response to disasters.

The aim of this chapter is to demonstrate the "patchwork" of cooperation between international institutions in relation to natural disasters or catastrophes of supranational reach. In the research, the elements of this "patchwork" of institutions and actions in matters of international cooperation, which included Poland, were identified. The objects of the research are Poland's actions aiming at the co-creation and implementation of disaster relief, and disaster risk-reduction related programmes and policies in Poland within the UN system—those undertaken individually or within the EU or NATO. Additionally, the importance attached by Poland to international cooperation in the COVID-19 context was examined. The analysis has been mainly conducted with the application of a legal-dogmatic and legal-comparative method.

1 International Disaster Response—legal institutions and regulations

Much of the discussion of International Disaster Response Law (IDRL) focuses on disaster response and relief: whether states are obliged to offer assistance in the case of disaster, whether states can force the "acceptance" of assistance without the consent of the government of the affected state, or whether an affected state is obliged to accept it. There is no convention currently governing these areas, although international humanitarian law is applied in wartime disasters (Eburn, 2010, pp. 162–163).

Consequently, different actors (both state and non-state) have turned their attention to exploring proper means of addressing these gaps in the field of disaster prevention, management, and recovery response.

One of the first attempts to develop a specific framework for international disaster response was undertaken in the 1920s under the auspices of the League of Nations, leading to the establishment of the (short-lived) International Relief Union (see: MacAlister-Smith, 1986). However, following the failure of the Union, mainly due to a lack of funds, further serious efforts to develop the legal framework for disaster prevention and response were not made until the 1970s when the UN Disaster Relief Organisation (UNDO), the predecessor to the UN Office for the Coordination of Humanitarian Affairs (OCHA), proposed a draft Convention on Expediting and Delivery of Emergency Assistance; however, it was never taken up by the UN General Assembly (see: the failure of the 1984 Draft Convention on Expediting the Delivery of Emergency Assistance, UN Doc. A/39/267/Add.2–E/1984/96/Add.2, 18 June 1984, elaborated at the initiative of the UN Disaster Relief Coordinator; United Nations, 1984).

In 1998, the OCHA was established as the primary entity responsible for humanitarian aid in the UN system to mobilise and coordinate humanitarian relief and ensure the coherence of the actions of all actors concerned.

In Poland, humanitarian aid is provided in accordance with the European Consensus on Humanitarian Aid (European Consensus on Humanitarian Aid,

2008) standards outlined by the UN and International Committee of the Red Cross (ICRC), as well Good Humanitarian Donorship. A significant part of Polish humanitarian aid is disbursed in two formats: by means of a bilateral channel, e.g., through Polish NGOs, diplomacy, educational institutions, etc., and by payments to specialised humanitarian organisations, among others, the UN, EU, ICRC, as well as by participation in special EU funds (Aspects of Humanitarian and Development Assistance, 2019).

The range of activities of the OCHA intertwines with the scope of work of the International Agency Standing Committee (IASC) as well as other UN agencies and international institutions, including the International Red Cross and Red Crescent Movement, which together constitute a "patchwork" of international coordination and cooperation in terms of disaster relief.

As a result of this cooperation, the International Federation of Red Cross and Red Crescent Societies (IFRC) in 2001 launched the International Disaster Response Law (IDRL) Programme (renamed in 2012 as the Disaster Law Programme to cover legal issues on recovery as well as disaster risk reduction; see Caron et al., 2014, pp. 47, 57), which was a comprehensive desk study of laws pertaining to international disaster relief. As a result, a complete set of laws comprising International Disaster Response Law (IDRL) was developed. In 2007, the IFRC introduced the "Guidelines for the domestic facilitation and regulation of international disaster relief and initial recovery assistance" (the "IDRL Guidelines"), unanimously adopted by all High Contracting Parties to the Geneva Conventions (International Federation of Red Cross and Red Crescent Societies, 2011). The IDRL Guidelines are not legally binding in the way that a treaty is, nor do they govern inter-state relations (International Federation of Red Cross and Red Crescent Societies, 2007). They serve as recommendations to governments on how to best structure their domestic laws relating to disaster management by promoting uniform legislation throughout the countries as a means of eliminating obstacles found in recent natural disaster responses (such as: barriers to entry of goods and people; legal recognition of organisations to operate; and coordination between organisations and governments).

One of the mechanisms of the development of an effective system of disaster response promoted in the IDRL Guidelines (Section 7 of Chapter II) are bilateral agreements on disaster response. Poland has concluded a number of bilateral agreements with its neighbours as well as other countries (e.g., with Croatia, Czechia, France, Germany, Hungary, Lithuania, Russia, Slovakia, Slovenia, and Ukraine) as well as understandings (e.g., with German Länder) to cooperate on forecasting, prevention, early warning, and elimination of effects of disasters. Poland is also a party to several international agreements on disaster response (e.g., the Tampere Convention on the Provision of Telecommunication Resources for Disaster Mitigation and Relief Operations, International Convention on the Simplification and Harmonisation of Customs procedures (Kyoto Convention) Annex J.5, Convention on Temporary Admission of 26 June 1990, Convention on Civil Aviation of 7 December 1944, Convention on the Safety of United Nations and Associated Personnel, Convention on Civil Protection, Food Aid Convention of 1999 and New Food Aid Convention (legally binding since 1 January 2013), Convention on Nuclear Accidents).

Poland also participates in numerous EU mechanisms referring to the IDRL Guidelines, such as the Union Civil Protection Mechanism (UCP) of 2001,[2] which is an EU tool for preparedness, prevention, and response to natural disasters in which 34 European states participate (the 27 EU Member States, the UK, Iceland, Norway, Montenegro, North Macedonia, Serbia, and Turkey, European Commission, 2020a). Another EU mechanism for responding to emergencies through which Poland and other EU Member States implement IDRL Guidelines is the *Emergency Response Coordination Centre* (ERCC). The ERCC coordinates assistance at the European level and ensures that it is efficient and effective (European Commission, 2020a). Additionally, Poland and other EU countries refer to the IDRL Guidelines through the implementation of the European Consensus on Humanitarian Aid (European Commission, 2019a) as well as the EU Host Nation Support Guidelines of 2012 (International Federation of Red Cross and Red Crescent Societies, 2012).

The main NATO mechanism serving the coordination of assistance to states affected by a natural disaster or catastrophe is the Euro-Atlantic Disaster Response Coordination Centre (EADRCC) (North Atlantic Treaty Organisation, 2020), which is responsible for administering the declared humanitarian aid, providing information, analysing experiences, organising seminars, and running field exercise and training for rescue services. The basis for cooperation between NATO and IGOs, NGOs, as well as civil authorities and local inhabitants in the case of natural disasters and catastrophes is Civil-Military Cooperation (CIMIC), an integral part of the NATO Host Nation Support (HNS)—Chapter 12 in the NATO Logistics Handbook (North Atlantic Treaty Organisation, 1997) October 1997. The assumptions related to the form of the HNS were adopted by the Polish Council of Ministers in 2001. HNS issues are discussed in the Regulation of the Council of Ministers of 15 June 2004 on the conditions and procedure of planning and financing the objectives pursued as part of the state defence preparations by government administration authorities and local government authorities (Regulation of the Council of Ministers, 2004) and in the documents of the General Staff of the Polish Armed Forces; in the Doctrine of support by the host state (DD/4.5) of 2005 and the Instruction Considerations, assumptions and procedures of pursuing support objectives by the host state (DD4.5.1A) of 2008.

2 Disaster Risk Reduction (DDR)—legal institutions and regulations

Nowadays, it is well accepted that the actions and decisions of individuals, communities, and nations make a significant difference as to whether or not a natural hazard turns into a disaster. Choices made with the aim of reducing the human impact of natural hazards can be described as Disaster Risk Reduction (DRR), in the broadest sense.

At the UN, actions have been undertaken to promote a global approach towards DRR, including the prevention of natural disasters, limitation of their consequences, and increasing the preparedness in case of their occurrence. In 1989, the UN established the International Day for Disaster Risk Reduction (13 October) to promote a global culture of risk-awareness and disaster reduction.

Another UN initiative in this field was the establishment in 1999 of the International Strategy for Disaster Reduction (UNISDR, the successor of the International Decade for Natural Disaster Reduction, IDNDR, declared by the UN for the decade 1990–1999) to promote actions aimed at reducing social vulnerability and the risks of natural hazards and related technological and environmental disasters, and the UN Office for Disaster Risk Reduction (UNDRR), which is its secretariat. In the framework of the UNISDR, governments have been requested to establish or strengthen national platforms, or focal points, for disaster reduction with a multisectoral and inter-disciplinary approach and the support of two international mechanisms: an Inter-Agency Secretariat in Geneva and an Inter-Agency Task Force on Disaster Reduction that represents 25 agencies and organisations from the UN, regional bodies, and civil society. Poland and other EU states cooperate with the UNISDR within the EU to reduce risk connected with natural disasters and catastrophes. The result, among others, is an increase in the number of cities developing suitable strategies in this field.[3]

In 2005, UNISDR compiled the Hyogo Framework for Action (HFA) 2005–2015: Building the Resilience of Nations and Communities to Disasters (International Strategy for Disaster Reduction, 2005). The HFA was a 10-year plan outlining the priorities and principles to enhance coordination among governments, organisations, and humanitarian actors in disaster prevention and response. The HFA was developed to accelerate the global work under the IDNDR of 1989, and the Yokohama Strategy for a Safer World: Guidelines for Natural Disaster Prevention, Preparedness and Mitigation and its Plan of Action, adopted in 1994, and the International Strategy for Disaster Reduction (ISDR) of 1999. The HFA aimed for a reduction in the number of victims of natural disasters by building the resilience of particular states, which were supposed to determine the course of action in case of a natural disaster. In these conditions, the Polish Act on crisis management did not stray significantly from the direction of actions in those days (Act of 26 April 2007, 2018). The successor instrument to the HFA, and simultaneously the newest initiative in terms of disaster reduction, is the Sendai Framework for Disaster Risk Reduction (SFDRR) for 2015–2030, which was adopted at the Third UN World Conference on Disaster Risk Reduction in Sendai, Japan, on 18 March 2015 (United Nations, 2015). The SFDRR, governed by the UNISDR, is the first global political framework of the UN programme designed for the post-2015 period constituting an element of a wider development programme and is reflected in the goals of the universal 2030 Agenda for Sustainable Development.[4] The EU played a leading role in the negotiations concerning the preparation of the SFDRR, and its many recommendations are based on existing EU policies and programmes in terms of risk management.

The main aim of the SFDRR is to achieve a substantial reduction in disaster risk and loss in life, livelihoods and health, and in the economic, physical, social, cultural, and environmental assets of persons, businesses, communities, and countries over the 15-year period. The SFDRR outlines four priority areas for action at all levels (local, national, regional and global) to lessen the risk of existing and future disasters[5]:

1 understanding disaster risk;
2 strengthening disaster risk governance to manage disaster risk;
3 investing in Disaster Risk Reduction for resilience; and,
4 enhancing disaster preparedness for an effective response, and to "Build Back Better" in recovery, rehabilitation and reconstruction.

Poland and other EU countries have been implementing the SFDRR within the EU through the Union Civil Protection Mechanism (UCPM). The first two priorities of the SFDRR—understanding the risk connected to disasters and the concept of disaster risk management fit well with the mechanism. The UCPM has imposed on the EU Member States the obligation to achieve in 2020 full risk-management capacity (Decision 2019/420/EU, 2019). Moreover, within the EU in 2016 a plan of action to implement the provisions of the Sendai Framework by the EU Member States was agreed (European Commission, 2016).

Poland is facing a few challenges connected with the implementation of the SFDRR, e.g., in the field of investment in disaster risk management—the third priority of the Sendai Framework assumes strengthening of efforts to build up the resistance of a state through investments, especially in critical infrastructure. In Poland, the Government Security Centre is the national contact point as far as the implementation of the SFDRR is concerned; one action that fits with these activities is the creation of a platform for the exchange of information about the national and international initiatives undertaken to reduce the risk of disasters. In the platform participate not only representatives of government administration and local authorities but also of science and research institutes, universities, NGOs, and the private sector. To implement the system of risk management in Poland, it was necessary to amend the Act on Crisis Management. The Council of Ministers adopted a draft amendment to the Act (Report of the Commission of Administration and Internal Affairs, 2020), under which critical infrastructure (of fundamental significance for society and the economy, such as ensuring electricity, fuel, food, and water) will be built at two levels—national and local. The Sendai Framework on actions for 2015–2030 concerning Disaster Risk Reduction will be implemented, as will the institution of a coordinator for all operators of critical infrastructure.

Along with the SFDRR priorities, there are a number of corresponding Polish projects in the field of natural disaster risk management, including:

- *Agricultural Drought Monitoring System* (ADMS)—a project led by the Polish Institute of Soil Science and Plant Cultivation (State Research Institute on behalf of the Polish Ministry of Agriculture and Rural Development), it corresponds to SFDRR Priority 1. The ADMS is designed to identify areas in Poland at the municipality level where there may be potential losses of crops due to drought conditions, and these are listed in the "Act on subsidies to insurance of agricultural crops and farm animals".[6]
- *IT System of the Country's Protection against Extreme Hazards* (ISOK). This is another project implemented in Poland that aims to contribute to the resolution or minimisation of several issues related to crisis resource management in Poland, with a particular focus on flood risks. These correspond to SFDRR Priorities 1 and 3. The main activities of the project are creating an inventory of available data resources, designing a systemic solution, compiling databases, drawing up risk and threat maps, and building and implementing a related IT system, and increasing public awareness of threats and crises. Achieving the project's goal should be assisted by the development of a flood hazard map, flood risk maps, maps of meteorological threats, maps of other hazards, and a map of Poland's hydrographic distribution.[7]
- *RescEU.* This the latest element introduced to the UCPM aimed at combating natural disasters. It establishes a new European reserve of resources, including airplanes, specialised water pumps, urban search-and-rescue facilities, field hospitals, and rescue teams. This corresponds to SFDRR Priority 4, although it only addresses preparedness for effective response and not the recovery phase. The force-reserves, designed to supplement domestic assets, are to be managed by the European Commission to support countries affected by disasters, including floods, forest fires, earthquakes, and epidemics. The long-term aim of the Polish project is to add further capacities and assets and build up a stronger *rescEU* reserve in Poland (European Commission, 2019b).
- *Urban Adaptation Plans* (UAP). This project, which includes 44 Polish cities, is intended to adapt those cities to both observed and predicted effects of climate change. Developed in cooperation with the Polish Ministry of the Environment, it covers about 30 per cent of the population of Poland. The project is designed to assess the vulnerability to climate change and plan adaptation activities to counter identified threats in cities with more than 100,000 residents. This corresponds to SFDRR Priorities 1 and 4. The project is the initiative in which the Ministry supports local authorities in coordinating activities adapting to the effects of climate change.[8]
- *Government Centre for Security Alert* (GCS Alert). Another programme in which Poland participates is the development of a population-based notification system, which is utilized when there is a high likelihood of life or health being threatened in a given area. The programme corresponds to SFDRR Priorities 2 and 4. A GCS Alert is generated based on information

about potential threats reported by ministries, emergency services (e.g., police, fire brigade, border guards), central offices, and relevant institutions (e.g., Institute of Meteorology and Water Management—National Research Institute or voivodeship offices) (Goniewicz and Burkle, 2019, p. 2574).

Moreover, on 4 June 2018, Poland joined—in the context of SFDRR—the UNISDR's Making Cities Resilient Campaign in Europe,[9] the primary aim of which is to raise awareness about Disaster Risk Reduction and gain commitments from local governments and political leaders. More than 4,300 cities have joined the campaign, demonstrating increased commitment to actions to ensure the safety and wellbeing of citizens from disasters and crises. As part of the project, the provincial government of Kujawsko-Pomorskie (in the north of Poland) has led the way, with 50 towns and cities having the opportunity to sign up to participate in the campaign, which has 3,800 members around the world. The city of Rypin and district of Powiat Tucholski in the region had already joined the campaign (UN Office for Disaster Risk Reduction, 2018).

3 UN response to COVID-19

Since the beginning of the pandemic, the UN, in its comprehensive response to COVID-19 has pursued a strategy based on three pillars:

- a large-scale, comprehensive health response guided by the World Health Organization (WHO) and the *Strategic Preparedness and Response Plan*. Within this response, the UN is supporting efforts to accelerate work towards a COVID-19 vaccine, diagnostics, and treatment, as well as establish international coordination and operational support at the global, regional and country levels in terms of preparedness and response to the pandemic.
- a wide-ranging effort to address the devastating socioeconomic, humanitarian, and human-rights aspects of the crisis with a focus on saving lives and the social, political, and economic impacts of the pandemic. This includes the immediate humanitarian response to support the most vulnerable people in the most vulnerable countries within the *Global Humanitarian Response Plan*.
- a recovery process, simultaneously addressing the climate crisis, inequalities, exclusion, gaps in social protection systems and the many other fragilities and injustices that have been exposed, referring to the 2030 Sustainable Development Agenda as a guide.

The UN is seeking funding through three main plans:

- *Strategic Preparedness and Response Plan* aimed at addressing immediate health needs (the required funding of the plan is $1.74 billion of which

$1.022 billion (59 per cent) was received or pledged as of 24 June 2020). The plan was produced by WHO and partners and is being financed through government budgets, the UN Central Emergency Response Fund (CERF) and WHO's *Solidarity Response Fund*, which is open to corporations and individuals (World Trade Organisation, 2020a, 2020b);

- *Global Humanitarian Response Plan* to ease the impacts in over 63 highly vulnerable countries (the required funding is $7.32 billion of which $1.44 billion (19.7 per cent) was received or pledged). The plan (regularly updated) is being coordinated by the OCHA with over 60 IASC partners, including WFP, FAO, WHO, IOM, UNDP, UNFPA, UN-Habitat, UNHCR and UNICEF, as well as the International Red Cross and Red Crescent Movement and NGOs (UN Office for the Coordination of Humanitarian Affairs, 2020);
- UN Framework for the immediate socio-economic response, which guides the actions to deliver rapid response and recovery in middle- and lower-income countries ($1 billion is required for the first 9 months of the response of which $ 49 million (5 per cent) was secured) (United Nations, 2020a).

The delivery of the response to COVID-19 within the UN system is mainly organisational in character. It is supported by different decision-makers (governments, partners and communities) whose supply chains, assets, expertise, and capacities are in use around the world. The entire UN system has been mobilised within the WHO-led health response to distribute medical supplies, train health workers, build testing and tracing capacities, prevent the spread of the virus, and support national response-planning and decision-making. Moreover, the Secretary-General is coordinating with world leaders on critical issues related to the pandemic, such as cooperation towards a vaccine, interim financing of economies, and debt relief. Peacekeeping missions are applying different mitigation measures to continue protecting vulnerable communities.

Humanitarian agencies, in turn, already support more than 100 million people around the world by providing life-saving help while also supporting the wider UN system's response to the pandemic (United Nations, 2020b).

Moreover, guided by the UN Framework for immediate socioeconomic response to COVID-19, the UN Country Teams (UNCT) have developed the socio-economic response plans that provide countries with their collective assistance in five main areas: health services, social protection, job, fiscal and financial stimulus, social cohesion, and community resilience. The UNCT are also supporting governments in the development of national response plans, 69 of which have been already finalized, and another 50 of which are being implemented (United Nations, 2020b).

Finally, the UN agencies are supporting governments and partners with recommendations and guidance on public health measures, aviation, shipping, tourism and many other areas impacted by the pandemic.

4 Poland's response to COVID-19

Cooperation within the EU

The EU and its Member States, acting together as "Team Europe",[10] are taking comprehensive and decisive actions to mitigate the destructive impact of COVID-19. The EU is adapting its priorities and programmes with partner countries to address the crisis. To support the COVID-19 response, the EU Member States cooperate in terms of:

- providing immediate support to the Response Plans of international organisations, including immediate humanitarian support in affected countries, in particular in the provision of healthcare, water, sanitation and hygiene, and logistics;
- increasing production in Europe of personal protective equipment (PPE) and medical devices to meet urgent needs in Europe and its partner countries;
- organising the supply of in-kind assistance to affected countries through the UCPM (European Commission, 2020b);
- providing guarantee and liquidity provisions to local banks via IFIs and European Development Finance Institutions, supported by the European Fund for Sustainable Development (European Commission, 2020c);
- supporting global efforts to ensure a sufficient supply of essential goods, food, and water, and enacting measures to combat export restrictions and ensure supply chains remain unaffected, especially those involving medical supplies and pharmaceuticals (European Commission, 2020d).

While the EU remains Poland's most important partner during the pandemic, the Polish government has continually demanded assistance from the EU, claiming that the Union is not doing enough to support the Member States. From the beginning of March 2020, Prime Minister Mateusz Morawiecki and Minister of Health Łukasz Szumowski have publicly criticised the EU for what they call a lack of European solidarity and indicated that Poland does not receive any material or financial support from the EU.[11] However, in several situations, Poland, at its own request, resigned from participation in European support mechanisms. For example, Poland was not a member of the EU Permanent Working Group of the Health Security Committee on Preparedness and Response Planning, which deals with the preparation of responses to health threats. This group has been developing an action strategy since January 2020, including planned, joint purchases of medical equipment. Eventually, Poland joined the joint procurement mechanism at the beginning of March, but after the tender for masks and gowns had already been set, so the country had to purchase this equipment independently, without discounts negotiated by the EU.

From the end of March, the Polish government began to actively cooperate with Brussels for EU funds. One element of this support is the Recovery Fund, which is intended to boost European economies after the pandemic passes (the fund is estimated at a total of EUR 2 trillion over 7 years) (see more: Chapter 5). Moreover, Poland has benefited from the financial support (the country received EUR 1 bn) under the European instrument for Temporary Support to Mitigate Unemployment Risks in an Emergency (SURE). The SURE instrument can provide the Member States with up to EUR 100 billion loans for salaries for employees who would normally be dismissed or worked on a smaller scale (European Commission, 2020e).

Support for EU Member States and non-EU countries

Poland has directly supported several EU countries faced with the pandemic, as well as other countries around the world. Poland has offered help via Polish doctors to areas heavily affected by the virus, including a group of healthcare workers and rescuers sent to Brescia on 30 March 2020 to support the Italian health service during the outbreak of COVID-19 in Lombardy (Italy), then considered an epicentre of the disease. In April, as part of the WHO mission, Polish doctors supported medical services in Kyrgyzstan and Slovenia, and in Tajikistan in June.

Additionally, Poland provided in-kind assistance to EU countries, such as a transport in April consisting of 20,000 litres of disinfectant produced by the Polish state-owned company *Polfa Tarchomin S.A.*, which was sent to Veneto in northern Italy and to the hospital in San Marino. Similar assistance was organised for Spain, amid its first wave of the coronavirus outbreak. On 16 April, an additional 20,000 litres of disinfectant were transported from Poland to Spain through the NATO Euro-Atlantic Disaster Response Coordination Centre (EADRCC).

Poland also sent large numbers of medical supplies to non-EU countries, including Armenia, Azerbaijan, Albania, Bosnia and Herzegovina, Belarus, Montenegro, Georgia, Jordan, Kazakhstan, Kosovo, Lithuania, North Macedonia, Moldova, Serbia, Ukraine, and The Vatican. Polish missions received additional funds (over ca. EUR 250 million) to support the fight against the coronavirus pandemic in Ukraine and Belarus (Ministry of Foreign Affairs Republic of Poland, 2020). On 23 April, a convoy with medical supplies under the banner of the Solidarity Foundation set off from Warsaw to the Republican Medical Response Centre in Minsk, Belarus.

In addition, Poland has been cooperating with the US on pandemic response. On April 18, presidents Andrzej Duda and Donald Trump discussed Polish–American cooperation and NATO's involvement in the fight against coronavirus, as well as medical cooperation. The presidents agreed on cooperation between their respective research institutes on vaccine and coronavirus research; however, these were exclusively political acts, and were not followed by either any agreements or specific actions. In the framework of medical cooperation, the presidents agreed to a Polish medical mission to Chicago, where one of the largest outbreaks in the US was occurring, to supplement the local health service and undergo practice in the treatment of patients infected with coronavirus.[12]

At the European Commission's coronavirus vaccine fundraising conference, Poland pledged EUR 750,000 for the development of a coronavirus vaccine and treatments. The same amount was pledged by the other states of the Visegrád Group (V4)—Czechia, Slovakia, and Hungary (all together, the V4 will provide a total of EUR 3 million). Major financial support was pledged by other European states: Germany (EUR 552 million), France (EUR 500 million), the UK (EUR 441.5 million), Switzerland (EUR 378 million), the Netherlands (EUR 192 million), Italy (EUR 140 million), and Spain (EUR 125 million).

Poland also supports multilateral mechanisms fighting the impact of the pandemic. It contributed about EUR 250,000 to the Central Emergency Response Fund of the UN Office for the Coordination of Humanitarian Affairs and the same amount to UNICEF actions in Palestine. Poland donated about EUR 100,000 for UNDP Belarus to carry out the project Preventing Non-communicable Diseases, Promoting Healthy Lifestyle and Support for Modernisation of the Health System in Belarus (BELMED). In addition, Poland made its annual contribution of about EUR 250,000 to UNRWA, the UN Relief and Works Agency for Palestine Refugees, and about EUR 500,000 to the UN High Commissioner for Refugees Fund to support Yemen and Syria. Poland contributed more than EUR 100,000 in total to the COVID-19 Preparedness and Response Plan fund run by UNICEF Ethiopia. It supported World Food Programme actions in Kenya to fight COVID-19 with a contribution of more than EUR 120,000 (Ministry of Foreign Affairs Republic of Poland, 2020).

Conclusions

Natural, as well as man-made, disasters are relatively commonplace and pose significant challenges and direct threats to people in affected states. Despite the prevalence of these events, the issue of international prevention and response to disasters is not addressed in an explicit and orderly way with universal and regional cooperation. There is no universal, specialised body of international law that can be applied to disaster prevention, response, and recovery. Disasters have no legally binding set of regulations to govern the actions of those involved in assistance and recovery and international disaster response is primarily governed by domestic legislation, as well as bilateral (even rarer, multilateral) agreements as well as, obviously, by international custom (based on humanitarian sentiment).

Faced with the lack of a coherent universal system, a "patchwork" of international institutions and mechanisms has emerged to deal with natural disasters and catastrophes. However, the actions are often duplicated, thus wasting resources, or leaving a vacuum in other areas.

Poland has been engaged in international cooperation in terms of disaster prevention and response by undertaking actions individually and within the EU and NATO. Poland has been implementing policies and programmes in terms of disaster protection and response. However, the Polish government remains oriented mainly toward emergency response (other phases of the disaster cycle, i.e., prevention, preparedness, recovery and rehabilitation, have rather been pushed to the background). Additionally, Poland has not fully embraced the SFDRR goals in the field of investment in disaster risk management—the country has yet to develop a risk-management plan at the national level that includes designations of areas of disaster risk and determines the current administrative and organisational capacity, as well as available technical and financial resources to accomplish this.

In the face of COVID-19, Poland is trying to maintain European solidarity and support for international cooperation. Its effect is material and human assistance for regions most affected by the pandemic. Poland has been playing an active role in helping mainly the Eastern Partnership countries and selected other European states to fight the COVID-19 pandemic. Poland has sent Polish doctors abroad to treat patients and offered in-kind assistance.

Nevertheless, in reality, it is difficult to assess the participation of particular EU Member States in international institutions and mechanisms of disaster prevention and response because the EU itself is the participating institution in global efforts to respond to natural disasters and catastrophes of supranational reach.

Notes

1 According to the report of the IFRC, in the last decade (2008–2017), more than 3,700 natural hazards were recorded, 2 billion individuals were affected by such events, around 700,000 people lost their lives as a result of disasters, and damage is estimated at $1.65 trillion. Such data do not include technological (man-made) hazards, armed conflict, or conflict-related famine; see: International Federation of Red Cross and Red Crescent Societies (2018, p. 168).

2 According to Decision 1313/2013/EU, one of the main purposes of the EU Civil Protection Mechanism is to protect people against all types of disasters, including acute health emergencies, occurring both inside and outside of the Union. This mechanism allows a Member State or third country to request assistance through the Emergency Response Coordination Centre (ERCC), which is part of the European Commission's Humanitarian Aid and Civil Protection department (ECHO). When a disaster occurs outside the EU, the United Nations, its agencies, or any relevant international organisation may also request assistance. EU Member States are not the sole contributors to the mechanism—it is also open to certain third countries. The mechanism has been widely activated in the context of the COVID-19 pandemic to support EU Member States as well as other countries (De Pooter, 2020).

3 https://samorzad.pap.pl/kategoria/komitet-regionow/pokonac-zywiol-onz-i-kr-chca-zmniejszyc-ryzyko-zwiazane-z-kleskami.

4 https://sustainabledevelopment.un.org/post2015/transformingourworld.

5 https://www.preventionweb.net/files/43291_sendaiframeworkfordrren.pdf.

6 http://www.susza.iung.pulawy.pl/en/.

7 https://isok.gov.pl/index.html.

8 http://44mpa.pl/urban-adaptation-plans/?lang=en.

9 Although, the Campaign is due to end in 2020, the Making Cities Resilient 2030 (MCR2030) will launch at the end of the year with the following main strategic

objectives: increase cities' understanding of risk and gain commitments to Disaster Risk Reduction and resilience; increasing cities' capacities to plan for risk reduction and resilience; increase cities' capacities to implement resilience actions and reduce risks; increasing vertical links with national governments and horizontal links amongst local partners to mainstream resilience across and between partners, functions and services, and foster city-to-city partnerships and sharing of experience (UN Office for Disaster Risk Reduction, 2020).

10 The support of the EU under "Team Europe" includes: responding to the immediate health crisis and the resulting humanitarian needs; strengthening health, water and sanitation systems, as well as partner countries' capacities and preparedness to deal with the pandemic; mitigating the immediate social and economic consequences, including support for the private sector with a focus on small and medium-sized enterprises (SMEs), and government reforms to reduce poverty (see: https://eeas.europa.eu/headquarters/headquarters-homepage/76341/coronavirus-latest-news-eu-actions-repatriation-efforts-and-solidarity-stories-around-world_en).

11 See: Pankowska (2020); Polska Times (2020); Gazeta.pl (2020); Rosati and Wiśniewski (2020).

12 https://china-cee.eu/2020/05/07/poland-external-relations-briefing-foreign-policy-and-the-fight-against-coronavirus.

Bibliography

Act of 26 April 2007 (2018) *Dziennik Ustaw*, Dz.U.2018.1401.

Aspects of Humanitarian and Development Assistance in 2015–2018 (2019) Print No 3405 of 11 April 2019. Available at http://orka.sejm.gov.pl/Druki8ka.nsf/0/2D8E44727C88E407C12583E70033FB79/%24File/3405.pdf (accessed: 23. 11. 20).

Caron, D. (2014) Preface, in Caron, D., Kelly, M. and Telesetsky, A. (eds), *The International Law of Disaster Relief.* Cambridge: Cambridge University Press.

Caron, D., Kelly, M. and Telesetsky, A. (eds) (2014) *The International Law of Disaster Relief.* Cambridge: Cambridge University Press.

De Guttry, A. (2012) Surveying the Law, in De Guttry, A., Gestri, M. and Venturini, G. (eds), *International Disaster Response Law.* Berlin: Springer.

De Pooter, H. (2020) The Civil Protection Mechanism of the European Union: A Solidarity Tool at the Test by the COVID-19 Pandemic, *American Society of International Law*, 24(7).

Decision 2019/420/EU of the European Parliament and of the Council of 13 March 2019 amending Decision 1313/2013/EU on a Union Civil Protection Mechanism (2019) *Official Journal of the European Union*, 20. 03. 2019, LI 77/1.

Eburn, M. (2010) International Law and Disaster Response, *Monash University Law Review*, 36 (3).

European Commission (2016) European Commission Launches Sendai Action Plan for Disaster Risk Reduction, 16 June. Available at https://ec.europa.eu/echo/news/european-commission-launches-sendai-action-plan-disaster-risk-reduction_en (accessed: 23. 11. 20).

European Commission (2019a) European Consensus on Humanitarian Aid. Available at http://ec.europa.eu/echo/policies/consensus_en.htm (accessed: 23. 11. 20).

European Commission (2019b) RescEU. Available at https://ec.europa.eu/echo/what/civil-protection/resceu_en (accessed: 23. 11. 20).

European Commission (2020a) EU Civil Protection Mechanism. Available at https://ec.europa.eu/echo/what/civil-protection/mechanism_en (accessed: 23. 11. 20).

European Commission (2020b) Emergency Response Coordination Centre (ERCC). Available at https://ec.europa.eu/echo/what/civil-protection/emergency-response-coordination-centre-ercc_en (accessed: 23. 11. 20).

European Commission (2020c) EU External Investment Plan. Available at https://ec.europa.eu/eu-external-investment-plan/about-plan/how-it-works-finance_en (accessed: 23. 11. 20).

European Commission (2020d) EU Global Response to COVID-19. Available at https://ec.europa.eu/international-partnerships/topics/eu-global-response-covid-19_en (accessed: 23. 11. 20).

European Commission (2020e) The European Instrument for Temporary Support to Mitigate SURE Unemployment Risks in an Emergency (SURE). Available at https://ec.europa.eu/info/business-economy-euro/economic-and-fiscal-policy-coordination/financial-assistance-eu/funding-mechanisms-and-facilities/sure_en (accessed: 23. 11. 20).

European Consensus on Humanitarian Aid (2008) Dziennik Urzędowy Unii Europejskiej, 2008/C 25/01.

Fisher, D. (2007) Domestic Regulation of International Humanitarian Relief in Disasters and Armed Conflict: A Comparative Analysis, *International Review of the Red Cross*, 89 (866), pp. 345–372.

Gazeta.pl (2020) Mateusz Morawiecki manipulował w Sejmie. "Unia Europejska nie dała eurocenta na walkę z koronawirusem" [Mateusz Morawiecki manipulated in Sejm. The European Union gave no single euro cent for the fight against the coronavirus"], 27. 03. 2020. Available at https://wiadomosci.gazeta.pl/wiadomosci/7,173952,25825335,mateusz-morawiecki-w-sejmie-unia-europejska-nie-dala-eurocenta.html (accessed: 23. 11. 20).

Goniewicz K. and Burkle, F.Jr. (2019) Challenges in Implementing Sendai Framework for Disaster Risk Reduction in Poland, *International Journal of Environment Research and Public Health*, 16(14).

http://44mpa.pl/urban-adaptation-plans/?lang=en (accessed: 23. 11. 20). http://www.susza.iung.pulawy.pl/en/ (accessed: 23. 11. 20).

https://china-cee.eu/2020/05/07/poland-external-relations-briefing-foreign-policy-and-the-fight-against-coronavirus (accessed: 23. 11. 20).

https://eeas.europa.eu/headquarters/headquarters-homepage/76341/coronavirus-latest-news-eu-actions-repatriation-efforts-and-solidarity-stories-around-world_en (accessed: 23. 11. 20).

https://isok.gov.pl/index.html (accessed: 23. 11. 20).

https://samorzad.pap.pl/kategoria/komitet-regionow/pokonac-zywiol-onz-i-kr-chca-zmniejszyc-ryzyko-zwiazane-z-kleskami (accessed: 23. 11. 20).

https://sustainabledevelopment.un.org/post2015/transformingourworld (accessed: 23. 11. 20).

https://www.preventionweb.net/files/43291_sendaiframeworkfordrren.pdf (accessed: 23. 11. 20).

International Federation of Red Cross and Red Crescent Societies (2007) Annotations to the Draft Guidelines for the Domestic Facilitation and Regulation of International Disaster and Initial Recovery Assistance, 26 October. Available at https://www.ifrc.org/PageFiles/125652/annotations.pdf (accessed: 23. 11. 20).

International Federation of Red Cross and Red Crescent Societies (2011) Introduction to the Guidelines for the Domestic Facilitation and Regulation of International Disaster and Initial Recovery Assistance, Geneva. Available at https://www.ifrc.org/

PageFiles/125652/1205600-IDRL%20Guidelines-EN-LR%20(2).pdf (accessed: 23. 11. 20).

International Federation of Red Cross and Red Crescent Societies (2012) The EU Approves New Host Nation Support Guidelines, 27 February. Available at www.ifrc.org/en/what-we-do/idrl/latest-news/disaster-law-newsletter-february-2012/host-nation-support-guidelines-approved-by-eu (accessed: 23. 11. 20).

International Federation of Red Cross and Red Crescent Societies (2018) World Disasters Report 2018: Leaving No One Behind, Geneva. Available at https://media.ifrc.org/ifrc/world-disaster-report-2018/ (accessed: 23. 11. 20).

International Strategy for Disaster Reduction (2005) Hyogo Framework for Action (HFA) 2005–2015: Building the Resilience of Nations and Communities to Disasters. Available at https://www.unisdr.org/files/1037_hyogoframeworkforactionenglish.pdf (accessed: 23. 11. 20).

MacAlister-Smith, P. (1986) The International Relief Union: Reflections on Establishing an International Relief Union of July 12, 1927, *Legal History Review*, 54, pp. 368–372.

Ministry of Foreign Affairs Republic of Poland (2020) Poland Shows Solidarity During COVID-19 Pandemic, 27 July 2020. Available at https://www.gov.pl/web/diplomacy/poland-shows-solidarity-during-covid-19-pandemic (accessed: 23. 11. 20).

North Atlantic Treaty Organisation (1997) *NATO Logistics Handbook*, Brussels, October 1997. Available at https://www.nato.int/docu/logi-en/logist97.htm (accessed: 23. 11. 20).

North Atlantic Treaty Organisation (2020) Euro-Atlantic Disaster Response Coordination Centre (EADRCC). Available at https://www.nato.int/cps/en/natohq/topics_52057.htm? (accessed: 23. 11. 20).

Organization of American States (1991) Inter-American Convention to Facilitate Disaster Assistance. Available at www.oas.org/juridico/english/sigs/a-54.html (accessed: 23. 11. 20).

Pankowska, M. (2020) Szumowski krytykuje UE: "Nie ma tej europejskiej solidarności". To wielopiętrowy fałsz [Szumowki is criticizing the EU: "There is no European solidarity". This is a multistoried falsehood], OKO.press, 26 March. Available at https://oko.press/szumowski-krytykuje-ue-nie-ma-tej-europejskiej-solidarnosci-to-wielopietrowy-falsz (accessed: 23. 11. 20).

Polska Times (2020) Polski rząd mówi jedno, a Unia Europejska robi drugie. Ogromna pomoc płynie do Polski z UE [The Polish government says one thing, and the EU does another. Enormous assistance is flowing to Poland from the EU], 26. 05. 2020. Available at https://polskatimes.pl/polski-rzad-mowi-jedno-a-unia-europejska-robi-drugie-ogromna-pomoc-plynie-do-polski-z-ue/ar/c1-14991273 (accessed: 23. 11. 20).

Regulation of the Council of Ministers of 15 June 2004 (2004) *Dziennik Ustaw*, No 152, Item 1599.

Report of the Commission of Administration and Internal Affairs on the Governmental Draft of the Act on Crisis Management and Some Other Acts (Print no 203) (2020) Print No 405. Available at http://orka.sejm.gov.pl/Druki9ka.nsf/0/EB479F3882335925C125857E003A53A2/%24File/405.pdf (accessed: 23. 11. 20).

Rosati, D. and Wiśniewski, P. D. (2020) Co nam, Unio, dasz w ten niepewny czas? [What will you, the Union, give us during this uncertain time?], Rzeczpospolita, 20. 04. 2020. Available at https://www.rp.pl/Opinie/304209897-Co-nam-Unio-dasz-w-ten-niepewny-czas.html (accessed: 23. 11. 20).

UN Office for Disaster Risk Reduction (2018) Poland Joins Resilient Cities Campaign, 4 June. Available at https://www.undrr.org/news/poland-joins-resilient-cities-campaign (accessed: 23. 11. 20).

UN Office for Disaster Risk Reduction (2020) Making Cities Resilient 2030 (MCR2030) – Initial Proposal. Available at https://www.unisdr.org/campaign/resilientcities/home/article/making-cities-resilient-2030-mcr2030-initial-proposal (accessed: 23. 11. 20).

UN Office for the Coordination of Humanitarian Affairs (2020) Global Humanitarian Response Plan COVID-19, April-December. Available at https://www.unocha.org/sites/unocha/files/Global-Humanitarian-Response-Plan-COVID-19.pdf (accessed: 23. 11. 20).

United Nations (1984) Draft Convention on Expediting the Delivery of Emergency Assistance, UN Doc. A/39/267/Add.2–E/1984/96/Add.2, 18 June 1984.

United Nations (2015) Sendai Framework for Disaster Risk Reduction 2015–2030. Available at https://www.preventionweb.net/files/43291_sendaiframeworkfordrren.pdf (accessed: 23. 11. 20).

United Nations (2020a) United Nations Comprehensive Response to COVID-19; Saving Lives, Protecting Societies, Recovering Better, June 2020. Available at https://www.un.org/sites/un2.un.org/files/un_comprehensive_response_to_covid-19_june_2020.pdf (accessed: 23. 11. 20).

United Nations (2020b) United Nations Comprehensive Response to COVID-19; Saving Lives, Protecting Societies, Recovering Better, September 2020. Available at https://www.un.org/other/afics/sites/www.un.org.other.afics/files/sg-pdf-20200916-un_comprehensive_response_to_covid-16_sep_2020_002_0.pdf (accessed: 23. 11. 20).

World Trade Organisation (2020a) COVID-19 Solidarity Response Fund. Available at https://www.who.int/emergencies/diseases/novel-coronavirus-2019/donate (accessed: 23. 11. 20).

World Trade Organisation (2020b) Strategic Preparedness and Response Plan, 4 February. Available at https://www.who.int/publications/i/item/strategic-preparedness-and-response-plan-for-the-new-coronavirus (accessed: 23. 11. 20).

4 Poland and EU cooperation—mechanism of joint public procurement (COVID-19)

Łukasz Dawid Dąbrowski

Introduction

The outbreak in 2009 of the H1N1 influenza pandemic highlighted weaknesses in the access and purchasing power of European Union (EU) countries to obtain related vaccines and medications (European Commission, 2015, p. 1). In an effort to prevent the risks arising from infectious diseases, Decision No 1082/2013/EU of the European Parliament and of the Council of 22 October 2013 on serious cross-border threats to health and repealing Decision No. 2119/98/EC (2013, pp. 1–15) was adopted. Article 5 of the Decision allowing the European Commission (10 April 2014) to accept the Joint Procurement Agreement to procure medical countermeasures (JPA) extended the previous approach beyond vaccines and antivirals against an influenza pandemic. JPA defines the principles of the mechanism's functioning and the decision-making process as to the selection of bidding procedures, offer evaluations, and requesting procurements. This agreement was concluded between the European Commission and Member States that agreed to participate in the mechanism. The emergence of the COVID-19 pandemic and the pressing need for pharmaceuticals, medical devices, and other healthcare supplies at fair prices, along with ensuring that access to drugs and vaccines will be reasonable and properly balanced, has triggered the need to focus on the public procurement system at both the EU and national levels.

The object of this study was actions taken by the Polish government regarding joint public procurement of preventive medical equipment and parallel actions supplemented or complemented by the mechanism (JPA). The aim of the study was to answer the question, whether the changes in Polish public procurement law as well as in policy regarding cooperation on acquiring protective and medical equipment from individual cases to actions within the framework of multilateral cooperation is appropriate and efficient from a legal standpoint. Thus, the chapter attempts to answer a few partial questions: how was the mechanism constructed with respect to legal regulations? Do the criteria applied to the division of procurement measures ensure the protection of Polish interests in equal measure to the interests of the other states participating in the mechanism? Which actions undertaken by Poland are complementary or

DOI: 10.4324/9781003144434-5

parallel to the mechanism? Are the measures that were taken in accordance with European public procurement principles? And finally, is the cooperation within the framework of the mechanism able to entirely substitute Poland's previous individual response to COVID-19?

1 Joint Procurement Agreement and actions taken on the EU level

The joint public procurement mechanism (JPP) was included in Article 5 of Decision No. 1082/2013/EU. The legal basis for those regulations was Article 168(5) of the Treaty on the Functioning of the European Union (2012, pp. 47–390), which provides for the European Council to adopt incentive measures designed to protect and improve human health and in particular to combat major cross-border health scourges (European Commission, 2014a). Article 5 of the Decision provides that the institutions of the EU and any Member States that so desire may engage in a joint procurement procedure (JPP) with a view to the advance purchase of medical countermeasures for serious cross-border threats to health. The JPP are subject to four conditions: 1) participation is open to all Member States, until the launch of the procedure; 2) the rights and obligations of States not participating in it should be respected, in particular those relating to the protection and improvement of human health; 3) the JPP does not affect the internal market; 4) it does not have any direct financial impact on the budget of States not participating in the mechanism.

The JPP is preceded by a Joint Procurement Agreement to Procure Medical Countermeasures (JPA) between the parties determining the practical arrangements governing that procedure, and the decision-making process with regard to the choice of the procedure, the assessment of the tenders, and the award of the contract. The JPA was signed by the European Commission on 10 April 2014 and was also signed by the majority of EU States (European Commission, 2015, p. 9). By the end of 2019, 24 countries had signed the JPA. Then, COVID-19 reached Europe in early 2020. On 6 March 2020, Poland signed up to the JPA. Poland was the next-to-last EU state acceding to the JPA. The agreement is now signed by all EU countries and covers 100 per cent of the Union's population.

States participating in the JPA made the decision about which medical countermeasures they would like to pursue in a specific procurement procedure for different categories of threats[1] unless the countermeasures can be considered a cross-border threat in the meaning of Article 3 (g) of Decision 1082/2013/EU.[2] When conducting the JPP, the European Commission has a coordinating role, which means that the Commission acts on behalf of all parties while the state parties purchase the goods. The JPP is based on actions by special committees. The JPA distinguishes two Steering Committees: a Joint Procurement Agreement Steering Committee (JPASC[3]) and one or more Specific Procurement Procedure Steering Committee (SPPSC[4]), and additionally evaluation committees, which are appointed to evaluate requests to participate, or tenders and opening committees, which are called to open requests to participate and tenders (European Commission, 2014a). SPPSC approves allocation criteria such as the frequency with which available medical countermeasures will be distributed among the participating countries. Participants in the tender receive all the reserved or ordered medical supplies. However, the delivery time depends on the contractor's capacity and generally applicable allocation criteria. At the same time, in case of legitimate reasons, such as problems encountered during delivery or due to urgent needs, it is possible to deviate from the generally applicable allocation criteria. Additionally, a derogation needs mutual approval of the SPPSC.[5]

The implementation of the arrangements negotiated and concluded in the framework contracts is carried out by means of specific contracts concluded between the individual parties participating in the tender and the contractors who are parties to the framework contracts. The parties to the framework contracts may conclude specific contracts up to the maximum number of medical countermeasures they have reserved within the framework contract. The contracting parties signing specific contracts are responsible for the performance of these contracts. JPA also provides for the possibility of redistribution (transfer) of ordered or purchased medical supplies through reallocation of reserved quantities, redirection of orders, resale of deliveries, or donation of medical countermeasures if it turns out that a country has a surplus of ordered or delivered medical countermeasures. So far, none of the countries, including Poland, has used any of the above possibilities.

Under the JPA, the Commission launched five different calls for tenders for medical equipment and supplies. First, on 28 February 2020, it called for medical gloves and gowns, and 20 countries participated, ordering several million gowns. A second tender, on 17 March 2020, for personal protective equipment (PPE) for eye and respiratory protection, in which 25 countries participated, 20 million goggles, 12 million face shields, and almost 400 million masks were ordered. The third tender, on 17 March 2020, requested medical ventilators and respiratory equipment, in which 26 countries participated, ordering 110,000. The fourth tender, on 19 March 2020, was for laboratory equipment, including testing kits, in which 20 countries participated, ordering 30 different lots. The last one, on 17 June 2020, covered intensive care medicine, in which up to 26 countries participated. Framework contracts following the first four JPP have been signed and states can place orders for ordered equipment. An evaluation of the JPA on intensive care medicine is ongoing.[6] A JPP for eye protection and respiratory protection equipment issued on 12 March 2020 failed.[7]

Poland did not take part in the tender for masks, gloves, safety glasses, surgical masks, and gowns because it had joined the JPA on 6 March 2020 (two days after the first case of coronavirus infection was detected in Poland). Although according to Article 49(3) of the JPA and Article 5(2)a of the Directive, after the launch of a JPP a country cannot participate in ongoing procurement procedures, on 24 March 2020, former European Council

President Donald Tusk appealed to the European Commission to allow equipment from the first tender to also go to countries that had not participated in it. It first went to Italy and Spain even though the latter wasn't on the list of countries that would have received medical masks through this instrument as it hadn't indicated its "interest in participating" in this JPP.

On 28 July 2020, the Commission signed a contract with a pharmaceutical company (Gilead) to secure treatment doses of the first medicine authorised at the EU level to treat COVID-19. Under this agreement, the medicine will be available to EU members as coordinated by the Commission. The Commission is now also preparing a JPP for further supplies of the medicine, expected to cover additional needs and supplies as of October 2020.[8] Additionally the European Commission is in negotiations with a number of pharmaceutical companies to purchase potential coronavirus vaccines. When a vaccine is proven safe, the Commission has agreed to purchase millions of doses on behalf of the Member States. The Polish Council of Ministers on 10 August 2020 adopted a resolution to participate in the early purchase of COVID-19 vaccines.[9]

2 Complementary (parallel) actions taken on the national level

On 1 April 2020, the European Commission published guidance on using the public procurement framework in the emergency situation related to the COVID-19 crisis ("Guidelines"). The Guidelines indicate how to use all the flexibility offered by the EU public procurement framework[10] in the pandemic emergency situation.[11] The Guidelines prioritise, in cases of urgency, the possibility to move up deadlines to accelerate open or restricted procedures.[12] Only in cases of extreme urgency, as a second option, can public buyers lead a procedure without publication and even allow a direct award to a preselected economic operator.[13] Contrary to the Guidelines, the Polish legislator decided to prioritise the non-application of Public Procurement Law (PPL) (Sołtysińska, 2020, p. 48). The Act of 2 March 2020 on special solutions related to preventing, counteracting, and combating COVID-19, other infectious diseases and crises caused by them (2020; so-called "Anti-crisis shield 1.0") introduced a regulation allowing the possibility of not applying PPL (Act of 29 January 2004, 2019) to contracts for "goods or services" necessary to counteract COVID-19. This possibility is permitted if there is a high probability of rapid and uncontrolled spread of the disease or if the protection of public health so requires (Article 6). The Act does not limit the application of regulations to entities operating in the area of health protection (e.g., hospitals) but can be applied to all those obliged to follow PPL (local government units or employers who purchase PPE for their employees) (Kittel and Kittel, 2020, pp. 30–35). To use the exemption from the application of PPL, the contracting authority must verify whether there is a high probability of rapid and uncontrolled spread of the disease. This condition may be considered fulfilled because the Minister of Health on 13 March 2020 announced the "state of epidemic emergency" in connection with the risk of occurrence of COVID-19 in order to take preventive actions (Ordinance of the Minister of Health of 13 March, 2020). The introduction of an indefinite state of epidemic risk and the related lockdown in many areas of state operation can undoubtedly be considered an exceptional situation not resulting from reasons attributable to the ordering party (Mazurek, 2020, pp. 8–13). Additionally, it is necessary to determine whether specific action is required for the protection of public health. The application of the provision is *ad hoc* and cannot be used to bypass the use of PPL (Wiktorowska, 2020). On 1 April 2020, the "Anti-crisis shield 1.0" came into force.

The Act of 31 March 2020 amending the "Anti-crisis shield 1.0" (Act of 31 March, 2020a; the so-called "special act") has given new wording. The term "goods or services" was replaced by "services or supplies". The exemption from the application of PPL cannot cover works contracts if they are the main subject of the contract (Jerka, 2020, pp. 18–25). An exemption from the PPL regime was also added for specific entities: Bank Gospodarstwa Krajowego, Polish Development Fund, and regional development funds (Article 6(2)) when undertaking actions related to the execution of the bank's entity contracts that concern support instruments necessary to counteract the negative economic effects of COVID-19 (Potemska, 2020). The regulations on PPL do not apply to orders for services or supplies granted by the Social Insurance Institution (ZUS) in connection with the performance of tasks related to the determination of rights or payment of compensation for loss of income from business activity (Article 15zza; see Falkowska, 2020). Simultaneously, a separate Act adopted on the same day as the "special act" (31 March 2020) on the amendment of certain acts regarding the health care system related to the prevention, counteracting and combating of COVID-19 (2020b) also introduced some changes to the "Anti-crisis shield 1.0". When public procurements aimed at making an investment consisting of the creation of a new therapeutic entity on the territory of a province whose activity consists of providing health services, the obligation to obtain an opinion on the advisability of such an investment issued by the voivode or the minister in charge of health was excluded (Article 6(3)).

The Act of 19 June 2020 on subsidisation of interest on bank loans granted to entities affected by COVID-19 and simplified arrangement approval proceedings due to COVID-19 (2020; Article 77(6), the so-called "Anti-crisis shield 4.0") made further changes to the "Anti-crisis shield 1.0". According to these regulations, the ordering party, within 14 days from the date of awarding the contract without the application of PPL, must place in the Public Information Bulletin (BIP) website information about the award of the contract, giving the company name or the name and surname of the entity with which it concluded the contract (Article 6(4)). This is a good regulation as it seeks to preserve the transparency and openness of public contracts, including those awarded outside PPL.

The regulations specifying the duration of the PPL exclusion have also been amended several times. Pursuant to the last amendment made by the Act of 24

July 2020 amending the Act on the posting of workers in the framework of the provision of services and certain other acts (2020; Article 4), the possibility of non-application of PPL expires 180 days from the date of entry into force (Article 36). Thus, as of 5 September 2020, it is not possible to not apply PPL with reference to COVID-19. The exclusion of PPL was possible during the period of the provisions of Article 6, i.e., between 8 March 2020 and 5 September 2020. The remaining regulations concerning the subjective orders of Bank Gospodarstwa Krajowego, Polish Development Fund, and regional development funds, covered by Article 6(2), expired on 1 January 2021, so as of that date, these entities have lost the possibility to award contracts without applying PPL. At the same time, Article 6(4) also ceased to apply. The grounds for non-application of PPL was provided also by law in Bulgaria and Latvia, direct award due to extreme urgency was granted in the United Kingdom, Ireland, Portugal, and Romania, and the possibility of applying the negotiated procedure without previous publication was allowed in Belgium, France, Germany, Italy, Malta, Spain, and also in Bosnia and Herzegovina, North Macedonia, Montenegro, and Serbia (OECD, 2020, pp. 8–16).

In addition, the Act of 31 March 2020 added to "Anti-crisis shield 1.0" the possibility to amend a public procurement contract in force (Article 15r). The law for "Anti-crisis shield 4.0" has made changes and clarifications in the wording of this provision. Currently, if it is found that the circumstances related to the occurrence of COVID-19 may (read: potentially) affect the proper performance of the contract, the buyer may, but does not have to, amend the contract. On the other hand, if it is found that such circumstances affect (in fact) the proper performance of the contract, the ordering party should agree with the contractor to amend it (see Szostak, 2020, pp. 2–20). In both cases, it is the contracting authority that determines and decides whether there are any circumstances that would entitle it to discuss a change of contract. This is a protection against abuse of the new regulations by contractors. Nevertheless, a contractor may in such circumstances have a claim to amend the contract (Article 15r(7)). The "Anti-crisis shield 4.0" also introduced the prohibition to deduct contractual penalties reserved in case of non-performance or improper performance of the contract from the contractor's remuneration or other claims. The contracting authority is also prohibited from seeking satisfaction from the security on due performance of a public procurement contract with regard to the contractual penalty reserved in the event of non-performance or improper performance of the contract by the contractor (Article $15r^1$). The provisions do not specify the duration of these regulations, which means that this provision is valid indefinitely as long as the "Anti-crisis shield 1.0" is in force or until a new PPL enters into force.[14] The "Anti-crisis shield 4.0" additionally abolished the obligation for ordering parties to demand a tender guarantee (bid bond) in procedures with a value equal to and higher than the EU thresholds. This means that in all procedures covered by PPL (regardless of their value) the requirement of a bid bond is optional (Article 15va). There is also an obligation to pay the remuneration in parts or to grant advance payments by the ordering parties in case of contracts concluded for a period longer than 12 months. Also, there is the possibility of a reduction of the maximum value of the performance bond to 5 per cent and partial return of the security (Article 15vb). "Anti-crisis shield 4.0" (Article 49) clarified that an announcement initiating an open tender procedure should be published on the initiator's website.[15] The above regulations are general in nature, i.e., they do not directly concern the fight against COVID-19, but allow for some remedial actions in response to problems that have arisen as a result of the pandemic.

The Act of 31 March 2020 amending certain acts (2020b) related to the "Anti-crisis shield 1.0" introduced Article 10c. This was a highly specific article assuring immunity for public officials who exceeded their powers or caused damage to commercial transactions, as well as from disciplinary tort for violation of public finance discipline, during the period of epidemic hazard when purchasing goods or services necessary for combating COVID-19, but in violation of their official duties or applicable regulations, if acting in the public interest and that without these violations the acquisition of these goods or services could not be secured or would be significantly threatened. By the Act of 24 July 2020 (2020), it was established that this regulation was in force for 180 days after the date of entry into force of the act. Thus, it expired on 5 September 2020.

After the entry into force of the "Anti-crisis shield 1.0" until 27 May 2020 (i.e., the approximate lockdown period in Poland) the Ministry of Health spent PLN 854 million and the Material Reserves Agency spent PLN 720 million based on statutory exclusion of PPL. The remaining ministries spent no more than several hundred thousand PLN each, and a few had not made any purchases. The Police informed that it had concluded 53 agreements, but did not indicate their value. Purchases were also made by voivodeship offices (e.g., Świętokrzyski—PLN 134,000, Mazowiecki—PLN 4.1 million).[16] In an analogous period, the UK awarded 115 contracts with a total value of just over £1 billion under fast-track rules bypassing competitive tenders.[17]

The purchases included masks, gowns, disinfectants, tests or swabs, and medical equipment, even laptops, allowing officials to work from home. The Polish national health service and the Ministry of Development purchased an information hotline service for businesses (contract worth PLN 676,000). The Lower Silesian Governor's Office paid to bring Poles home from abroad by plane (PLN 1.8 million) while the Mazovian Governor's Office paid for transport of people to quarantine facilities (PLN 130,000).[18] In the announcement of 24 March 2020, the Public Procurement Office stated that the exemption under Article 6 of the "Anti-crisis shield 1.0" was possible not only for purchases of medical equipment but also the supply of IT equipment or services in the field of IT and necessary equipment for the workplace (e.g., purchases of laptops, telephones) for remote work, or adaptation of IT infrastructure to introduce and perform remote work. In each case, however, it was necessary to analyse whether the other prerequisites required by the law had been fulfilled.[19] As part of the fight against COVID-19, the Ministry of Health purchased respirators from a Polish company owned by a motorised hang-glider manufacturer and organiser of flights to hard-to-reach regions of the world, that in the past had been involved in the illegal arms trade, and which the UN has blacklisted for arms smuggling to Angola and Liberia.[20] The purchase was made at a high price. For 1.2 thousand respirators, Poland paid EUR 44.5 million (PLN 200 million). This is an average of PLN 165,000 per unit compared to, for example, a high-grade respirator from another company costing PLN 70,000–90,000. The price of respirators with additional options and accessories is usually about PLN 110,000–120,000.[21] At the time of writing, the respirators still had not been delivered, and the ministry is making efforts to recover the funds already paid.[22] At the same time, attempts by representatives of the parliamentary opposition to review the agreements are encountering difficulties with access to the relevant documents concluded by the Ministry of Health.[23] This suggests that it will be difficult to control all public institutions that, during the exemption period, concluded contracts without PPL. Therefore, a lot of emotions and controversy have been stirred up in Poland by the proposal of another amendment to the "Anti-crisis shield 1.0" through proposed Article 10d. Unlike its predecessor (Article 10c), it exempts public officials from *any* criminal liability, not only for exceeding the official's powers or causing damage to commercial transactions. The regulation as proposed refers to a state of higher necessity. If it enters into force, authorities who made decisions in this period will be able to count on immunity for all unlawful actions, whether real or only apparent connections to the fight against the pandemic and other infectious diseases.[24] It is therefore extremely capacious and undefined. Terms such as "counteracting COVID-19", "in the public interest", "significantly impeded" are not precise enough and their meaning can be wide. This may additionally lead to the exclusion of liability not only for officials' crimes but also for all crimes, even common ones affecting life, health, or freedom.[25]

Conclusions

It is expected that the JPP will strengthen the Contracting Parties' negotiating power, e.g., by obtaining advantageous prices and order flexibility with regard to a given product (European Commission, 2011, p. 13) and ensuring equitable access to medical countermeasures against serious cross-border threats to health. Nevertheless, the parties are allowed to carry out any national procurement procedures even if the subject of such orders is medical products that are the remit of a JPP (framework agreement) or concern suppliers participating in a JPP. In this respect, public buyers should first fully exploit the flexibilities of the EU procurement framework. Then, as a secondary, complementary tool, they should take part in a JPP. This means that the JPP mechanism could have a complementary character to the actions undertaken by Poland or any other state individually. The complementary character is possible assuming Poland's early reaction to the legal mechanism launched within the JPP, but only in the case of possible further waves of the COVID-19 pandemic or the appearance of similar new threats. It can be difficult for a single state to have full access to medical resources, particularly vaccines against COVID-19 when they became available. JPP can help states representing smaller markets overcome economic and other imbalances in access to suppliers.

The measures that different governments have undertaken has been very decisive (Caduff, 2020, p. 1), also in the area of PPL. This could be part of a broader discussion about whether such a far-reaching legal solution like non-application of PPL is actually necessary in a situation in which the same law also allows the use of effective methods of negotiation, such as not requiring the need for prior publication, according to Article 32 of Directive 2014/24/EU (Sołtysińska, 2020, pp. 48). Currently, the use of this exclusion has expired, and even when available it was used only exceptionally, as exceptions are to be interpreted restrictively (Sołtysińska, 2020, pp. 48). In any case, it seems that the basic needs have already been met, even though the pandemic is ongoing. Further purchases should therefore be made on a competitive basis. It is true that in an emergency, the need to act quickly is crucial, but acting through secret COVID-19 contracts awarded without competition is not desirable[26] because transparency, competitiveness, and objective criteria when making decisions are European public procurement principles.

Notes

1 Any JPASC member may propose the launch of a procurement procedure, which can be activated if at least five contracting parties, including the Commission, vote in favour of starting such a procedure.

2 In the above situation, any "medical countermeasures", understood as medicines, medical devices, other goods or services that are aimed at combating serious cross-border threats to health, can be contracted. It means that the JPA may cover, for example, laboratory tests, diagnostic tools/kits for seasonal or pandemic influenza, influenza vaccines, antivirals, ancillary products, and protective equipment for healthcare workers such as decontamination products, masks, and personal protective equipment or other goods and services depending on the need triggered by a serious cross-border threat to health (European Commission, 2014b, pp. 4, 5).

3 JPASC is responsible for: decisions on the type of medical countermeasures to be procured and on the order in which such procurements will be organised in time, any legal proceedings under the JPP that concern all parties, the process necessary to address any lack of compliance with a particular JPA by a party, the amicable settlement of disagreements between two or more parties, and for amendments to a JPA (Article 5(1) JPA).

4 SPPSC is responsible for matters relating to the subject matter of the specific procurement, including: the specific JPP, any legal proceedings under the framework contract, the determination and application of allocation criteria and temporary deviations from the allocation criteria (Article 5(2) JPA). JPASC and SPPSC adopt decisions by common accord but when agreement cannot be reached Committees vote (JPA provides precise rules for voting).

5 The JPA also provides for the possibility for two or more parties to agree on a temporary derogation from the generally applicable allocation criteria for their framework contracts in respect of the amounts to which they are entitled on the basis of those criteria. In that case, these parties shall inform the SPPSC of any such

agreement, including the duration of the agreed temporary derogation. The terms of a temporary derogation from the generally applicable award criteria are agreed between the contractor and the contracting parties.

6 Available at https://ec.europa.eu/info/live-work-travel-eu/health/coronavirus-response/public-health_en (accessed: 24.9.2020).

7 COVID-19 Procurement Actions (25 May 2020), MedTech Europe, Available at https://www.medtecheurope.org/resource-library/covid-19-procurement-actions/ (accessed: 27.9.2020).

8 Available at https://ec.europa.eu/commission/presscorner/detail/en/ip_20_1416 (accessed: 24.9.2020).

9 Available at https://bip.kprm.gov.pl/kpr/bip-rady-ministrow/prace-legislacyjne-rm-i/prace-legislacyjne-rady/wykaz-prac-legislacyjny/r5999908,Projekt-uchwaly-Rady-Ministrow-w-sprawie-przystapienia-do-porozumienia-dotyczace.html (accessed: 4.10.2020).

10 See Directive 2014/24/EU of the European Parliament and of the Council of 26 February 2014 on public procurement and repealing Directive 2004/18/EC (2014, p. 65).

11 Available at https://ec.europa.eu/info/live-work-travel-eu/health/coronavirus-response/public-health_en (accessed: 20.9.2020).

12 Under the open procedure, the deadline for the submission of tenders may be reduced from 35 to 15 days in cases of duly justified urgency (Article 27(3) of Directive 2014/24/EU). Under the restricted procedure, the deadline to submit a request for participation may be reduced from 30 to 15 days (Article 27(3) of Directive 2014/24/EU) and the time to submit an offer from 30 to 10 days (Article 28(6) of Directive 2014/24/EU). This allows for the speedy award of the contract.

13 This possibility is restricted by four conditions, which must be fulfilled cumulatively: events have to be unforeseeable by the contracting authority that plans to carry out the public procurement, extreme urgency making compliance with general deadlines impossible, a causal link exists between the unforeseen event and the extreme urgency, can be used only temporarily in order to cover the gap until more stable solutions can be found.

14 The provision of the "Anti-crisis shield 1.0" refers in its content to the Public Procurement Law of 29.1.2004, which was replaced on 1.1.2021 by the new Public Procurement Law of 11.9.2019. Since that date, the provision ceased to apply to COVID-19, as the "Anti-crisis shield 1.0" has not been amended by reference to the new law.

15 From 1.1.2021 (entry into force of the new act of the Public Procurement Law of 11.9.2019), the same solutions apply with respect to the deposit, maximum value of the security, advance payments, partial payments and announcements of planned tenders.

16 Available at https://biznes.gazetaprawna.pl/artykuly/1485057,koronawirus-zamowienia-bez-przetargu.html (accessed: 20.9.2020).

17 Available at https://www.theguardian.com/world/2020/may/15/firms-given-1bn-of-state-contracts-without-tender-in-covid-19-crisis (accessed: 20.9.2020).

18 See https://biznes.gazetaprawna.pl/artykuly/1485057,koronawirus-zamowienia-bez-przetargu.html (accessed: 20.9.2020).

19 Available at https://www.uzp.gov.pl/baza-wiedzy/interpretacja-przepisow/informacje-dotyczace-zamowien-w-zwiazku-z-covid-19/komunikat-w-sprawie-art.-6-tzw.-ustawy-o-covid-19 (accessed: 20.9.2020).

20 Available at https://www.termedia.pl/mz/Resort-zdrowia-kupil-1-2-tys-respiratorow-za-200-mln-zl-Nie-dostal-ani-jednego,38305.html (accessed: 20.9.2020).

21 Available at https://wyborcza.pl/7,75398,26027396,poslowie-szukaja-umowy-na-respiratory-od-handlarza-bronia-ministerstwo.html (accessed: 20.9.2020).

22 Available at https://tvn24.pl/polska/koronawirus-w-polsce-lukasz-szumowski-o-zakupie-maseczek-i-respiratorow-od-handlarza-bronia-4669033 (accessed: 20.9.2020).
23 Available at https://www.polityka.pl/tygodnikpolityka/kraj/1960024,1,respiratorow-nie-widac-pieniadze-poszly-dokumenty-wyszly.read (accessed: 20.9.2020).
24 Available at https://prawo.gazetaprawna.pl/artykuly/1489262,ustawa-abolicyjna-urzednicy-koronawirus-ziobrysci-zjednoczona-prawica.html (accessed: 20.9.2020).
25 Available at https://www.prawo.pl/samorzad/bezkarnosc-urzednicza-co-dalej-z-nowelizacja-ustawy-covidowej,503174.html (accessed: 20.9.2020).
26 Available at https://www.theguardian.com/commentisfree/2020/jul/15/coronavirus-contracts-government-transparency-pandemic (accessed: 20.9.2020).

Bibliography

Act of 29 January 2004 on Public Procurement Law PL (2019) *Dziennik Ustaw*, item 1843.

Act of 2 March 2020 on special solutions related to preventing, counteracting, and combating COVID-19, other infectious diseases and crises caused by them (2020) *Dziennik Ustaw*, item 374.

Act of 31 March 2020 amending the Act on special solutions related to preventing, counteracting, and combating COVID-19, other infectious diseases and crises caused by them (2020a) *Dziennik Ustaw*, item 568.

Act of 31 March 2020 on the amendment of certain Acts regarding the health care system related to the prevention, counteracting and combating of COVID-19 (2020b) *Dziennik Ustaw*, item 567.

Act of 19 June 2020 on subsidisation of interest on bank loans granted to entities affected by COVID-19 and simplified arrangement approval proceedings due to COVID-19 (2020) *Dziennik Ustaw*, item 1086.

Act of 24 July 2020 amending the Act on the posting of workers in the framework of the provision of services and certain other Acts (2020) *Dziennik Ustaw*, item 1423. https://bip.kprm.gov.pl/kpr/bip-rady-ministrow/prace-legislacyjne-rm-i/prace-legislacyjne-rady/wykaz-prac-legislacyjny/r5999908,Projekt-uchwaly-Rady-Ministrow-w-sprawie-przystapienia-do-porozumienia-dotyczace.html (accessed: 4. 10. 2020). https://biznes.gazetaprawna.pl/artykuly/1485057,koronawirus-zamowienia-bez-przetargu.html (accessed: 20. 9. 2020).

Caduff, C. (2020) What Went Wrong: Corona and the World after the Full Stop, *Medical Anthropology Quarterly*, July. Available at https://anthrosource.onlinelibrary.wiley.com/doi/full/10.1111/maq.12599 (accessed: 27. 09. 2020).

Communication from the Commission Guidance from the European Commission on using the public procurement framework in the emergency situation related to the COVID-19 crisis 2020/C 108 I/01 (2020) OJ C 108I, 1. 4. 2020.

Decision No 1082/2013/EU of the European Parliament and of the Council of 22 October 2013 on serious cross-border threats to health, and repealing Decision No 2119/98/EC (2013) OJ L 293, 5. 11. 2013.

Directive 2014/24/EU of the European Parliament and of the Council of 26 February 2014 on public procurement and repealing Directive 2004/18/EC (2014) OJ L 94 of 28. 3. 2014.

European Commission (2011) Explanatory Memorandum to the Decision of the European Parliament and the Council on serious cross-border threats to health Brussels, 8. 12. 2011, COM(2011) 866 final, 2011/0421 (COD).

European Commission (2014a) Considerations on the legal basis and the legal nature of the Joint Procurement Agreement, Luxembourg. Available at https://ec.europa.eu/health/preparedness_response/key_documents_en (accessed: 1. 07. 2020).

European Commission (2014b) Medical countermeasures that could be procured in common under the Joint Procurement Agreement, Luxembourg, December, Available at https://ec.europa.eu/health/preparedness_response/key_documents_en (accessed: 1. 7. 2020). https://ec.europa.eu/info/live-work-travel-eu/health/coronavirus-response/public-health_en (accessed: 24. 9. 2020). https://ec.europa.eu/commission/presscorner/detail/en/ip_20_1416 (accessed: 24. 9. 2020). https://ec.europa.eu/info/live-work-travel-eu/health/coronavirus-response/public-health_en (accessed: 20. 9. 2020).

European Commission (2015) Explanatory Note on the Joint Procurement Mechanism, Luxembourg, December, Available at http://www.ec.europa.eu/health/preparedness_response/docs/jpa_explanatory_en.pdf+&cd=1&hl=pl&ct=clnk&gl=pl&client=firefox-b (accessed: 1. 07. 2020).

European Commission (2020) Explanatory Note Decision Process in the Steering Committees Managing the Joint Procurement Mechanism, Luxembourg. Available at https://ec.europa.eu/health/preparedness_response/key_documents_en (accessed: 1. 07. 2020).

European Commission (2014) Joint Procurement Agreement to Procure Medical Countermeasures, 10 April. Available at https://ec.europa.eu/health/sites/health/files/preparedness_response/docs/jpa_agreement_medicalcountermeasures_en.pdf (accessed: 1. 7. 2020).

Falkowska, M. (2020) Wpływ "tarczy antykryzysowej" na zamówienia publiczne, *LEX.pl.*

Jerka, J. (2020) Rozwiązania szczególne wynikające z COVID-19, *Monitor Zamówień Publicznych*, no. 3–4.

Kittel, M. and Kittel, R. (2020) Wyłączenia stosowania przepisów Prawa zamówień publicznych w związku ze stanem zagrożenia epidemicznego, *Zamówienia Publiczne Doradca*, no. 3.

Mazurek, G. (2020) Udzielanie zamówień w sytuacji zagrożenia epidemicznego, *Monitor Zamówień Publicznych*, no. 3–4.

OECD (2020) Application of public procurement rules during the COVID–19 crisis from the perspective of the European Union's Procurement Directives and the Government Procurement Agreement, 8 April. Available at http://www.sigmaweb.org/publications/Public-procurement-COVID-19-crisis-SIGMA-April-2020.pdf (accessed: 5. 11. 2020).

Ordinance of the Minister of Health of 13 March 2020 on the declaration of an state of epidemic emergency in the Republic of Poland (2020) *Dziennik Ustaw*, item 433.

Potemska, B. (2020) Wpływ specustawy koronawirusowej na funkcjonowanie jednostek samorządu terytorialnego, *LEX.pl.* https://www.polityka.pl/tygodnikpolityka/kraj/1960024,1,respiratorow-nie-widac-pieniadze-poszly-dokumenty-wyszly.read (accessed: 20. 9. 2020). https://www.prawo.pl/samorzad/bezkarnosc-urzednicza-co-dalej-z-nowelizacja-ustawy-covidowej,503174.html (accessed: 20. 9. 2020). https://prawo.gazetaprawna.pl/artykuly/1489262,ustawa-abolicyjna-urzednicy-koronawirus-ziobrysci-zjednoczona-prawica.html (accessed: 20. 9. 2020).

Sołtysińska, A. (2020) Zamówienia publiczne w czasie epidemii COVID-19, *Europejski Przegląd Sądowy*, no 6.

Szostak, R. (2020) Zmiana umowy o zamówienie publiczne w okolicznościach zagrożenia epidemicznego, *Zamówienia Publiczne Doradca*, no 5.

Treaty on the Functioning of the European Union (2012) OJ C 326, 26. 10. 2012, pp. 47–390. https://www.theguardian.com/world/2020/may/15/firms-given-1bn-of-state-contracts-without-tender-in-covid-19-crisis (accessed: 20. 9. 2020). https://www.termedia.pl/mz/Resort-zdrowia-kupil-1-2-tys-respiratorow-za-200-mln-zl-Nie-dostal-ani-jednego,38305.html (accessed: 20. 9. 2020). https://www.theguardian.com/commentisfree/2020/jul/15/coronavirus-contracts-government-transparency-pandemic (accessed: 20. 9. 2020). https://tvn24.pl/polska/koronawirus-w-polsce-lukasz-szumowski-o-zakupie-maseczek-i-respiratorow-od-handlarza-bronia-4669033 (accessed: 20. 9. 2020). https://www.uzp.gov.pl/baza-wiedzy/interpretacja-przepisow/informacje-dotyczace-zamowien-w-zwiazku-z-covid-19/komunikat-w-sprawie-art.-6-tzw.-ustawy-o-covid-19 (accessed: 20. 9. 2020).

Wiktorowska, E. (2020) Wyłączenie z obowiązku stosowania p.z.p. dla zakupu towarów lub usług niezbędnych do przeciwdziałania COVID-19, 8. 03. 2020, Available at https://sip.lex.pl/#/procedure/1610619152 (accessed: 1. 7. 2020). https://wyborcza.pl/7,75398,26027396,poslowie-szukaja-umowy-na-respiratory-od-handlarza-bronia-ministerstwo.html (accessed: 20. 9. 2020).

5 The EU funds for addressing the consequences of the COVID-19 pandemic

Implications for Poland

Elżbieta Kawecka-Wyrzykowska

Introduction

On 21 July 2020 the EU leaders agreed on a record-high EUR 1.82 trillion financial package (European Council, 2020a).[1] The final budgetary deal was reached in December 2020. The unprecedented financial package combines the standard 7-year budget for 2021–2027 (the Multiannual Financial Framework—MFF) and an emergency recovery program, Next Generation EU—NGEU (called also the Recovery Programme). This stimulus package is to pull the European economy out of the deep recession following the COVID-19 pandemic. Furthermore, it should support Member States' efforts to achieve the EU's development priorities having been implemented under the Europe 2020 strategy. Coordination of actions of EU Member States is also necessary to avoid possible competition distortions in the internal market and increased inequalities in the EU in the future, since wealthier states with larger budgetary reserves are able to provide greater financial support to their businesses.

The objective of the study is to: a) identify how the pandemic has affected the reorientation of spending in the EU budget for 2021–2027, b) assess the EU budgetary decisions from the point of view of interests of Poland's economy, c) identify the factors which determine the role of EU assistance in the Polish economy. For the purpose of this evaluation, various indicators were calculated to illustrate the scale and type of financing relative to other comparable measures. Some figures for Poland are estimates, indicating the order of magnitude rather than specific appropriations. However, they allow us to conclude on the likely allocation of funds and their possible importance.

The structure of the chapter is as follows. First, brief information on *ad hoc* financial measures introduced by the EU in 2020 is presented. Next, the funds offered to Poland within the NGEU programme are discussed and assessed against the background of total EU funds of this type, their goals and conditions of their use. That part is followed by an overview of the size and composition of the MFF for the EU and for Poland. The chapter ends with conclusions offering some policy-oriented reflections.

DOI: 10.4324/9781003144434-6

1 EU financial response to the consequences of COVID-19 in 2020

In early 2020, the EU took *ad hoc* actions to mitigate the consequences of the pandemic and to ensure the Member States' coordinated approach.[2] The measures comprised more flexible state aid rules (cf. Chapter 6), the mobilisation of unused structural funds from the 2014–2020 MFF to address the most pressing needs, and increased flexibility in the use of these funds. In the framework of the last initiative, Poland was able to spend EUR 7.4 billion. To preserve jobs in the period of the pandemic, the Commission launched an initiative for a Support to Mitigate Unemployment Risks in an Emergency—SURE, worth EUR 100 billion, in the form of low-interest loans. Within the programme, Poland has access to EUR 11.2 billion. In October 2020 the first tranche of EUR 1 billion was transferred to the country.

2 The framework and purpose of Next Generation EU (NGEU) in 2021–2023[3]

The general overview of the NGEU funds for the EU and for Poland

The NGEU programme provides exceptional and one-off funds. It is not a part of the MFF, mostly due to the manner of its establishment. NGEU constitutes "other revenue"[4] and will be funded from long-term bonds issued by the European Commission. The standard budget is financed from the EU's own resources. The new funds need to be repaid, while transfers from own resources are non-repayable. The idea and scale of the extraordinary NGEU programme are unprecedented in the EU's history. The agreed package, worth EUR 750 billion, represents an impressive 70 per cent of the regular MFF. The money should be spent relatively quickly (commitments should be made by the end of 2023, and payments by the end of 2026), thus allowing for stronger effects. One factor reducing the impact of the programme is the fact that only a portion of the funds will be allocated in the form of grants (EUR 384.4 billion) and guarantees (EUR 5.6 billion) which carry the largest fiscal impulses. The remaining EUR 360 billion will be available as low-interest loans.[5] See Table 5.1.

Under NGEU, Poland may receive EUR 29.0 billion in the form of grants (7.4 per cent of the total amount), which is the sum of the further mentioned individual program items. Poland will be the fourth largest beneficiary of the Programme in absolute terms. More money will go to bigger countries which at the same time have been harder hit by the pandemic: Italy—21 per cent, Spain—19 per cent and France—12 per cent. From the point of view of importance to beneficiaries, it is more rationale to compare the scale of funds *per capita*. Such a list shows that Poland may obtain per capita around EUR 760, whereas higher appropriations will be assigned to the following Member States (in brackets—the respective support *per capita* in EUR): Italy, Spain, Croatia, Greece (from 1400 to 1800); Latvia, Lithuania, Bulgaria and other

Table 5.1 Funds agreed at the July 2020 summit under NGEU (EUR billion, 2018 prices)

1. Grants	**390.0**
In that:	
Recovery and Resilience Facility (incl. Technical Support)	312.5
Cohesion Policy (ReactEU)	47.5
Horizon Europe	5.0
InvestEU Fund, of which under the Union Recovery plan	5.6
Union Civil Protection Mechanism (Resc-EU)	1.9
Pillar II of CAP (Rural Development)	7.5
Just Transition Fund	10.0
2. Loans: Recovery and Resilience Facility	**360.0**
3. Total	**750.0**

Source: Based on European Council (2020a).

(above 1000), while the EU average level is EUR 870. The other comparable point of reference for evaluation of the scale of funds for each EU Member is fund's share in GDP of the beneficiary. Countries with the highest coefficient (based on the 2019 GDP) are: Greece, Bulgaria, Croatia (12–13 per cent of their GDP); Lithuania, Latvia, Portugal, Romania (6–7–7 per cent), Italy, Poland, Spain (5–6 per cent). The average share of NGEU in the 2019 GDP of the EU-27 is 2.8 per cent. These comparisons reveal that Poland is among the biggest beneficiaries of the EU recovery support, both in absolute and relative terms.

The use of funds under NGEU and the MFF depends on meeting a number of general conditions, three of which are the most essential: allocating a minimum of 30 per cent of the total expenditure to climate actions, compliance with the European Semester procedure and respecting the rule of law. Those are described in more detail in subsequent points.

The size and objectives of NGEU instruments

Recovery and Resilience Facility

Table 5.1 shows that the most funds will go to the Recovery and Resilience Facility (RRF)—EUR 672.5 billion, i.e. 90 per cent of the total amount available under NGEU. Out of that, EUR 312.5 will be in form of grants (Figure 5.1). 70 per cent of these grants from the RRF will be committed in 2021 and 2022, the years in which recovery-related needs will be the most significant, whereas the remaining 30 per cent will be allocated by the end of 2023. The Facility is intended to support the implementation of projects necessary to ensure sustainable recovery and prevent the widening of socio-economic divergences between the EU Member States. Therefore, its objectives are very wide, including support for employment, education systems, and health care. Assistance is focused on the areas

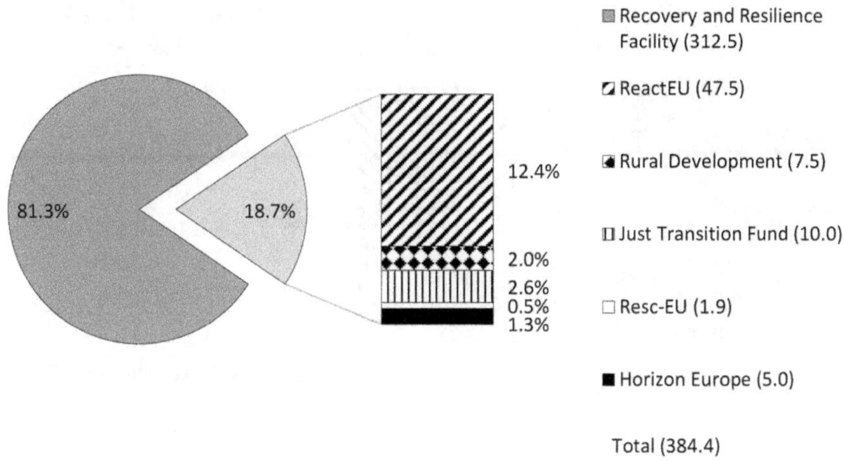

Figure 5.1 Distribution of NGEU grants in the EU (% & EUR billion).
Source: Figure based on https://ec.europa.eu/info/strategy/eu-budget/long-term-eu-budget/eu-budget-2021-2027_en (Accessed: 13 October 2020).

most affected by the pandemic and with the greatest resilience needs (European Commission, 2020a). According to Commission's estimates, Poland's part of the RRF grants will be EUR 23 billion, i.e. 7.4 per cent of the total RRF funds (Figure 5.2). The Member States to receive more than Poland, as in the case of NGEU as a whole, will be Italy, Spain and France (moreover, Germany will get almost the same amount of money as Poland).

The RRF will be channelled in accordance with the country-specific recommendations of the European Semesters for 2019 and 2020. The Polish government will need to prepare a national recovery and resilience plan as part of the standard national reform programme presented annually under the European Semester cycle. This Plan will have to contain Poland's investment and reform agenda for 2021–2023. It must also be consistent with national energy and climate plans, just transition plans, partnership agreements and operational programmes within the MFF funds. The Commission will assess the plan very quickly (within 2 months of the submission). The basis of the opinion will be "consistency with the country-specific recommendations". Other prerequisites for a positive assessment will be "effective contribution to the green and digital transition" and "the respect of the rule of law" (see also below). The Commission's evaluation of the recovery and resilience plans will be approved by the Council, by qualified majority. The solution adopted is a novelty in EU action for the approval or rejection of an economic recovery plan of one Member to be decided by other EU Members. Till now, recommendations addressed to the Member States within the European Semesters have been formally non-binding. In practise, the whole procedure has involved significant peer pressure on the states to act on such recommendations (Kawecka-

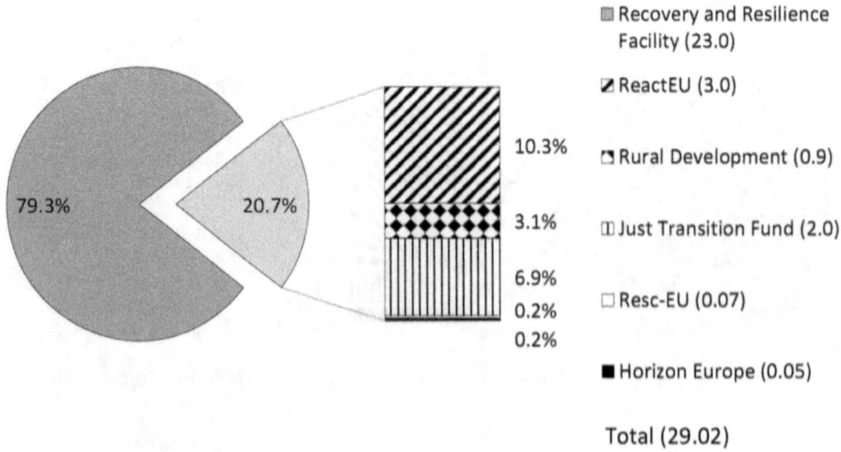

Figure 5.2 Distribution of NGEU grants in Poland (% & EUR billion).
Source: Figure based on https://ec.europa.eu/info/strategy/eu-budget/long-term-eu-budget/eu-budget-2021-2027_en (Accessed: 13 October 2020).

Wyrzykowska, 2017). A new, more demanding mechanism may repeatedly contribute to fierce disputes between Member States about whether or not to accept a plan. As regards the execution of the recovery plan, it will also be assessed within the European Semester. All this means high requirements for the RRF beneficiaries, with regard to both the very concept of using the funds in line with the EU priorities and their practical implementation.

Recovery assistance for cohesion and the territories of Europe (REACT-EU)

The assistance worth EUR 47.5 billion is provided to supplement the ongoing 2014–2020 cohesion policy programmes. It aims to facilitate overcoming the consequences of the economic crisis in the early and most difficult period. Such support is intended notably for workers, small and medium-sized enterprises and health care systems. Also in this case, funding is supposed to support remedy measures in the sectors that are crucial to economic recovery and for a green, digital and more resilient economy. Programmes within this assistance scheme can be financed entirely from the EU budget, i.e. no co-financing is necessary (European Commission, 2020b, p. 3) That principle is advantageous to the budgets of all beneficiaries, which is of particular importance at a time when regional and local authorities and firms struggle to maintain financial liquidity. The funds are intended to be used in 2020–2022. Poland may obtain approx. EUR 3 billion, i.e. 6.3 per cent of the programme appropriations. Much higher amounts will go to the Member States most hit by the crisis, with highest unemployment rates i.e. Italy and Spain: 30.2 per cent and 26.0 per cent respectively, as well as to France—7.9 per cent of the total funds of the programme.[6]

JUST TRANSITION FUND

In order to address the social and economic consequences of the objective of achieving climate neutrality by 2050[7] a *JUST TRANSITION FUND* (JTF) will be created (European Commission, 2020c). It will be worth in total EUR 17.5 billion, out of that EUR 10 billion will come from NGEU and the rest from MFF. Poland can receive EUR 2.0 billion (20 per cent) from the NGEU envelope.[8] In practice, however, the actual amount may be reduced by 50 per cent. The reduced share is foreseen for countries which refrain from committing to climate neutrality by 2050. As the only EU Member State, Poland has not declared it will implement this objective. The Polish government supported the objective as a goal for the Union as a whole but not necessarily for each state. The government argued that Poland could not afford its practical implementation due to specific historical and structural conditions. Poland's objection was the main reason why the July European Council conclusions did not include a roadmap for achieving the objective at both the EU and national levels. As a result, such a solution left room for different interpretation.

The JTF is intended to support the economic and social transformation of the mining regions and industrial sectors most affected by the transition, given their dependence on fossil fuels or greenhouse gas-intensive industrial processes. The Fund can be spent on the reskilling of workers, support for SMEs in the creation of new economic opportunities, as well as on promoting economic diversification in the most affected regions. The JTF aims at targeted assistance towards a cleaner, healthier and stronger industry without CO_2 emissions. The underlying assumption is that the post-pandemic recovery must not be based on obsolete pre-pandemic technologies polluting the environment. The funds are supposed to foster climate transition rather than maintaining the status quo. The first beneficiaries in Poland include nine sub-regions (NUTS level 3 regions) strongly dependent on coal: Katowice, Bielsko-Biała, Tychy, Rybnik, Gliwice, Bytom, Sosnowiec, Konin, Wałbrzych. Poland has more such locations. So far, however, the European Commission found that there were on-going transition planning efforts only in those regions (European Commission, 2020d, p. 59). In order to obtain the money, the Polish government will need to prepare the territorial just transition plans consistent with the EU climate policy. Those must include not only a commitment to achieve real transition but also the presentation of its stages, with reliable goals and milestones. All energy transition projects must refer to the National Energy and Climate Plan covering the period 2021–2030. Although Poland submitted the document to the Commission in December 2019, it excluded achieving the EU's common objectives by 2030. In the February 2020 report on Poland's implementation of the European Semester, the Commission assessed that "[a] clear energy decarbonisation strategy to foster investment and the energy transition in Poland is lacking" (European Commission, 2020d, p. 42). Also, the draft document "Poland's energy policy until 2040", presented by the government in September 2020, does not indicate a specific date to abandon coal. Unless it is changed quickly, Poland will not be able to use EU funds to the full. And without such funds, a country will be left alone to deal with various energy-related problems. The most important challenges include: very strong dependence on coal,[9] high employment in the coal-mining sector,[10] high greenhouse gas emissions in Poland,[11] high energy intensity of the industry and the low energy efficiency of buildings.

Missing Poland's swift consent to achieve the EU climate targets will also undermine Poland's position in any talks on the use of other EU funds. Also, such government's stance reduces the willingness of energy producers to introduce necessary changes in the energy sector and strengthens the position of those opposing the phasing out of coal. Therefore, the preparation of a strategic plan for the country as a whole (and for specific regions) is extremely urgent. A big problem is also to find huge money necessary for energy transformation (for new climate-friendly investments and compensation of social costs). Moreover, delivering climate strategies (plans for reducing emissions and for switching production towards sustainable development) and the accompanying requirements, e.g. with regard to reporting for progress evaluation reasons, will be mandatory for large business CO_2 emitters, most probably as from 2021. The majority of Polish firms are not ready for this and have no emission reduction strategies.[12]

INVESTEU

In the context of NGEU, the already existing InvestEU programme was increased by EUR 5.6 billion (guarantees). It is the EU's flagship investment programme to mobilise private investment in strategic projects across the Union. Its main pillar will be the Strategic Investment Facility whose precursor was the European Fund for Strategic Investments. The Fund was a successful investment support instrument in the difficult period of the EU's recovery from the deep crisis of 2008–2009 and the resulting high investment risk. The InvestEU Programme is intended to mitigate projects risks and to crowd in private financing worth much more than the Programme itself. By increasing the risk-taking capacity of firms (due to guarantees), it will be possible to mobilise long-term investments without the need to use budget appropriations of the Member State in question, thus without generating public debt. The programme mainly targets the private sector, but public undertakings are eligible as well. In particular, it is intended to help finance investments in key value chains (as many projects are cross-border) crucial for Europe's future economic resilience and strategic autonomy, which is consistent with the new industrial policy presented by the Commission in early 2020 (Kawecka-Wyrzykowska, 2020). The investment examples indicated by the Commission include the industrial internet of things, low-CO_2 emission industry and cybersecurity. So far, Polish enterprises have had limited experience in implementing such projects and may encounter problems with using this type of fund.

Agriculture

Apart from significant appropriations for the common agricultural policy within the MFF, NGEU provides for an extra EUR 7.5 billion. The funds are intended to support farmers and rural areas in structural changes necessary to implement the European Green Deal. Poland can receive ca. EUR 0.9 billion which accounts for 12 per cent of the total support. The offer is very advantageous (even if financially modest), considering the substantial needs of Polish agriculture with regard to structural catching-up with the most competitive EU Members. An important aspect is also the nature of the offer: this money has to be used for investments resulting in long-term changes rather than for agricultural income support, and lead to the discontinuation of assistance.

Other funds within NGEU

In addition to the above-mentioned appropriations, NGEU comprises two more instruments. One, worth EUR 1.9 billion, is RescEU (part of the existing EU Civil Protection Mechanism), aimed at enhancing the protection of citizens from disasters and the management of emerging risks. Poland can obtain EUR 0.07 billion, i.e. 3.7 per cent of the total amount. Most of the funds will go to Germany (25.8 per cent), France (17.9 per cent) and Italy (12.6 per cent).[13]

The other instrument supplements the Horizon Europe programme with EUR 5 billion, to increase European support for health and climate-related research and innovation activities. With a share of 1 per cent in the programme (EUR 0.05 billion), Poland ranks among the smallest beneficiaries. Probably, it reflects the limited engagement of Polish entities in the present EU research programme, since Poland has received from Horizon 2020, the predecessor of the new Horizon Europe, EUR 620 million, i.e. 1.2 per cent of the total appropriations. More funds from the programme will go to Member States much smaller than Poland in terms of population, e.g. Belgium, Hungary, i.e. 12.8 per cent and 1.8 per cent respectively. However, those countries have been able to receive and apply more money than Poland from the Horizon 2020, respectively: 5.5 per cent and 0.6 per cent.[14]

After analysis of the NGEU let us note that the programme is no novelty in terms of objectives to be achieved. On the contrary, the funding is oriented towards investing in the EU's common priorities through the existing programmes. It is intended to strengthen the European Green Deal, the digital single market as well as economic and social cohesion. But the initiative is new as regards the impressive scale of extra funds and the innovative capital raising method. The financial assistance under NGEU gives the EU Members mostly hit by the crisis an opportunity to avoid deeper divergences and at the same time to speed up the environmental and digital transformation, making the economies more resilient, environment-friendly and innovative.

3 The Multiannual Financial Framework for 2021–2027

An overview of the budget

According to the July 2020 Conclusions and to the related regulation adopted by the Council on 17 December 2020 (following the European Parliament's consent; Council Regulation, 2020), the MFF arrangement for 2021–2027 provides for EUR 1,074.3 billion. Poland can obtain ca. EUR 96 billion from the total amount (ca. 9 per cent)[15] The multiannual budget introduces significant changes in expenditure priorities relative to the MFF for 2014–2020. On the one hand, those include a marked reduction in funds for the traditional objectives (i.e. the cohesion policy and the common agricultural policy—CAP): down from 71 per cent of the MFF for 2014–2020 to 62 per cent in 2021–2027. On the other hand, appropriations for new goals have increased substantially, although from a low base. The most significant increase in expenditure will concern measures alleviating the problem of migration and border protection (by a factor of 2.6); youth programmes (mostly ERASMUS+; by 2.2 factor); security improvement (1.8 factor); climate action (1.7 factor); research and innovation (1.6 factor). As in the case of NGEU, spending must be largely linked to the climate and digital transformation and disbursed in accordance with the "rule of law" principle.

Cohesion policy funds for Poland

According to Conclusions, the MFF—as NGEU—should aim to support the fastest possible recovery from the recession and to counteract widening divergences in the EU. On account of its magnitude and previous functions, those tasks will mostly be implemented through cohesion policy. Poland can receive ca. EUR 66.4 billion in cohesion policy appropriations, as the largest beneficiary in the EU: 20 per cent of the total structural funds of EUR 330.2 billion. The amount will only be EUR 2.3 billion lower than that to be received by Italy and Spain combined—the second and third largest cohesion policy beneficiaries respectively.[16]

The cohesion policy funds imply a significant reduction relative to the previous multiannual budget—by ca. 10 per cent. Poland's allocation is much higher—by 20 per cent. The new allocation of appropriations between Member States partly results from modified distribution criteria: the existing criteria of low income (determining 81 per cent of the whole allocation for the Member State concerned) and the labour market and education situation (15 per cent of the allocation) were supplemented with those related to migration (non-EU net migration—3 per cent of the allocation) and the Member State's engagement in climate protection (greenhouse gas emissions in sectors excluded from the ETS—1 per cent). The reduced amount for Poland also reflects the fact that several Polish regions exceeded the GDP *per capita* threshold for less developed regions (with GDP *per capita* below 75 per cent of the EU-27 average; in terms of GDP measured in purchasing power standards—PPS).

Therefore, they will benefit from lower support funds intended for wealthier regions in transition (with GDP *per capita* between 75 per cent and 100 per cent of the EU-27 average: the Dolnośląskie and Wielkopolskie voivodships). Furthermore, the region of the capital city of Warsaw, statistically separated from the Mazowieckie voivodship, will be eligible for lower funding provided for more developed regions (GDP *per capita* above 100 per cent of the EU-27 average).

Another factor driving down cohesion funding is a decrease in the maximum transfer level (the so-called "capping") from the funds to individual Member States, depending on GDP *per capita* in PPS. For Poland, it will be 1.5 per cent of its GDP, whereas it has been 2.35 per cent of GDP until 2020.

There is a dramatic fall in the Cohesion Fund size as compared to the previous MFF (by 33 per cent). It will reduce the possibility to meet the still significant investment needs in the cohesion countries, including Poland, in the two areas in which Cohesion Fund investments are implemented, i.e. transport infrastructure and environmental protection. The needs are particularly big in the latter area considering the EU's pressure to achieve ambitious climate objectives and high dependence on coal as well as low energy efficiency in Poland.

Certain priorities of cohesion policy measures have changed. No financing will be available to projects in areas such as airport infrastructure, fossil fuels and rolling stock for rail transport (European Commission, 2018, Article 6). At the same time, relatively more funds will be spent on projects related to EU priorities: innovation, environmental protection, green transport and clean energy. Those changes are consistent with Polish needs. The preparation and implementation of such projects requires, however, more knowledge and experience than Polish entities tend to have. A positive decision for Poland is maintaining the decommitment rule at N+3, which means that the annual allocation of EU appropriations to the programme must be spent within 3 years following the year of its commitment (except for 2027, the year for which the N+2 rule will apply).

As in the case of NGEU, there will be a stronger link between the whole EU budget and the implementation of EU-wide policy objectives—throughout the European Semester framework. It means that projects financed from the structural funds will depend more on Council's country-specific recommendations (prepared by the Commission) and will be subject to more thorough surveillance procedures.

The role of the structural funds in public investment in Poland

The EU cohesion policy arrangements (which are pro-investment and not pro-consumption instruments) can be assessed not only with regard to their scale and rules (as discussed in the previous point) but also against the background of all investment expenditure in the economy. The rate of overall investment (especially of private investment) in Poland has been low for years. The 2019 figure was 18.6 per cent of GDP (with the EU-27 average at 22.1 per cent), among the lowest indicators in the region.[17] At the same time, Poland is a country whose public investment as a percentage of GDP significantly exceeded the EU average and the respective rates for most regional peer economies: in 2018 it was 4.7 per cent, whereas the EU average—2.9 per cent of GDP (European Commission, 2020d, p. 32). To a significant degree, it was fuelled by EU funds. In recent years, Poland has ranked among the Member States characterised by the highest shares of EU funds in financing public investment (61 per cent, fourth place), behind Portugal (84.2 per cent of public investment), Croatia—79.6 per cent and Lithuania—74.4 per cent.[18] Another indicator showing the scale of the dependence on the EU cohesion policy funds is a considerable share of these funds in Poland's GDP. In 2014–2020, the proportion was 2.7 per cent of GDP annually (total amount, EUR 90.6 billion, including national co-financing) (European Commission, 2020d, p. 17).

From the point of view of the economic growth prospects, both the magnitude and the structure of investment are of importance. In advanced economies, a major share of investment is allocated to the production of intellectual property products—IPP,[19] i.e. to research and development, computer programs, etc. Such investment enhances the innovation capacity of economies. In the last few years, there has been a rapid increase in innovation-related investments, but it has taken place from a very low level and Poland is still staying well below the EU average. According to the most recent data, in 2016, the percentage of IPP investments in total investment reached a record high of 62 per cent in Ireland, ahead of Denmark and Sweden with shares of 26 per cent. At the same time, the respective figure for Poland was below 8 per cent while the average for the EU was 21 per cent.[20] Most public funds in Poland, including from the EU, are allocated to simple regional investments, road and rail infrastructure development rather than to innovative environmental and energy projects.[21] Such a structure results in a very weak position of Poland in the EU in terms of innovation. According to the European Innovation Scoreboard, by 2019 Poland slightly advanced, moving up to 59 per cent of the EU average. But it still ranked fourth to last in the ranking (ahead of Romania, Bulgaria and Croatia). The EU's innovation leaders were Sweden, Finland and Denmark (exceeding 130 per cent of the EU average) (European Commission, 2020e, p. 91). The above data show the distance that Poland needs to cover in terms of innovation, a prerequisite of sustainable economic growth and improving the competitiveness of any economy.

The MFF money for financing agriculture in Poland

Due to the special nature of the Common Agricultural Policy (with approx. 70 per cent of funds allocated to income support for farmers in the form of direct payments, largely to be spent freely, thus not necessarily on investment-related measures), this section only indicates selected aspects of CAP financing, material from the point of view of the main subject of this chapter. The 2021–2027 CAP allocation for Poland (within the MFF) is EUR 27.8 billion, i.e. 8.3 per cent of the total CAP appropriations for EU-27 (EUR 336.5 billion). More EU funds will go to France—in EUR billion (54.7), Germany (37.6), Spain

(37.2) and Italy (31).[22] As in the EU as a whole, a major share (70 per cent) will be received by Polish farmers in the form of direct payments (EUR 19.5 billion), whereas the remaining 30 per cent will be spent on rural development, the so-called Pillar II of the CAP (EUR 8.3 billion). For Poland as well as for the whole EU, it means a significant reduction in the CAP funds: in both cases, by approx. 12 per cent relative to the 2014–2020 amounts. Particularly unfavourable are cuts in Pillar II, considering that this money finances a wide range of rural and agricultural development objectives. The reduction will be partly compensated with an extra EUR 0.9 billion from NGEU. Funds within MFF can be transferred between pillars.[23] However, it is unrealistic to expect that the government will decide to increase the amount for rural development at the expense of decreased funds for direct payments. That would meet with fierce opposition from the strong and well-organised agricultural lobby that requested equal payments in all the EU Member States in the budget negotiation period.[24] More probably, the government will decide to transfer funds in the opposite direction, as in 2014–2020, in order to compensate farmers for a modest increase in the amount of payments per hectare.

The new CAP places greater emphasis on farmers' implementing measures aimed to achieve environmental- and climate-related objectives. As indicated in the European Council Conclusions of July 2020, "[t]he share of the CAP expenditure that is expected to be dedicated to climate action shall be 40 per cent". Therefore, it is a more ambitious target than in other areas where climate-related measures should account for a minimum of 30 per cent of expenditure. In addition, some direct payments will be conditional on meeting more stringent environmental and climate requirements. Beneficiaries of payments will be obliged not only to comply with good agricultural and environmental condition (already in place) but also to satisfy additional requirements such as the protection of wetlands and peat bogs, a focus on crop rotation instead of previous crop diversification. Support for young farmers will be given a priority. A very favourable co-financing rate of 85 per cent for less developed regions (the majority of Polish regions) was introduced in the case of public expenditure.

The rule of law conditionality

In line with the July 2020 summit Conclusions, one condition for benefiting from the EU funds (NGEU and the MFF) is that "[t]he Union's financial interests shall be protected in accordance with the general principles embedded in the Union Treaties, in particular the values of Article 2 TEU". Thus, "[t]he European Council underlines the importance of the respect of the rule of law". A mechanism was to be adopted to allow suspending or cutting EU funds if a Member State breaches the rule of law. The idea of this proposal was a response to accusations made in recent years by certain Member States and the European Commission against Hungary and Poland of failing to uphold EU values and undermining the independence of the judiciary. According to the

July 2020 Conclusions, the Commission was to "[p]ropose measures in case of breaches for adoption by the Council by qualified majority".

However, later when the Commission's proposal of a respective regulation was discussed, Poland and Hungary protested against its content and declared to veto the MFF and NGEU. Both countries argued that the new instrument represented an intrusion into their national sovereignty, and feared that it could be used against them on other issues, such as migration or LGTBI rights. In spite of Hungary's and Poland's opposition, the regulation of the European Parliament and of the Council on a general regime of conditionality for the protection of the Union budget was agreed in November by the required qualified majority in the Council (Regulation, 2020). It contains the definition of the rule of law, principles, measures and procedures of its execution. The objective of the Regulation is to protect the EU budget against any kind of fraud, corruption and conflict of interest. Also, "Independence and impartiality of the judiciary should always be guaranteed" to protect "[a]gainst unlawful and arbitrary decisions by public authorities that could harm the financial interests of the Union".

Despite adoption of this Regulation, Poland and Hungary continued their opposition to the rule of law mechanism, threatening to veto the adoption of laws on MFF and NGEU (these documents require unanimous voting in the Council), necessary to start quickly the new long-term budget and recovery program. A compromise on the financial packages and rule of law procedure was achieved only during the EU summit on 10–11 December 2020 (European Council, 2020b), three weeks before the beginning of the new budgetary period. The December Conclusions kept the mechanism of the rule of law intact, but added several elements (European Council, 2020b). First of all, the Commission—in consultation with Member States—will adopt guidelines on the way it will apply the Regulation. The Commission will not activate a procedure against any country until the Court of Justice of the EU rules on the conformity of the mechanism with EU law (which will delay the activation of mechanism). The Regulation will apply only in relation to the new MFF and Next Generation EU. Thus, it excludes spending within the MFF 2014–2020 (to be continued till the end of 2023 in the area of cohesion policy). These additional rules were sufficient to convince Poland and Hungary to vote for the adoption of MFF and NGEU. The political agreement reached in December by the EU leaders paved the way to the adoption of the legal acts necessary for MFF and NGEU to enter into force.

Conclusions

Based on the still incomplete data, currently it is only possible to indicate certain elements of the assessment of the importance of EU funds for the recovery of the Polish economy from the COVID-19 pandemic. An important aspect of the evaluation is the fact that most appropriations from the EU multiannual budget, as well as from NGEU, will be investment oriented. It concerns first of all such budgetary items as cohesion, rural development, research and development, amounts for economic recovery from the RRF. Moreover, in the programming period 2021–2027, expenditure financed from the EU budget and NGEU should focus on structural reforms that are expected to have lasting effects on growth and employment. In particular, an enormous focus will be on the financing of green and digital projects, i.e. on areas where Poland lags significantly behind the EU's top performers. The actual importance of all EU funds will largely depend on the concrete structure of the use of EU appropriations. The question is whether Poland maintains its current attitude and uses EU financial resources mainly for traditional investments in transport infrastructure and "hard projects" or rather actively implements EU development priorities. Despite significant backwardness, in the programming period 2014–2020, modest funds from the EU budget have been spent in Poland on the environmental protection. In the largest national Operational Programme covering such activities, "Infrastructure and Environment", the latter area accounted for a mere 31 per cent of the total funds of the Programme, whereas infrastructure received 64 per cent.[25] Poland will not avoid climate transition, whether due to its EU membership or major negligence in the past.[26] Poland's objection to the climate package will not stop the EU's further work in that area. Action taken at the EU level will result in acts of secondary law impossible for Poland to veto independently, but whose provisions will still apply to Poland as the EU Member. Furthermore, for failure to respect the EU's common objectives and to comply with the relevant legislation, Poland may be subject to financial sanctions. The non-adoption of EU solutions also poses a risk that Polish products manufactured with the use of "dirty" technologies will no longer be accepted in the EU market. It is a matter of time. As a matter of equal importance, the (necessary) low-carbon transition not only involves costs, but also offers an opportunity to boost economic growth, competitiveness and innovation. This is a consequence of rising demand for eco-products, green technologies and the related increase in employment. Undoubtedly, due to relatively high coal mining employment, the well-organised lobby in this sector and the necessity to ensure safety of energy supply, improving Poland's environmental sustainability will require a broad political consensus.

A particularly significant role is to be played in the process of structural changes in the economy by digitisation. The COVID-19 outbreak highlighted its importance across all areas of the economy and society. New technologies have helped businesses and public services to keep functioning and have ensured the continuation of international trade. In the long term, the pandemic is expected to trigger permanent changes: more remote working, e-learning, e-commerce. It has, therefore, become an imperative for undertakings and governments to invest in digitisation. This requirement offers a chance that the digitisation of the Polish economy will accelerate and result in increased innovativeness of many businesses. The country's present position in this area is very weak: Poland ranks low (last but five) among the Member States in terms of the EU's Digital Economy and Society Index.[27]

Given the investment-oriented nature of majority of EU funds, it is possible to better appreciate and assess their positive impact on the Polish economy in the next years. The very appropriations from the new NGEU funds imply significant supplementation of funds for the country's development and modernisation: the amount of EUR 29.0 billion (grants) available to Poland is equivalent to 5.5 per cent of Poland's 2019 GDP. It translates into average annual investment of 1.8 per cent of GDP to be committed in three years. Furthermore, Poland will be offered investment funds under the MFF (almost all transfers without those for direct payments, i.e. EUR 75.5 billion) equal to 14.2 per cent of its 2019 GDP, i.e. almost 2.0 per cent of GDP per year during the 7-year period of the MFF.[28] Almost all these amounts will have to be supplemented by national co-financing, thus increasing the total funds invested. In comparison with a low rate of investment in the past years, the EU funds offer a major additional development stimulus that should facilitate post-pandemic recovery as well as long-term reinforcement of the development foundations of the Polish economy. Due to the NGEU grants the allocation from the MFF will increase by 26 per cent, which should provide real support for economic recovery. Also, Poland will get access to NGEU cheap loans worth about EUR 34 billion. The impact of the appropriations employed will be reflected in both demand growth (additional amounts spent in the market and creating demand in other sectors through the investment multiplier mechanism) and more sustainable supply-side effects (new technologies, new goods and services, more efficient products, etc.). The significance of the financial transfers is strengthened by elements such as: the predictability of support and the stability of the conditions to obtain it in the next few years, the synergy of effects, a focus on the agreed priorities, etc.

In general, the pandemic response is a chance for Poland and the whole EU to radically restructure the economy by focusing on prospective innovative investments related to climate protection and broad digitisation. It is also a chance for quicker and less costly overcoming the heritage of a fossil (mainly coal) economy's energy mix, as well as for enhancing its innovative capacity. The other side of the coin is, however, that Poland faces a risk of huge debt which will put a burden on the next generations.

The scope of actual changes and their significance will depend on meeting quite difficult conditions for using the funds. The starting point is the preparation of a good national recovery and resilience programme taking account of the Commission guidelines and the Union's priorities, to guarantee a development-oriented structure of expenditure. It also involves significant implementation capacity (including good cooperation between public administration institutions and regional and local authorities). In certain cases, new strategies have to be adopted, e.g. with regard to Poland's joining the implementation of the EU climate neutrality programme. Recall that the cuts agreed in certain programmes affecting Poland partly result from Poland's previous disrespect of EU agreements regarding solutions on current pressing challenges like withdrawal from the refugee allocation system or weak implementation of EU climate policy so far. It would be very unfavourable for Poland to continue taking up such stance. A good uptake of EU appropriations also entails the need to find funds for national co-financing. This may, however, prove problematic for beneficiaries under the conditions of rising general government debt and impaired liquidity of enterprises in the aftermath of the pandemic. It is also indispensable to overcome the opposition of certain influential business groups in Poland (especially the coal-mining lobby) to the implementation of ambitious climate plans of the EU (cf. Chapter 7). Furthermore, it is necessary to assign significant funds for supporting the transformation and to mitigate the social costs of change.

The EU funds offer an opportunity to increase investments, but they will not finance all measures related to addressing the consequences of the pandemic and the simultaneous implementation of EU objectives.[29] With the current very low level of investment, the Polish economy has little chance to further develop quickly and to boost innovation, especially given the fact that the working-age population is on the decline as a consequence of its ageing society and R&D investment is very low. Neither should substantial public funds for investment be expected in the coming years. This opinion is based on two factors. One reason is rising public deficit and debt which reflects huge expenditures to fight pandemic consequences and reduced revenue. The other reason is huge social transfers from the state budget introduced in recent years, which are of fixed character. The indebtedness will further grow if Poland decides to raise loans from NGEU. Therefore, to maintain or, even better, to increase the rate of investment, it is necessary to quickly introduce instruments mobilising greater private funds, including foreign investment. Also regulatory measures are required to improve business environment, incentives for innovations, etc.

In conclusion, it is worth emphasising that the NGEU programme will have major EU-wide effects. It is a truism that benefits will be derived by all EU Member States, considering their enormous interdependence in the functioning of the EU's internal market. Perhaps, however, it is more important than the benefits themselves that the potential costs of the lack of support and the absence of joint action at the EU level would be greater: especially the risk of the euro area collapsing (as the crisis has hit particularly hard the weakest euro-area countries in South Europe, already considerably indebted) and of increased income inequalities between EU Member States. Aside the economic impact, NGEU is of a very political significance to the EU as well. At the beginning of the pandemic, the EU was criticised for its non-action. The proposal for non-budget support (NGEU), on a scale unknown in history, put forward relatively quickly (in a few months) by the European Commission, enhances the EU's perception in the Member States' societies and worldwide. It also strengthens intra-EU solidarity as all the Member States have agreed to provide significant financial aid to those affected the most by the pandemic. Further, solidarity among the EU Member States is an important indication for financial markets, demonstrating the strength and potential of the European Union and attracting non-EU investors. Lastly, NGEU program provides an antidote against anti-EU sentiment having risen recently not only in the south of the EU, but also across the whole bloc.

Notes

1 Unless otherwise mentioned, all figures are expressed in constant 2018 prices.

2 The list of the most important initiatives is presented at: https://ec.europa.eu/info/live-work-travel-eu/health/coronavirus-response/jobs-and-economy-during-coronavirus-pandemic_en (Accessed: 5 September 2020).

3 Figures come from https://ec.europa.eu/info/strategy/eu-budget/long-term-eu-budget/eu-budget-2021-2027_en (Accessed: 15 October 2020) and own calculations.

4 Unless otherwise explained, citations come from the July 2020 Conclusions (European Council, 2020a).

5 With a very strong credit rating, the Commission will be able to raise loans in financial markets on conditions more favourable than market terms. Only countries that borrow at a rate higher than the EU borrowing rate would benefit from an EU loan.

6 https://www.bruegel.org/2020/07/having-the-cake-how-eu-recovery-fund/ (Accessed: 15 October 2020) and the author's calculations.

7 The EU objective of climate neutrality means that by 2050 the European Union Member States should only emit such quantities of greenhouse gases (including carbon dioxide) as their economies are capable of absorbing. Its implementation should follow a roadmap called the European Green Deal, presented by the Commission in December 2019.

8 An additional sum at EUR 1.5 billion may be available within MFF, providing Poland meets all requirements.

9 Around 90 per cent of electricity is still generated in conventional power plants, mainly using domestic hard coal and lignite. Solid fossil fuels also play a large role in household energy consumption, especially in heating (European Commission, 2020d, p. 41).

10 Coal mining and the coal-based energy sectors provide employment to ca. 112,000 people in Poland (European Commission, 2020d, p. 39).

11 Total emissions in Poland have been increasing gradually since 2014 contrary to the general downward trend in the EU. In recent years, emissions have grown substantially in the building and transport sectors, in contrast to declining emissions in the energy sector (European Commission, 2020d, p. 41).

12 As analysed by Nobili Partners, a mere 1 per cent of listed companies in Poland have reported carbon dioxide emissions along their value chains, https://300gospodarka.pl/300klimat/gpw-spolki-gieldowe-niegotowe-zmiany-klimatu (Accessed: 14 September 2020).

13 https://www.bruegel.org/2020/07/having-the-cake-how-eu-recovery-fund/ (Accessed: 14 September 2020) and own calculations.

14 https://www.bruegel.org/2020/07/having-the-cake-how-eu-recovery-fund/; https://ec.europa.eu/research/horizon2020/index.cfm?pg=country-profiles (Accessed: 16 October 2020) and own calculations.

15 https://ec.europa.eu/info/strategy/eu-budget/long-term-eu-budget/eu-budget-2021-2027_en (Accessed: 15 October 2020). Thus, total funds for Poland from the NGEU programme (EUR 29 billion) and under the MFF (EUR 96 billion) should be ca. EUR 125 billion.

16 https://ec.europa.eu/info/strategy/eu-budget/long-term-eu-budget/eu-budget-2021-2027_en (Accessed: 15 October 2020).

17 The Member States with shares of investment in GDP lower than that of Poland included: Portugal and Bulgaria (18.3 per cent), Italy (18.1 per cent), Luxembourg (16.9 per cent) and Greece (11.4 per cent). At the same time, the percentage was the highest for Ireland (45.6 per cent!), followed by Hungary (28.6 per cent), the Czech Republic (26.2 per cent) and Estonia (26.1 per cent). https://ec.europa.eu/eurostat/databrowser/view/tec00011/default/table?lang=en (Accessed: 9 September 2020).

18 In the absence of comparable data, EU funds intended for rural development are excluded. https://cohesiondata.ec.europa.eu/Other/Share-of-Cohesion-Policy-per-Member-State-to-publi/drqq-sbh7/data (Assessed: 15 September_2020).

19 Intellectual property products are defined as produced non-financial assets which are the result of research, development, investigation or innovation which lead to knowledge that the developers can market or use for their own benefit in production.

20 https://data.oecd.org/gdp/investment-by-asset.htm#indicator-chart (Accessed: 14 September 2020). A more composite measure of R&D expenditure as a share of GDP indicates that although in 2018 the figure for Poland had doubled from EU accession, it still represented a mere half of the EU average (1.2 per cent of GDP in Poland against 2.2 per cent in the EU-27) (European Commission, 2020e, p. 83).

21 For more on this subject, see: Ambroziak, 2020, pp. 103–124.

22 https://300gospodarka.pl/news/znamy-wyliczenia-rzadu-polska-ostatecznie-4-najwiekszym-beneficjentem-srodkow-z-ue-na-odbudowe-po-pandemii (Accessed: 14 September 2020).

23 Up to 15 per cent of their annual national ceilings, for both rural development measures and direct payments.

24 It was agreed to reduce the disparities in the amounts of direct payments per hectare but on a scale significantly below Poland's expectations.

25 Author's calculations based on: Ministerstwo Infrastruktury i Rozwoju (2014, pp. 23–24 and 26–27).

26 According to a report prepared by three non-governmental organisations, Poland ranks last in the EU in terms of climate change performance. The composite indicator for the assessment, the Climate Change Performance Index, covers four areas: GHG Emissions, Renewable Energy, Energy Use and Climate Policy (Burck et al., 2020, p. 9).

27 The DESI reflects a Member State's performance in five areas: Connectivity, Human Capital, the Use of Internet, Integration of Digital Technology and Digital Public Services (European Commission, 2020f, pp. 11, 14).

28 Author's calculations based on: https://ec.europa.eu/eurostat/databrowser/view/tec00001/default/table?lang=en (Accessed: 20 September 2020).

29 As estimated by the European Commission, the energy transition in Poland will cost EUR 240 billion https://www.gov.pl/web/fundusze-regiony/polska-chce-sprawiedliwej-transformacji (Accessed: 19 September 2020).

References

Ambroziak, A.A. (2020) State aid in Poland following accession to the EU. In: A. Visvizi, A. Matysek- Jędrych and K. Mroczek-Dąbrowska (eds.), *Poland in the Single Market: Politics, Economics, The Euro*, London: Routledge, 103–124, doi:10.4324/9780429285301.

Burck, J., Hagen, U., Höhne, N., Nascimento, L. and Bals, C. (2020) *Climate Change Performance Index, Results 2020*, Bonn: Germanwatch, NewClimate Institute & Climate Action Network, 1–32.

Council Regulation (EU, Euratom) 2020/2093 of 17 December 2020 laying down the multiannual financial framework for the years 2021 to 2027, OJ L 433.

European Commission (2018) Proposal for a Regulation of the European Parliament and of the Council on the European Regional Development Fund and on the Cohesion Fund. COM(2018) 372 final.

European Commission (2020a) Corrigendum to Annexes to the Proposal for a Regulation of the European Parliament and of the Council establishing a Recovery and Resilience Facility. COM(2020) 408 final/3 Annexes 1 to 3.

European Commission (2020b) Proposal for a Regulation of the European Parliament and of the Council amending Regulation (EU) No 1303/2013 as regards exceptional additional resources and implementing arrangements under the Investment for growth and jobs goal to provide assistance for fostering crisis repair in the context of the COVID-19 pandemic and preparing a green, digital and resilient recovery of the economy (REACT-EU). COM(2020) 451 final.

European Commission (2020c) Amended proposal for a Regulation of the European Parliament and of the Council establishing the Just Transition Fund. COM(2020) 460 final.

European Commission (2020d) Commission Staff Working Document Country Report Poland 2020 Accompanying the document Communication from the Commission to the European Parliament, the European Council, the Council, the European Central Bank and the Eurogroup. 2020 European Semester: Assessment of progress on structural reforms, prevention and correction of macroeconomic imbalances, and results of in-depth reviews under Regulation (EU) No 1176/2011. SWD(2020) 520 final.

European Commission (2020e) Innovation Scoreboard 2020.

European Commission (2020f) Digital Economy and Society Index (DESI) 2020.

European Council (2020a) Conclusions of the European Council. July 21. EUCO 10/20.

European Council (2020b) Conclusions of the European Council. December 11. EUCO 22/20.

Kawecka-Wyrzykowska, E. (2017) Coordination of EU member states' economic policies and the industrial development environment. In A.A. Ambroziak (ed.), *The New Industrial Policy of the European Union*, Switzerland: Springer, 241–265, doi:10.1007/978-3-319-39070-3-11.

Kawecka-Wyrzykowska, E. (2020) A new industrial policy in the EU: in search for a new paradigm of public intervention. In A.A. Ambroziak (ed.), *New Challenges for the European Union's Industrial Policy: Climate Change, Servitisation, Digitalisation*, Warsaw: SGH Publishing House, 11–36.

Ministerstwo Infrastruktury i Rozwoju (2014) Program Operacyjny Infrastruktura i Środowisko 2014–2020, Warsaw.

Regulation (EU, Euratom) 2020/2092 of the European Parliament and of the Council of 16 December 2020 on a general regime of conditionality for the protection of the Union budget, OJ L 433. https://www.bruegel.org/2020/07/having-the-cake-how-eu-recovery-fund/

https://cohesiondata.ec.europa.eu/Other/Share-of-Cohesion-Policy-per-Member-State-to-publi/drqq-sbh7/data.https://data.oecd.org/gdp/investment-by-asset.htm#indicator-chart

https://ec.europa.eu/info/live-work-travel-eu/health/coronavirus-response/jobs-and-economy-during-coronavirus-pandemic_en. https://ec.europa.eu/info/strategy/eu-budget/long-term-eu-budget/eu-budget-2021-2027_en

https://ec.europa.eu/eurostat/databrowser/view/tec00001/default/table?lang=en

https://ec.europa.eu/info/sites/info/files/about_the_european_commission/eu_budget/recovery_and_resilience_facility_.pdf

https://ec.europa.eu/research/horizon2020/index.cfm?pg=country-profiles

https://300gospodarka.pl/news/znamy-wyliczenia-rzadu-polska-ostatecznie-4-najwiekszym-beneficjentem-srodkow-z-ue-na-odbudowe-po-pandemii

https://300gospodarka.pl/300klimat/gpw-spolki-gieldowe-niegotowe-zmiany-klimatu https://www.gov.pl/web/fundusze-regiony/polska-chce-sprawiedliwej-transformacji.

6 Financial measures adopted in Poland in the light of COVID-19 state aid EU framework

Adam A. Ambroziak

Introduction

State aid is deployed to support entrepreneurs faced with unexpected events unrolling in the marketplace that could not have been duly considered in their business plans but, at the same time, it implies interfering with normal (market) operations pursued by economic entities. Such interventions are the more welcome, the more fierce the external competition; they are also expected in times of crisis when enterprises lose liquidity and are deprived of access to the sources of funding. Under such circumstances demand drops dramatically which, in combination with the growing number of incomplete transactions, increases uncertainty about future market developments. This is the reality that European entrepreneurs, including the Polish ones, have had to cope with since the Q2 2020. However, the COVID-19-induced crisis is completely different from all previous crisis experiences. The exceptionality of what we are witnessing today results from the fact that the rapid slowdown in economic activity has been triggered by a non-economic factor, which spread to almost all countries across the globe within a relatively short period of time. Today's economic crisis is not the effect of erroneous monetary or fiscal policy, trade wars, inflation shocks, overproduction, or financial sector problems but stems from the economy (enterprises and consumers) being brought to a near-standstill motivated by health related issues. As a result, the traditional approach of viewing market failure as the only reason for triggering state intervention has partly lost its *raison d'etre*. COVID-19-induced government intervention is, in a way, a compensation for market distortions (economic lockdown) resulting from governments' decisions to protect the health and lives of their citizens. Therefore, the Commission, based on a principle according to which aid can be justified by the scope and depth of the crisis but, at the same time, it needs to be proportional to the scale of the phenomenon so that the distortion of competition in the domestic market were the least possible (EC, 2012), introduced new provisions concerning admissibility of state aid during the COVID-19 pandemic.

The aim of the study was to identify: a) changes in the principles regarding state aid in the EU in relation to COVID-19, and b) to assess the state aid

DOI: 10.4324/9781003144434-7

measures (schemes) offered by Poland from the perspective of their potential impact on competition within the EU Internal Market. An analysis will be carried out not only of changes in the EU legislation but also of aid schemes introduced in Poland compared to instruments available in other Member States.

To this end, Polish COVID-19 state aid schemes were examined together with decisions taken by the EC by 30 September 2020 in light of the Temporary rules on state aid introduced in the EU (EC, 2020s). The assessment discussed in this chapter focuses exclusively on new aid schemes put in place by the end of September 2020. We need to bear in mind, however, that many public institutions have introduced additional facilitations and reliefs for entrepreneurs by slightly modifying the tools they already had at their disposal (used in cases of a "traditional" downturn). They did it without amending the earlier approved aid schemes or these tools have not been considered state aid in the light of Art. 107 of the Treaty on the Functioning of the European Union (TFEU). That was the case of, inter alia, projects previously programmed and financed by the European funds, as well as instruments offered by the National Economy Bank (Bank Gospodarstwa Krajowego—BGK) before the COVID-19 outbreak (PFR, 2020a). As a result, we cannot unambiguously identify the impact of only new COVID-19 state aid schemes on economy and competition, as many additional actions have been taken in this area between the government and entrepreneurs.

Moreover, we compared Polish state aid schemes to schemes available in other EU Member States and analysed their actual disbursement performance in Poland by the end of September 2020. We based our findings on the EC's decisions on state aid schemes, as well as on Polish programmes under which COVID-19 support is offered to entrepreneurs. Considering wide and multi-directional support offered to entrepreneurs by the Member States in relation with COVID-19 and the sectoral specificity, this analysis does not cover the airline industry (aid to airports and airlines) and agriculture, as well as aid to research and development dedicated to fighting the pandemic.

Data used in statistical analysis are continuously collected in Poland by the Office of Competition and Consumer Protection (OCCP), however, we found many inconsistencies, errors, and delays in providing information on state aid received from local, regional, and central authorities. This study covers aid granted in Poland and committed in aid schemes by other Member States as at 30 September 2020. Therefore, values presented in the chapter reflect general trends rather than the exact final outcomes of COVID state aid granted in Poland in the first 6 months of the COVID-19 era.

1 Reasons behind COVID-19 state aid in the EU

In principle, pursuant to Art. 107.1 of the TFEU any aid granted by a Member State or through State resources in any form whatsoever which distorts or threatens to distort competition by favouring certain undertakings or the production of certain goods shall, in so far as it affects trade between Member States, be incompatible with the internal market. The EU law provides for mandatory and facultative exemptions from the general ban on granting state aid. Their goal is to ensure the so-called level playing field within the framework of the EU Single Market. Granting state aid in one Member State without limitations could distort competition within the entire EU. Taking the above into account and in connection with the need to notify and obtain an approval from the European Commission for putting in place state aid schemes compliant with the internal market, the EU worked out guidelines for different categories of state aid. Their goal is to ensure transparency in the work of the Commission and to make it easier for public authorities to draft programmes compliant with the EU regulations (Ambroziak, 2014, 2017).

As already mentioned above, decisions made by the Member States to impose a freeze on their economies have produced strongly negative effects. A powerful supply shock was observed triggered by the disruption of supply and production chains resulting from the closure of not only external borders but also of the internal frontiers within the EU. At the same time, demand shocks took place as a response to a rapid drop or even total loss of consumer demand for some goods and services (in industries such as: transport, tourism, hotel, culture, events, catering, as well as shoemaking and tailoring services). However, one needs to bear in mind that demand for other goods (medical products, including personal protection equipment, disinfectant and cleaning products, food, and computers) and services (e-commerce, courier services, access to the Internet and Internet platforms used for virtual/remote work) dramatically increased.

Another consequence for the economy, this time experienced relatively equally by all, was drastic downsizing of investment plans by economic operators as well as households in the face of an uncertain future: potential increase in unemployment, lack of access to certain goods and services, changing consumer patterns and habits, cooperation between enterprises, being dependent on external partners, diversification of suppliers and customers, changes in the length of value chains.

The above economic phenomena led to the loss of financial liquidity of many entrepreneurs. The reasons underpinning it include the lack of cash flows from consumers, the lack of transactions and settlements between enterprises, uncertainty and higher risk, and impeded access to external finance.

In its first COVID-19 Communication the European Commission, as the guardian of the treaties which include state aid rules, stressed that Member States may adopt diverse support measures consistent with the EU legal framework. These measures, which do not constitute state aid, include: measures that apply to all entrepreneurs (e.g., tax allowances, wage subsidies, or subsidies to social insurance premiums that apply *erga omnes*) and direct support to consumers (EC, 2020d).

In the face of intensifying negative effects of the pandemic and further freezing of economies, already in March 2020 the Commission adopted the Temporary Framework, a document which since that time has been amended many times as the circumstances and demands of the Member States evolved (EC, 2020a, 2020b, 2020c, 2020t). Primary provisions provided for granting the above mentioned support until the end of December 2020, however, the fourth amending exercise of 13 October 2020 extended this period until 30 June 2021 (EC, 2020u). The need to adopt these guidelines which are enshrined in the existing Treaty foundations resulted from the wish to ensure transparency in activities and decisions swiftly issued by the Commission. It is assumed that the conditions for granting state aid are used as assessment criteria by the Commission in the light of impact on competition in the EU internal market.

With regard to the connection between COVID-19 pandemic and consequences to entrepreneurs, the Commission considered Art. 107.2b of the TFEU referring to aid to make good the damage caused by exceptional occurrences appropriate for the assessment of aid to entrepreneurs in industries particularly affected by the pandemic. At the same time, the Commission highlighted that the aid must compensate damage directly resulting from restrictions imposed on economic activity by the governments of the Member States. Such aid may not be granted to maintain or restore profitability, liquidity or solvency of an institution or economic operator. In addition, the assessment of individual aid schemes should be made on a case-by-case basis, based on the jurisprudence of the Court of Justice of the European Union and considering previously issued decisions based on criteria such as: unpredictability, difficulties to predict, significant scale and economic impact, and extraordinariness.

Ultimately, Member States have notified aid targeting event and media businesses, tour operators but also airports, ferry carriers, and transport companies invoking this treaty basis. Like Denmark, Sweden, Hungary, Slovenia, and Austria, Poland received approval for its scheme to compensate large enterprises and certain small and medium-sized enterprises (SMEs) providing them with direct liquidity through loans (EC, 2020k).

Besides Art. 107.2.b of the TFEU, the European Commission cited in the Temporary Framework a catalogue of categories of lawful aid based on Art. 107.3.b of the TFEU which provides for facultative exemptions from the general ban on granting state aid.[1] It provides for granting aid when there are distortions in the economies of the Member States. The European Commission explained that the situation has been triggered by economic downturn resulting from the coronavirus outbreak. Thus, the goal was to support businesses, mainly micro enterprises and SMEs that have found themselves in unpredictable economic and social circumstances. The catalogue of categories of allowable aid originally drafted rather widely and extended on numerous occasions provided for granting aid or benefits restricted as to the maximum amount and type of instrument (borrowings, guarantees, capitalization) or the goal for which the support is granted (R&D aid).

2 Poland against the background of COVID-19 state aid in the EU

According to available data, the European Commission agreed to grant COVID-19 state aid in the EU up to EUR 1.7 trillion by 30 September 2020 (excluding aid to agriculture, transport, and R&D not covered by this chapter).

However, it must be stressed that there are several aid schemes (three from Germany, one from Italy and one from Belgium) which were approved at the beginning of the pandemic in March 2020 but reported no data about their respective budgets of proposed measures (Figures 6.1 and 6.2). It means that the below presented rankings of these Member States are clearly underestimated, but, even without these resources, these countries are leaders when it comes to nominal value of declared aid budget. The total budget of aid schemes under research proposed by Poland and approved by the European Commission exceeds EUR 51.96 bn, which is very little compared to nominal and relative values made available by Germany and France. These countries' budgets are estimated to represent much more than 60 per cent of the total amount of state aid granted within the EU (with their cumulated share in GDP of 35 per cent in 2019) while resources planned in Poland account for 3 per cent.

Looking at the relationship between aid offered by a Member State and its GDP in 2019, the biggest donors of aid will be France (15.8 per cent) and Germany (18.8 per cent) with Poland's share of 9.8 per cent (slightly higher than in Austria and Portugal). However, it is worth noting, that for the Polish budget rather heavily burdened with social welfare programmes put in place in recent years, this aid (if paid out in full) may be dangerous for public finances.

The structure of COVID-19 state aid in the EU Member States notified to the Commission is the reflection of three factors: availability of financial resources in the budget, administrative culture and its readiness to embrace more advanced financial instruments (from direct grants to repayable instruments), and government's approach to public interventions. State aid comes in diverse forms, such as direct grants, advance payments, soft loans, guarantees, including guarantees on loans and equity instruments.

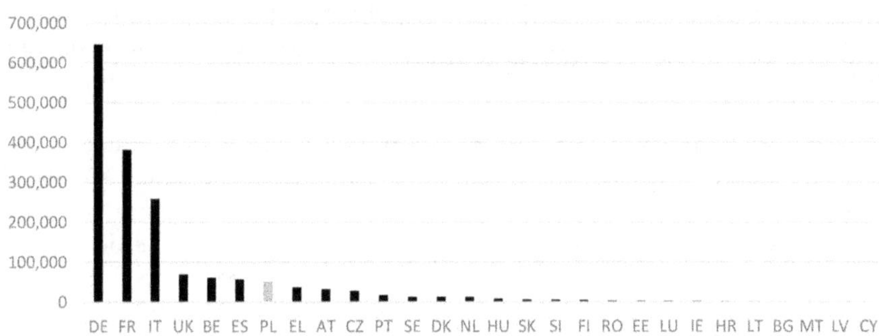

Figure 6.1 COVID-19 state aid approved by the European Commission in national schemes by 30 September 2020 (in millions of EUR).

Note: In case of Germany, France, Italy, and Belgium values are underestimated due to the lack of data in certain Commission's decisions on their state aid schemes.

Source: Own calculations based on own analysis of the European Commission decisions on COVID-19 state aid schemes (EC, 2020v).

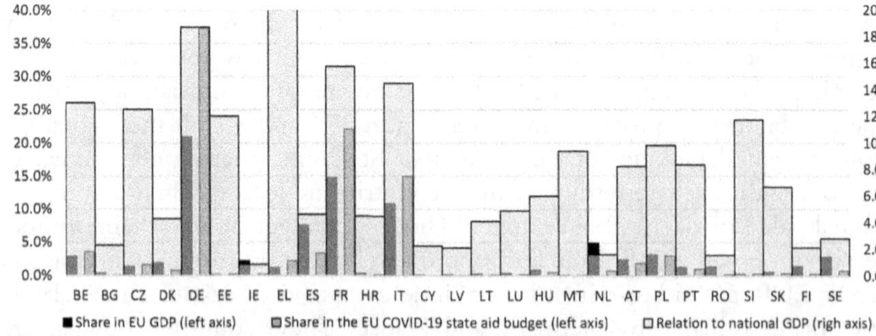

Figure 6.2 COVID-19 state aid budgeted in schemes adopted by the EC by 30 September 2020 (in relation to GDP).

Note: See Figure 6.1.

Source: Own calculations (EC, 2020v).

Poland (together with Italy, the Netherlands, Greece, France, and Latvia) has found itself in the group of states which were rather economical in planning state aid in the form of direct grants (6.9 per cent of the total budgeted amount) but it increased the share of payment advantages (4.9 per cent) more than other countries (with the exemption for Cyprus). Notably, the latter cover a wide and diverse range of financial instruments that are in fact allowances of various type (exemptions, write-off of tax arrears, tax waivers, reduction of the tax base or of the amount of tax and charges, payment deferrals, and payment in instalments) that apply to all charges, payments, and taxes payable to public authorities (national and local). These instruments do not engage public funding but increased losses in revenues to the central government and local government budgets (like in Italy, Cyprus, and Hungary). They provide enterprises with short-term liquidity, however, are not of investment nature. From the viewpoint of the central budget, advance payments mean drops in income and lower future public investment in Poland. On the other hand, however, one may expect that in the new financial perspective public investment projects will get support from the EU funds.

According to available data, Poland is also one of the Member States which decided to rely on preferential loans (42.5 per cent of notified COVID-19 resources in Poland), similarly to Hungary (45.4 per cent). Latvia (87.5 per cent), Croatia (83.5 per cent), and Cyprus (73 per cent) were leaders in this ranking. It is a consequence of the importance of direct payments from public institutions, which were used to lower interest rates or even make loans unrepayable.

When investigating the structure of COVID-19 state aid and what it is earmarked for, one may observe that the key role is played by various guarantees (74.4 per cent of total budget of all Member States). Moreover, it needs to be stressed that German and Italian state aid schemes, for which no data have been reported about their budgets, focused on providing diverse guarantees. Their goal is to support state loan schemes, help to ensure the circulation of funds between private entities while the actual deployment of aid—in the form of loan repayment in the event of default by a debtor—is relatively rare. Therefore, it does not cause problems for the budget at the time when guarantees are provided and carries potential disbursements over to a later period.

When it comes to Poland, since the outbreak of the pandemic until late September 2020 the Commission issued 16 positive decisions concerning proposed COVID-19 aid schemes totalling EUR 51.96 bn (originating from the state budget, local government budgets, and unused resources of the cohesion policy at the disposal of the Polish government). They provided for the implementation of 37 different instruments of financial support (Figure 6.3). From the point of view of capital that would potentially be mobilised, preferential loans (42.5 per cent) and loan guarantee schemes represented the biggest proportion among notified measures and included not just loan but also factoring guarantees (42.4 per cent). Direct payments (6.9 per cent), as well as widely understood payment advantages (4.9 per cent), and equity instruments (3.2 per cent) have a much smaller share in budgeted COVID-19 aid. It does not mean, however, that these funds have already been injected to the Polish economy. The assessment of the real scale of support is hindered by some elements. First, the time between the approval of a specific measure by the Commission and the actual launching of the support is usually several weeks as a system of distribution must be prepared underpinned by institutional structure, legal and procedural instruments, possibly signing agreements with financial intermediaries, training the staff dealing with the reviewing of applications for aid and applying entrepreneurs. Second, aid donors are obliged to input data into the system and data available for the end of September 2020 are incomplete.

In fact, as at 30 September 2020, the total COVID-19 aid granted in Poland amounted to EUR 17.9 bn, which represented 34.4 per cent of funds earmarked for this purpose. The highest level of support granted within the

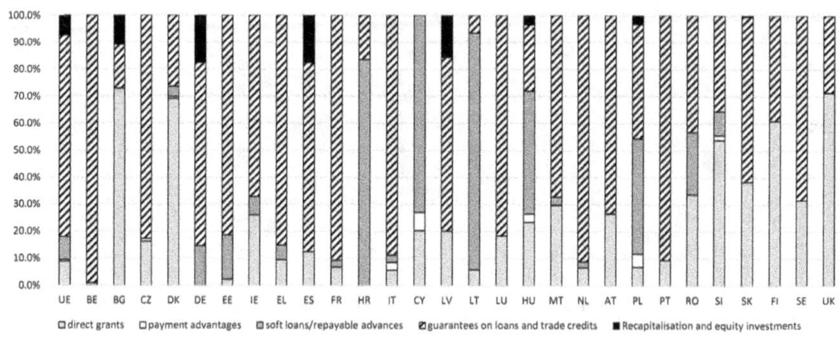

Figure 6.3 Structure of COVID-19 state aid in Member States broken down by forms.
Note: See Figure 6.1.
Source: Own calculations (EC, 2020v).

investigated period compared to the plans approved by the European Commission was reported for payment advantages (70.1 per cent), repayable instruments (67.7 per cent), and direct grants (26.6 per cent). These forms of state aid were available at the earliest moment and offered by several instruments provided by some schemes.

3 General COVID-19 state aid schemes limited by amount

The basic allowable aid consistent with the Temporary Framework based on Art. 107.3.c included the support not higher than EUR 800,000 per business granted in the form of direct grants, tax allowances and exemptions, as well as reductions in charges, preferential guarantees, repayable advances, and borrowings (Figure 6.4). The first amended version of the Temporary Framework was expanded with tax payment deferrals or deferred payment of social insurance contributions, as well as subsidising employees' salaries and wages to avoid lay-offs during the COVID-19 pandemic (EC, 2020a, 2020t). The approval for wage subsidy schemes running for not more than 12 months was conditioned by the declaration to maintain jobs and to keep subsidies at the maximum level of 80 per cent of monthly gross remuneration paid for the subsidised job.

Polish grant schemes

Direct grants are direct transfers to entrepreneurs in the form of subsidies or refunds, but they also take the form of subsidised interest rates on loans. Main instruments introduced by the COVID Law with a view to subsidise current business operations included subsidies to remuneration and social insurance contributions (Art. 15zzb COVID Law, 2020a), subsidies to businesses run by

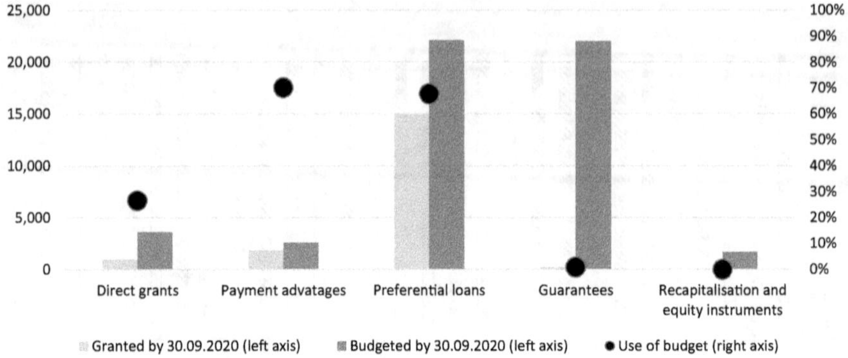

Figure 6.4 Structure of budgeted and granted COVID-19 state aid in Poland by 3Q2020 (in million EUR and %).

Source: Own calculations based on OCCP Data (EC, 2020v).

private individuals (Art. 15zzc), and subsidies to the remuneration of employees of NGOs (Art. 15zze) (EC, 2020h) offered by heads of poviats (counties).

Subsidies to employees' remuneration could be granted for the maximum period of 3 months within which the beneficiary had to maintain the initial number of jobs. The fundamental reason for receiving the subsidy from the head of poviat was coronavirus-related turnover drop by at least 30 per cent.[2]

Private individuals who run businesses (primarily self-employed) can receive support from the budget of up to EUR 0.36 bn, heads of poviats, through the Poviat Labour Offices, offered subsidies (in proportions identical to the above ones) to cover some costs involved in economic activity. Maximum ceilings for subsidies to the remuneration of employees of NGOs were the same, however, the budget of the programme, because of the scale of the problem, was much lower and amounted to EUR 17.3 million.

The above solutions were quite popular with other EU Member States. However, we need to observe that salaries and wages in Poland are amongst the lowest in the EU (Figure 6.5), which is why the scale of subsidies in other Member States, such as Luxembourg, Ireland, or the Netherlands was much greater. For these instruments the ceiling of EUR 800K would be next to unattainable to Polish businesses, especially from the SME sector.

A separate group of aid instruments, typical of Poland, addressed current operations of businesses which employ the disabled. Pursuant to the Rehabilitation Law (1997) PFRON (Polish abbr. for State Fund for Rehabilitation of Disabled People) offered reimbursement of costs incurred by businesses employing the disabled which in the Polish law have a special legal status and offer workplaces to people with disabilities. The same measure was offered to other businesses for the training, recruitment, and adaptation of workplaces to the needs of the disabled (EC, 2020h). We need to bear in mind that back in 2018, aid granted by the President of the State Fund for Rehabilitation of Disabled People to the amount of EUR 708 million represented the biggest share (14.7 per cent) in total aid distributed in Poland before COVID-19 (UOKiK, 2019). Comparing this data with

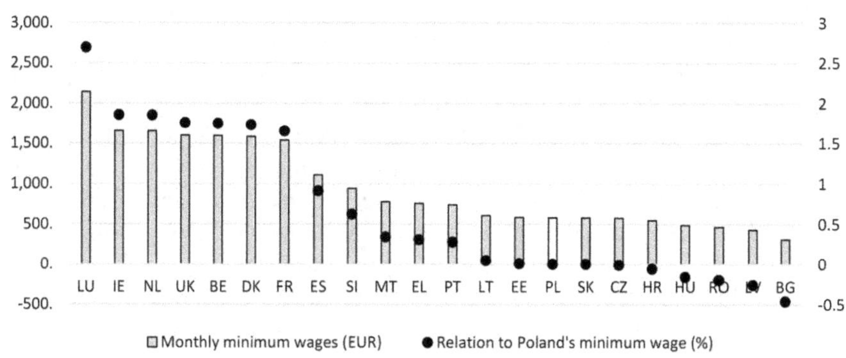

Figure 6.5 Minimum remuneration in the EU member states in 2020.

the planned budget of the discussed aid scheme amounting to EUR 780 million we may conclude that it *de facto* consumes all resources remaining at the disposal of PFRON in 2020. Thus, these are not new funds but existing funds which would have anyway ended up in the hands of strictly identified operators.

Direct grants for entities rendering services in the culture sector made up a specific category of aid measures. In this case, aid was supposed to help entities which due to lockdown suffered from total loss of demand for their services and after the decision to defrost the economy continued to experience very limited interest in their offer. By virtue of COVID Law (2020a), in the state of the risk of pandemic or the state of pandemic emergency and within 12 months following any of the two, the Minister for Culture and National Heritage could earmark resources from the state budget to grant aid to private individuals, legal entities, or organisational units without legal personality if their creative or cultural activities could not be continued in the previous format during the state of pandemic risk. Budget allocated for this purpose was set at EUR 17.51 million (Art. 15m COVID Law, 2020a; EC, 2020o). By the end of September 2020 the Ministry of Culture did not report on state aid granted within the programme, yet. Similar schemes were notified by Croatia, Lithuania, Sweden, the Czech Republic, and Denmark whose scheme worth EUR 12 million had been approved before the adoption of the Temporary Framework based on the Art. 107.2.b of the TFEU.

Besides domestic resources, within the examined period Poland used EU funds from the Multiannual Financial Framework 2014–2020 to support businesses with grants. Some funds were transferred to subsidise working capital in medium-sized enterprises whose turnover dropped by 30 per cent since 1 February 2020. The goal of the subsidy was to meet current and urgent needs of businesses (paying for utilities, rent, purchases of goods, or buying insurance for the company, however, excluding the payroll) for a maximum of 3 months. The scale of support depended on the size of employment, which, according to the schemes, translated into the maximum ceiling for micro businesses reaching EUR 15.6 K, for small enterprises EUR 36.7 K, and for medium-sized ones ca. EUR 95.6 K. Aid was distributed by the Polish Agency for Enterprise Development under two national Operational Programmes and by self-governments under their own regional operational programmes (MFiPR, 2020b; EC, 2020j).

Subsidies to interest rates paid on loans available from the Fundusz Dopłat do Oprocentowania (Interest Subsidy Fund) of the BGK were another form of aid selected much less frequently. Based on the COVID Law (2020b), BGK could subsidise interests paid on loans granted to all categories of businesses for 12 months. The scheme was joined by the largest banks in Poland: Bank Pekao SA and PKO BP S.A. and some commercial and cooperative banks with a wide network of branches not only in big cities but also in small towns and villages, which significantly improved access to it. Aid mechanism consisted in the obligation of an entrepreneur to pay back only a fraction of interests: subsidies to SMEs amounted to 2 percentage points while to large enterprises to 1 percentage point (COVID Law, 2020b; EC, 2020g). As at the end of

September 2020 the estimated utilisation of the instrument was less than 1 per cent out of the total budget of EUR 115 million. This very little impressive performance can be explained by the fact that bank interest rates at that time were relatively low and many competitive loans were available on preferential terms (at zero interest rate or as grants) under other schemes offered in Poland.

Polish payment advantages schemes

Not only direct grants but also the launching of payment advantages were sources of immediate support to businesses in the first stage of COVID-19 pandemic. Aid scheme including the above measures was notified by Poland relatively quickly in early April 2020 (EC, 2020h).

In this group, the suspension of the duty to pay mandatory social security and health contributions was the most widely used tool of support to businesses. Pursuant to the COVID Law (Art. 31zo, COVID Law, 2020a), micro businesses could be exempted from the payment of mandatory social security and health insurance, Labour Fund, Solidarity Fund, Guaranteed Employee Benefits Fund or Bridge Pension contributions due for the period running from 1 March 2020 to 31 May 2020. According to plans, the maximum value of aid granted in this area was anticipated to reach EUR 2.1 bn (Figure 6.4).

In addition, pursuant to COVID-19-related regulations (Art. 15zzze; COVID Law, 2020a) heads of poviats, city mayors, city councils (depending on who was the owner of the real estate) could cancel, fully or partially, defer the payment of or divide into instalments payables to the State Treasury due for the tax on rental income, lease or using real estate. Budget of the scheme was estimated at EUR 100 million.

Another aid instrument consisted in local authorities' waiving the payment of rent, leasing, and use charges due on real estate owned by territorial self-government by virtue of an autonomous decision (Art. 15zzzf and 15zzzg, COVID Law, 2020a). This aid was estimated at EUR 77.8 million.

Acting in the same spirit, municipality councils could adopt resolutions to offer exemptions from property tax on land, buildings, and structures used for business-related activities for parts of 2020. In this case, the budget was estimated at EUR 86.3 million (Art. 15p, COVID Law, 2020a). Another instrument with the budget of ca. EUR 6.7 million, approved by the Commission provided for property tax deferrals up to 30 September 2020 (EC, 2020h, 2020t).

In late July 2020, further financial reliefs were put in place: a reduction of the annual fee for perpetual usufruct, and an exemption of the fees for rent, lease or usufruct due by undertakings for conducting their business activities on real estate owned by public authorities (for 3 consecutive months in 2020 following the month in which an entrepreneur has applied for being covered with such aid measure) (COVID Law, 2020b). It is worth noting that the measure applied to real estate owned by the State Treasury and could be extended on property owned by local authorities by virtue of their autonomous decisions. The estimated budget of the measure was: for the reduction of the annual fee for perpetual usufruct: EUR 33.8 million from the State budget, EUR 29.3 million from the budgets of cities, and EUR 5.6 million from municipality budgets, while for the exemption from rental, lease, or usufruct charges it amounted to EUR 54.1 million from the local government budgets. It is worth noting that the Polish government assumed that only 30 per cent of undertakings whose activities are carried out in property owned by the state would eventually benefit from the measure (EC, 2020r).

Using direct grants and payment advantages

All the above discussed grant-related instruments (direct grants and payment advantages) were used mainly by micro (47.5 per cent), small (21.2 per cent) and medium (30.6 per cent) businesses. That was primarily the effect of the specificity of these measures addressed to businesses whose savings and margin for cost reduction were extremely narrow. In many cases these were family businesses or one-man businesses where labour cost reduction would mean a closure and a dramatic increase in unemployment in Poland. By helping them to survive through funding their current operational costs, the government was seeking to maintain jobs. Other instruments linked with allowances and reliefs in charges provided quite substantial assistance to craftsmanship services and catering. It needs to be stressed, however, that local governments, although authorised to grant reliefs, did not always decide to do so. The problem is that recently, local governments in Poland have become increasingly indebted (sometimes as a result of ill considered investment projects, e.g. aquaparks, co-financed from the EU funds which, after having been completed, need to be permanently subsidised). In addition, in recent years many tax allowances have been introduced in personal income tax which reduced the revenue of local governments (revenue from PIT is shared between the central and local budgets). On top of that, during the pandemic, local governments are heavily burdened with the cost incurred by some health care units and hospitals engaged in combating COVID-19.

The total amount of grants and payment advantages used by these measures reached 1.17 per cent of the Polish GDP (respectively 26.6 per cent and 70.1 per cent of amounts earmarked for aid schemes were used up). Some of the discussed schemes were launched in the Q3 2020 while others, as already mentioned, largely depend on the affluence and financial stability of local budgets.

4 Repayable COVID-19 state aid schemes

The next group of aid measures in the catalogue of allowable aid laid down by the Temporary Framework of March 2020 included repayable instruments (mainly loans), two *quasi*-grant instruments: repayable advances and conditional loan write-off programmes, as well as soft loans. These measures could be granted at interest rates reduced to at least the base rate applicable on 1 January 2020 plus credit risk margin (EC, 2020t). According to data at the end of September 2020, the value of repayable advances accounted for 89.8 per cent of the value of all repayable measures with loans covered by conditional write-off option ca. 10.14 per cent, and the rest for soft loans.

Repayable advances

Repayable advances were offered by the Polish Development Fund, Polski Fundusz Rozwoju (PFR) to micro, small, and medium-sized enterprises. Its budget amounted to EUR 16.6 bn. Financing for this group of enterprises relied on interest-free advances (which, should certain conditions be met, became subsidies) available from selected commercial and cooperative banks. The measure aimed to adjust the amount of financial support to the scale of potential loss in income due to a decrease in revenue caused by COVID-19. The higher the employment—the higher the financial subsidy. The estimated average amount of aid per micro- enterprise was set at around EUR 16,000 and up to a maximum of EUR 72,000, while for SME respectively: EUR 0.42 million and EUR 0.77 million (EC, 2020i). To be eligible for 75 per cent redemption of a repayable advance, a business had to continue its operations and maintain an average employment for 12 months while SMEs had to provide evidence for cumulated cash loss on sales. Repayable part of advances had to be paid back in 24 equal monthly instalments following the date when the subsidy was paid (PFR, 2020c). Since terms on which loans were offered were rather generous and because businesses *de facto* continued to operate, substantial proportion of the loan has been redeemed. However, if this condition is not met, the loan should be paid back at no additional cost. As a result, many businesses used this instrument as a cost-free annual loan. Therefore, in late September 2020, it was estimated that over 80 per cent of the total budget of EUR 16.6 bn would be disbursed.

Conditionally redeemed loans

The second repayable instrument, in terms of provided amounts, especially in the first period of the COVID-19 pandemic, were loans offered by the heads of poviats (PL: starosts) through the Poviat Labour Offices under the COVID Law (Art. 15zzd COVID Law, 2020a) from the Labour Fund. These were one-off loans in the amount of EUR 1,110 intended to cover the current costs of running a micro-business. The loan interest rate was fixed at 0.05 of the rediscount rate for bills of exchange accepted by the National Bank of Poland, and the repayment period was set at 12 months with a grace period of 3 months from its granting. The attractiveness of this instrument was determined by its redemption at the request of a micro-entrepreneur, provided that within 3 months of its granting he did not cut the number of jobs. According to preliminary data, the entire budget of the program of over EUR 300 million was used up at the end of September 2020 (EC, 2020h, 2020t).

Preferential loans

Preferential loans were offered primarily under aid schemes financed from the EU resources. Aid in the form of loans with subsidised interest rates for micro businesses and SMEs was granted by BGK through financial intermediaries (local funds and development foundations (MFiPR, 2020a; EC, 2020f). The Temporary Framework binding at that time provided for only reduced interest rates on preferential loans (soft loans) not for total elimination of interest rates. That is why, Poland has developed a separate aid scheme with a budget of ca. EUR 145 million to reduce interest rates on these loans to 0 per cent (MFiPR, 2020b; EC, 2020j). Repayment period of such a loan is set at 6 years, with a grace period of up to 6 months from the date of its granting and no fees or commissions apply to it. An entrepreneur could obtain more than one liquidity loan, provided that their total amount does not exceed EUR 3.33 million and 25 per cent of the total turnover in 2019 or twice the annual payroll (BGK, 2020c).

After the catalogue of state aid forms was expanded and a threshold of EUR 800 K per business was laid down in the Temporary Framework (EC, 2020a) Poland worked out an additional simplified loan scheme that was offered by the BGK but, above all, by regional institutions dealing with the distribution of EU funds. This scheme intended for 7 K beneficiaries offered soft loans granted to the amount not exceeding the above mentioned threshold (MFiPR, 2020d; EC, 2020n). On the one hand, it facilitated the building of a loan instrument (although not accompanied by programmes that would reduce the interest rate to zero) but, on the other hand, the loan could not exceed EUR 800 K per beneficiary. According to data provided by the OCCP at the end of September 2020 the value of loans reached only 1.4 per cent of the total budget of EUR 450 million (only 136 beneficiaries out of 7 K intended).

Another soft loan scheme was offered mainly by local authorities and institutions channelling the distribution of EU funds (its budget was earmarked for loans amounted to ca. EUR 77 million and EUR 33 million were allocated to guarantees). Amounts duly used on repayable instruments granted under the financial perspective 2007–2013 were partly re-injected into the system to be used to combat the effects of COVID-19 (MFiPR, 2020c; EC, 2020m). By the end of September 2020 only one institution based in Lublin running an aid scheme at the regional level offered a loan to micro, small, and medium-sized enterprises ranging between EUR 2,200 and EUR 110,000 with 0 per cent interest rate to entrepreneurs eligible for *de minimis* aid, to which no fees or commissions applied (OIC, 2020).

The next instrument is a Liquidity Shield worked out by the PFR targeting large enterprises with the budget reaching ca. EUR 2.2.bn Aid is offered in the form of repayable loans with no write-off option granted for the period of 4 years. Its value may not exceed EUR 221 million per enterprise and cannot be higher than the double annual payroll and 25 per cent of the company's total turnover in 2019. In justified cases the financing can be increased to meet the corporate demand for liquidity over the forthcoming 12 months for large enterprises or for 18 months for SMEs. Write-off as non-refundable financing is intended to cover up to 75 per cent of the actual damage suffered by the company as a result of COVID-19 (PFR, 2020b; EC, 2020p).

The PRF Financial Shield is one more aid scheme addressed to large enterprises which has not been launched by the end of September 2020. Its declared budget circulates around EUR 1.6 bn and is expected to be distributed to ca. 150–200 beneficiaries. The aid scheme provides for aid in the form of a loan granted at subsidised interest rates and is limited to a maximum of 4 years. Write-off as non-refundable financing is intended to cover up to 75 per cent of the actual damage suffered by the company as a result of COVID-19 and may not exceed 75 per cent of the loan. It means that the remaining amount must be paid back by the beneficiary in accordance with the loan agreement. It is important to underline that as it was impossible to define precisely the actual damage, the measure provides that the loan beneficiary will receive a partial capital rebate (equivalent to a non-reimbursable grant) on the loan at the latest by 30 September 2021. The loans under the measure should be granted at reduced interest rates which would be at least equal to the base rate applicable on 30 April 2020 plus the credit risk margins. Therefore, preferential funding is granted up to the amount of estimated damage suffered by the enterprise as a result of COVID-19 outbreak and it may not exceed EUR 166 million, double annual payroll of the company for 2019, and 25 per cent of total company's turnover in 2019 (PFR, 2020b; EC, 2020k).

Summing up, at the end of September 2020 the list of principal beneficiaries of the above listed schemes included micro (47.8 per cent), small (34.5 per cent), and medium-sized (17.7 per cent) enterprises. Both the latter and the former programmes for large companies were launched only in September 2020, therefore, the number of beneficiaries and state aid granted were limited.

5 Guaranteed COVID-19 state aid schemes

State guarantees for investment or working capital loans are a financial instrument which serves to secure the repayment of the loan to a creditor. The idea was to encourage the financial sector (creditors) to grant loans despite the highly uncertain current situation and future of business. Their goal was to ensure the liquidity of the real sphere of economy. The European Commission limited the guarantee period to a maximum of 6 years and its value to 90 per cent of the principal of the loan if the losses were borne proportionately and under the same conditions by the credit institution and the State; or 35 per cent if the losses were first attributed to the State and only then to the credit institutions (i.e. first-loss guarantee).

In Poland, BGK has been authorised to grant sureties and guarantees for the repayment of loans taken by medium-sized and large entrepreneurs (Art. 15zzzd.1, COVID-law, 2020a). Entrepreneurs could obtain guarantees in commercial and cooperative banks on relatively preferential terms: up to 80 per cent of the loan for a period of up to 27 months and no longer than the loan period extended by 3 months. The amount of the guarantee was set between PLN 3.5 million and PLN 200 million, while the amount of the loan covered by the guarantee was dependent on the company's payroll or total turnover, or on a justified declaration of the entrepreneur about corporate demand for liquidity and, anyway, could not exceed PLN 250 million in total. (PFR, 2020a).

Polish authorities estimated the budget of the aforementioned programme at EUR 4.8 bn which should allow BGK to issue guarantees amounting up to ca. EUR 22 bn. That amount of guarantee can be used to cover the total of loans of up to EUR 27 bn (EC, 2020e). At the end of September, guarantees granted by Poland amounted to EUR 38 million, which shows that the instrument has only just started to be used.

A specific guarantee instrument that has been introduced in Poland in connection with COVID-19 is factoring. This instrument is important because it is a financial service providing an alternative source of working capital. It should facilitate the increasing of the sales of products at limited creditworthiness, problems in settlements with business partners or extended payment terms. Reducing the risk of delayed or non-payment for company's products should have a stabilizing effect on the position of companies particularly exposed to such situations during the COVID-19 pandemic. On the basis of the amended COVID Law, BGK was authorised to grant, on its own behalf and on its own account, sureties and guarantees for the repayment of loans and other liabilities incurred by entrepreneurs (Art. 15zzzd COVID Law, 2020b). Factoring guarantees introduced in Poland concerned recourse and reverse factoring for a maximum period of 24 months. The amount of a single guarantee of repayment of a factoring credit limit (up to 80 per cent) may not exceed EUR 49 million (BGK, 2020a). In assessing the instrument's attractiveness, it is worth noting that Poland ranked 8th in Europe in terms of turnover covered by factoring in 2019. (EU 66.1 bn, or 3.3 per cent of the European market share). At the same time, the turnover of Polish factors has been growing increasingly faster in recent years (BGK, 2020b). The estimated budget of the measure was approx. EUR 2.6 bn with 4–5 thousand users of factoring products (EC, 2020q), however, by the end of September 2020 this kind of support was not yet provided in Poland.

Another aid measure provided for in Poland targets exports by businesses active in international trade. At the outset of the pandemic, the European Commission observed dramatically shrinking opportunities to successfully apply for insurance for any export credit in the private market. Therefore, it proposed to cover also marketable risks with export credit insurance. In fact, the Commission considered all commercial and political risks (with a maximum risk period of less than 2 years) related to exports to a specific group of countries to be temporarily non-marketable until the end of 2020. This was the case for EU Member States, but also Australia, Canada, Island, Japan, New Zealand, Norway, Switzerland, and the USA (EC, 2020c).

6 COVID-19 recapitalisation state aid schemes

A separate support formula provided for in the Temporary Framework, which was introduced by its next amendment in May 2020, is aid for recapitalisation of companies affected by COVID-19 (EC, 2020b). The Commission has considered such aid as a "second best tool" to mitigate the effects of the pandemic, as it has the greatest potential negative impact on competition in the single market. It should therefore be used if other instruments have proved ineffective or inadequate to the needs of the beneficiary. In the case of this measure, the Commission stressed that the recapitalisation must not exceed the minimum necessary to ensure the viability of the beneficiary and should be limited to restoring the capital structure of the company from before the COVID-19 outbreak. Moreover, potential beneficiaries, i.e. large companies, are required to plan not only for their future viability, but also for the achievement of the EU objectives connected with green and digital transformation.

The PFR has been involved in the implementation of such an instrument in Poland, offering the Capital Shield with a budget of EUR 1.65 bn. The main purpose of this instrument was to restore a stable financing structure, which was shaken by COVID-19. The aim was to provide companies with capital to finance their investment projects, among others, funds for current operations, including working capital financing. The financing could be offered either in the form of acquisition or purchase by PFR of capital instruments of companies on market terms, with the acquisition or purchase taking place after meeting the private investor test or on a *pari passu* principle with new investors; or under the state aid regime, provided that the amount of PFR financing serves to restore the capital structure affected by the COVID-19 epidemic (PFR, 2000b; EC, 2020l). Given that this instrument causes quite a significant distortion of competition, the Commission indicated in its Temporary Framework that the state should be remunerated as close to the market as possible and that the beneficiary should not engage in aggressive commercial expansion financed by state aid. In addition, an exit strategy for the state from the supported entrepreneur should be prepared, together with a plan to continue his business operations. By the end of September 2020, this instrument was not applied in Poland (Figure 6.4).

Conclusions

The COVID-19 outbreak forced the European Commission to adjust EU state aid law to a new situation. It, in principle, has not changed its orthodox approach to granting state aid, however, it has singled out many categories of aid that it considered acceptable. In its Temporary Framework, the Commission referred to undefined exceptional occurrences (Art. 107.2.b TFEU) and to a serious disturbance in the economy of a Member State (Art. 107.3.b TFEU), which allowed it to develop a set of criteria for acceptable categories of aid. The TFEU turned out to be flexible enough to be used as a stepping-stone to regulations corresponding to the exceptional circumstances that could not have been predicted when the Treaty was drafted. In this approach, however, it is difficult to find a reference to market failure as a factor justifying granting state aid recognised in the theory of economics. The problem encountered by entrepreneurs consists in the total loss of demand, suppliers, sometimes the labour market as a result of governments' decisions on lockdown caused by COVID-19 pandemic. Thus, the aid programs that have been launched are a kind of compensation for the freezing of the economy rather than support aimed at improving their competitiveness.

In the Temporary Framework, the Commission has clearly defined the criteria for admissible state aid beyond the already existing rules. This means that, *de facto*, it did not make the existing rules more flexible, but created a new, temporary channel through which the Member States may exercise financial intervention in various forms and categories of state aid in the economy.

When it comes to the acceptable categories of COVID-19 aid proposed by Poland and other Member States, their diversity should be assessed positively as it takes into account the different effects of the pandemic on companies as well as the capacity of national budgets. The main objective of these instruments was to meet the current (in the first wave of COVID-19 of Spring 2020) urgent needs of enterprises with regard to ensuring the payment of salaries and wages to employees, complying with public, legal, and commercial liabilities and commitments, paying infrastructure maintenance costs, and current liabilities.

Apparently, the most controversial provision is the one limiting state aid amount granted in diverse forms to EUR 800 K per business affected by the pandemic. Together with the *de minimis* state aid of EUR 200 K (accounted for over 3-year periods), each entrepreneur in the EU, who suffered from the COVID-19 outbreak, could count on aid amounting to EUR 1 million. It is very difficult to capture this cause-and-effect relationship and schemes put in place both in Poland and in other more developed Member States, however, it can be expected that, as a Member State was able to bear the burden of financing aid to such an amount, virtually all smart entrepreneurs applied for such maximum support.

The potential distortion of competition within one country is not likely to be great, as all entrepreneurs could receive the same support in all regions. However, differences in the nominal values of aid granted between Member States may be significant. Of course, the amount of aid was a derivative of the level of economic development of the country in question, and thus of its wealth. However, the prices of components and raw materials for all European operators are similar. The same is true for the cost of employment of highly qualified specialists. Therefore, it can be expected that richer countries (Germany, France) will subsidise their economies much more strongly, providing their entrepreneurs with higher liquidity than Poland with less financial resources at its disposal. Therefore, it is quite likely that the conditions of competition will be seriously distorted and the competitive position of companies from Poland and other less affluent countries will decline in favour of more developed countries which can grant aid more generously. The factor limiting excessive "profligacy" of governments in this respect should be the EU fiscal rules (including the budget deficit limit). However, in view of the willingness of the states to provide real support (which required a significant increase in spending) and the magnitude of the negative consequences of the pandemic, on 23 March 2020 the EU Council relaxed its fiscal approach thereby agreeing to exceed the current budget deficit and public debt limits (Council, 2020).

As for the instruments used in Poland to combat the effects of the pandemic, according to the data as at the end of September 2020, loans enjoyed the largest share. This means financial liquidity was ensured, especially to the SME sector. The instrument was seen as attractive by entrepreneurs, because some schemes provided for the write-off or only partial reimbursement of obtained amounts when a business is discontinued. From the point of view of Poland, subsidy instruments were also important, including subsidies to salaries and wages, as well as allowances in the payment of compulsory social security contributions. This support was used primarily by micro and small businesses which otherwise would not be able to reduce their operating costs in any other way than by laying off their employees or even closing the company. The problem is, however, that in many cases such support was provided to companies that did not need it or were not eligible to receive it. Such cases will probably be gradually revealed and examined.

In general, it should be concluded that according to the data available at the end of September 2020, Polish entrepreneurs did not make significant use of the aid schemes approved by the Commission with three exemptions (out of total 37 instruments of financial support accepted by the Commission) concerning specific repayable advances, payment advantages, and certain preferential (unrepayable) loans. The under-utilization of support is partly due to protracted works on the procedures involved in granting new aid, as well as, perhaps, to the state's withholding of aid instruments for fear of even greater demand in the future (during the next pandemic waves). The country's budget, which has been severely overburdened with social programs, may not be able to provide adequate support to entrepreneurs in the future that would be comparable to what their competitors receive in other EU Member States.

It is also worth noting that aid granted to businesses comes from three sources. The first one is the waiving of a number of fees, charges, taxes, and social security contributions. From the point of view of the central budget this may be an acceptable move, but to local governments it may pose a serious problem (most of these charges flow to local governments' budgets, which, among other things, are responsible for local investment projects and some health care facilities which are extremely needed during the COVID-19 pandemic). The second source is the EU funds from both financial perspectives 2007–2013 and 2014–2020, which had already been used once as repayable instruments in Poland and were at the disposal of institutions managing European funds (including, among others, EUR 7 bn from the cohesion policy for 2014–2020, not used by Poland—for more see Chapter 5). Initially, they were supposed to be spent on activities within the cohesion policy, however, redirecting them to COVID-related support means a reduction of funds for innovation and development. Therefore, we can say that no new funds were received for COVID-related support directly from EU funds. The third source is bonds issued by the Polish Development Fund to provide funding underpinning a series of anti-crisis shields for large companies, but also for the SME sector. They will be bought out in subsequent years and increase the indebtedness of the public sector in Poland.

The EU Temporary Framework was again amended in mid-October, both in terms of new aid categories and new conditions that were introduced. A separate issue is the extension of its application until 30 June 2021, although many countries have indicated the advisability of extending it until the end of 2021. This shows that the Commission has got reservations regarding admissible aid. Moreover, the current limit of up to EUR 800,000 has not been changed, despite requests for an increase voiced by the largest and the richest Member States. It seems, however, that the implementation of the latter suggestions would lead to even greater differentiation in the EU when it comes to granting state aid. From Poland's point of view, with public debt growing dramatically fast, a significant increase in financial interventions should not be expected, which will result in an unfavourable competitive position of domestic enterprises in the internal market compared to economic operators from countries generously distributing public funds. This imbalance may lead to an upsetting of the level playing field within the internal market, to a reduction or elimination of the benefits resulting from the functioning of Polish (and other) entrepreneurs in the EU Single Market, and, consequently, to serious tensions in the EU and legitimate questions about the future of the European integration project.

At the end, one should also be aware that the situation of pandemic does not really mean the collapse of the entire economy. We can observe a clearly uneven distribution of benefits and losses between individual operators. Just as the entrepreneurs offering some traditional services have suffered huge losses (e. g. tourism industry), the companies from the digital industries have recorded significant increases in profits. The trend may deepen the longer the pandemic stays with us and the more society gets used to new sanitary requirements which are the standards of our future functioning. The current Temporary Framework is only responding to short term actions of Member States' governments. We need to develop regulations, above all for state aid, which will take into account the long-term needs of accelerated digital transformation, change of consumer habits, and new approach of entrepreneurs. These aspects, no doubt, require further research.

Notes

1 There is also an exemption based on Art. 107.3.c. of the TFEU which enabled granting state aid for concrete activities pursued by entrepreneurs in relation with the pandemic, including, e.g., R&D works and the implementation of results obtained while fighting the pandemic.

2 Subsidy for which an employer may apply depending on the number of employees and turnover drop by at least:

-30 per cent, the maximum subsidy of 50 per cent of minimum wage (580 EUR), i.e., for a full-time worker EUR 290 plus social insurance premiums paid by the employer,

-50 per cent, the maximum subsidy of 70 per cent of minimum wage,

-80 per cent, then the maximum subsidy amounts to 90 per cent of minimum wage.

References

Act of 4 July 2019 on the System of development institutions, as amended, OJ 1572/2019 as amended.

Ambroziak, A.A. (2014) *New Cohesion Policy of the European Union in Poland. How It Will Influence the Investment Attractiveness of Regions in 2014–2020*, Cham, Heidelberg, New York, Dordrecht, London: Springer.

Ambroziak, A.A. (2017) State Aid Policy and Industrial Policy of the European Union In: A.A. Ambroziak (ed.) *New Industrial Policy of the European Union*, Cham, Heidelberg, New York, Dordrecht, London: Springer.

BGK (2020a) Warunki uzyskania w Banku Gospodarstwa Krajowego gwarancji spłaty limitu faktoringowego w ramach portfelowej linii gwarancyjnej LGF FGP (Terms on which BGK grants factoring credit limit payment guarantees under portfolio guarantee LGF FGP), Warszawa. Available at: https://www.bgk.pl/files/public/Pliki/Przedsiebiorstwa/Gwarancja_splaty_limitow_faktoringowych/Warunki_uzyskania_gwarancji_splaty_limitu_faktoringowego_w_BGK_09_2020.pdf (Accessed: 20 October 2020).

BGK (2020b) Briefing prasowy BGK I PZF. Nowatorskie rozwiązania BGK w tarczy antykryzysowej, 7 września 2020 r (BGK and PZF press briefing: new BGK solutions in anti-crisis shield). Available at: https://www.bgk.pl/files/public/Pliki/Przedsiebiorstwa/Gwarancja_splaty_limitow_faktoringowych/BGK_-_Gwarancje_limitow_faktoringowych_-_prezentacja_po_briefingu_7-09-2020.pdf (Accessed: 20 October 2020).

BGK (2020c) Pożyczki Płynnościowe POIR (Liquidity loans) Available at: https://www.bgk.pl/przedsiebiorstwa/pozyczki-plynnosciowe-poir/ (Accessed: 20 October 2020).

Council (2020) Statement of EU ministers of finance on the Stability and Growth Pact in light of the COVID-19 crisis, Press Release, 23. 03. 2020.

COVID Law (2020a) Act of 31 March 2020 amending the act on specific solutions related to the prevention, counteracting and combating COVID-19, other infectious diseases and crisis situations caused by them and some other acts, OJ 568/2020.

COVID Law (2020b) Act of 19 June 2020 on interest subsidies on bank loans granted to businesses affected by COVID-19 and on simplified procedure for the adoption of the arrangement related to COVID-19, OJ 1423/2020.

EC (2012) EU State Aid Modernisation (SAM), COM(2012) 209 final, 8. 05. 2012.

EC (2020a) Amendment to the Temporary Framework for State aid measures to support the economy in the current COVID-19 outbreak, OJ C 112, p. 01.

EC (2020b) Amendment to the Temporary Framework for State aid measures to support the economy in the current COVID-19 outbreak, OJ C 164, p. 03.

EC (2020c) Communication from the Commission amending the Annex to the Communication from the Commission to the Member States on the application of Articles 107 and 108 of the Treaty on the Functioning of the European Union to short-term export-credit insurance, OJ C 101, I/01.

EC (2020d) Coordinated economic response to the COVID-19 Outbreak, COM(2020) 112 final, 13. 03. 2020.

EC (2020e) State Aid SA.56876 (2020/N) – Poland COVID-19: Liquidity guarantee fund, C(2225) final, Brussels, 3. 4. 2020.

EC (2020f) State Aid SA.56896(2020/N) – Poland COVID-19: anti-crisis measures in the form of loans and guarantees financed from EU funds, C(2020) 2340 final, Brussels, 8. 4. 2020.

EC (2020g) State Aid SA.56979 (2020/N) – Poland COVID-19: Interest rate subsidy scheme, C(2000) 2362 final, Brussels, 10. 04. 2020.

EC (2020h) State Aid SA.56922 (2020/N) – Poland. Polish anti-crisis measures – direct grants, repayable advances, tax and payments advantages, tax deferrals and wage subsidies schemes related to COVID-19, C(2020) 2686 final, Brussels, 23. 04. 2020.

EC (2020i) State Aid SA.56996 (2020/N) – Poland COVID-19: repayable advance scheme for micro, small and medium-sized enterprises, C(2020) 2822 final, Brussels, 27. 04. 2020.

EC (2020j) State Aid SA.57015 (2020/N) – Poland. State aid in the form of grants or repayable assistance under operational programmes for 2014–2020 to support the Polish economy in connection with the occurrence of the COVID-19 pandemic outbreak, C(2020) 2782 final, Brussels, 24. 04. 2020.

EC (2020k) State Aid SA.57054 (2020/N) – Poland. COVID-19: The Polish anti-crisis measures – aid for damage compensation and to improve the liquidity of undertakings affected by the COVID-19 outbreak, C(2020) 3656 final, Brussels, 29. 05. 2020.

EC (2020l) State Aid SA.57055 (2020/N) – Poland - anti-crisis measures - COVID-19 – equity instruments, C(2020) 4036 final, 11. 06. 2020.

EC (2020m) State Aid SA.57065(2020/N) – Poland COVID-19: anti-crisis measures in the form of loans and guarantees financed from the re-use of resources returned from 2007–2013 financial instruments, C(2020) 2634 final, Brussels, 22. 04. 2020.

EC (2020n) State Aid SA.57191 (2020/N) – Poland. State aid in the simplified repayable form from financial engineering instruments resources subject to re-use and from financial instruments under operational programmes for 2014–2020 perspective to support the Polish economy in connection with the COVID-19 pandemic outbreak, C(2020) 3163 final, Brussels, 11. 05. 2020.

EC (2020o) State Aid SA.57282 (2020/N) – Poland. Amendment to the scheme SA.56922 (2020/N) – Polish anti-crisis measures – direct grants, repayable advances, tax and payments advantages, tax deferrals and wage subsidies schemes related to COVID-19, C(2020) 3268, Brussels, 13. 05. 2020.

EC (2020p) State Aid SA.57306 (2020/N) – Poland COVID-19: Financial shield for large enterprises: Liquidity loans, C(2020) 3535 final, 25. 05. 2020.

EC (2020q) State Aid SA.57452 (2020/N) – Poland COVID-19: Guarantees on Factoring, C(2020)5165 final, Brussels, 23. 07. 3030.

EC (2020r) State Aid SA.57726 (2020/N) – Poland COVID-19: State aid in the form of reduction of the annual fee for perpetual usufruct and relief in rent, lease and usufruct fees to support entrepreneurs affected by the COVID-19 pandemic outbreak, C(2020) 5290 final, Brussels, 28. 07. 2020.

EC (2020s) State Aid SA. 58481 (2020/N) – Poland. Amendment of the scheme SA.56922 (2020/N) concerning Polish anti-crisis measures – direct grants, repayable advances, tax and payments advantages, tax deferrals and wage subsidies schemes related to COVID-19, C(2020)6175 final, Brussels, 3. 09. 2020.

EC (2020t) Temporary Framework for State aid measures to support the economy in the current COVID-19 outbreak and its amendments C(2020) 2215 of 3 April 2020, C(2020) 3156 of 8 May 2020 and C(2020) 4509 of 29 June 2020, OJ C 91 I/1.

EC (2020u) 4th Amendment to the Temporary Framework for State aid measures to support the economy in the current COVID-19 outbreak and amendment to the Annex to the Communication from the Commission to the Member States on the application of Articles 107 and 108 of the Treaty on the Functioning of the European Union to short-term export-credit insurance, OJ C 340 I/01.

EC (2020v) State aid rules and coronavirus: https://ec.europa.eu/competition/state_aid/what_is_new/covid_19.html).

MFiPR (2020a) Regulation of the MFiPR of 14 April 2020 on granting aid from repayable instruments under Operational Programmes for 2014–2020 to support Polish economy affected by COVID-19 pandemic, OJ 670/2020.

MFiPR (2020b) Regulation of the MFiPR of 28 April 2020 on granting state aid in the form of subsidies or repayable aid under Operational Programmes 2014–2020 to support Polish economy affected by COVID-19, OJ 773/2020.

MFiPR (2020c) Regulation of the MFiPR of 29 April 2020 on granting aid from reusable financial engineering resources to support Polish economy affected by COVID-19 pandemic, OJ 783/2020.

MFiPR (2020d) Regulation MFiPR of 27 May 2020 on granted state aid in a simplified repayable form from reusable financial engineering resources under Operational Programmes 2014–2020 to support Polish economy affected by COVID-19 pandemic, OJ 949/2020.

OIC (2020) "Pożyczka płynnościowa" dla firm dotkniętych negatywnymi skutkami gospodarczymi wynikającymi z COVID-19 (title in English: "Liquidity Loan" for businesses affected by COVID-19) https://www.oic.lublin.pl/aktualnosci/pozyczka-plynnosciowa-dla-firm-dotknietych-negatywnymi-skutkami-gospodarczymi-wynikajac))ymi-z-covid-19/)

PFR (2020a) *Przewodnik Antykryzysowy dla przedsiębiorców, Tarcza Antykryzysowa, Wersja 6.0, 20 lipca 2020 r* (title in English: Anti-Crisis Guidebook for Businesses, Anti-Crisis Shield, Version 6.0, 20 July 2020)

PFR (2020b) Regulamin ubiegania się o udział w Programie Rządowym Tarcza Finansowa Polskiego Funduszu Rozwoju dla dużych firm (title in English: Regulations for applying for participation in the Government Program Financial Shield of the Polish Development Fund for large companies), Warsaw.

PFR (2020c) Regulamin ubiegania się o udział w Programie Rządowym Tarcza Finansowa Polskiego Funduszu Rozwoju dla małych i średnich firm (title in English: Regulations for applying for participation in the Government Program Financial Shield of the Polish Development Fund for small and medium-sized enterprises), Warsaw.

Rehabilitation Law (1997) Act of 27 August 1997 on vocational and social rehabilitation and employment of persons with disabilities as amended, OJ 1997, No 123, item 776.

RPP (2020) Komunikat po posiedzeniu Rady Polityki Pieniężnej, 17 marca 2020 r (Communication following the meeting of the Monetary Policy Council, 17 March 2020).

UOKiK (2019) Raport o pomocy publicznej w Polsce udzielonej przedsiębiorcom w 2018 roku (title in English: Report on State Aid Granted to Enterprises in Poland in 2018), Warszawa.

7 Poland and the European Green Deal amidst the pandemic

Marzenna Błaszczuk-Zawiła

Introduction

As early as 1991, Poland adopted an environmental policy based on sustainable development assumptions, co-creating a group of countries initiating the implementation of its principles (IOŚ-PIB, 2019, p. 35). Limited budget appropriations and the lack of a firm and clear energy policy were barriers to achieving adopted objectives. Successive strategic documents, adopted by changing ruling teams, did not always take into account the achievements of the previous policy. Instability has not served the development of the energy sector in Poland, and delays in adopting the necessary laws have slowed down many investment processes (Paska and Surma, 2013, p. 18). The conditions changed after accession to the European Union in May 2004. Poland had to adjust its law to the Union's environmental requirements[1] but also gained access to new financing sources. Since then, the main stimulus to environmental changes in Poland have been climate and environmental protection laws adopted at the EU level as well as EU funds provided to Poland. However, the country still had delays in implementing the necessary changes.

In the coming years, further changes will be forced by laws resulting from the new EU growth strategy—the European Green Deal (EGD)—adopted in December 2019. Among the EGD objectives, the top priority for the EU is to become a climate-neutral area by 2050 (European Commission, 2019, p. 4). To achieve this goal the EU and its Member States should, primarily, accelerate greenhouse gas (GHG) emission reduction; improve energy efficiency; and develop renewable energy sources (RES) faster.

The EU Member States adopted the ambitious goals set by the Commission, but Poland chose not to commit to achieving climate neutrality by 2050 at the national level. The European Council accepted that position but decided to raise the issue again in June 2020 (European Council, 2019, p. 1).

Although the outbreak of the COVID-19 pandemic became an opportunity for Poland and some other countries (the Czech Republic, Romania) to put forward postulates questioning the validity of the implementation of ambitious climate objectives in a situation of economic crisis, the European Commission

DOI: 10.4324/9781003144434-8

received the "green light" for preparing the implementation of the EGD and making it the main pillar of the recovery of the EU economy.

This chapter aims to answer the question about possible achievement of the EGD objectives in Poland, in particular climate neutrality by 2050, especially during the pandemic. The starting point is an analysis of Poland's position against other EU Member States. It is followed by a presentation of selected factors hindering Poland's achieving the EGD goals and the positions taken by the Polish government and businesses towards the EGD. The chapter ends with a summary and conclusions. The focus is on issues related to CO_2 emission reduction and the transition of the Polish energy sector and energy-intensive industries. Transition in those areas is widely regarded as the greatest challenge.[2] The study is based on desk research and statistical data analysis. It covers an examination of the literature, government documents, expert commentaries, interviews with public officials and business representatives, strategic documents and annual reports of companies as well as the available positions taken by firms and their associations.

1 Starting point—Poland's position compared to the other EU Member States

Against the backdrop of the other Member States, Poland's environmental protection performance has not been very impressive. As far as emissions of CO_2—the main greenhouse gas in Poland (81.8 per cent share of total emissions in 2018)—is concerned, in 1990–2018 the country managed to cut emissions by a mere 9 per cent (reaching 344 $MtCO_2$), whereas Germany—the EU-27's largest emitter—by nearly 28 per cent (to 759 $MtCO_2$) (Figure 7.1). Significant changes also occurred in France and Italy, as a result those countries fell behind Poland in terms of total

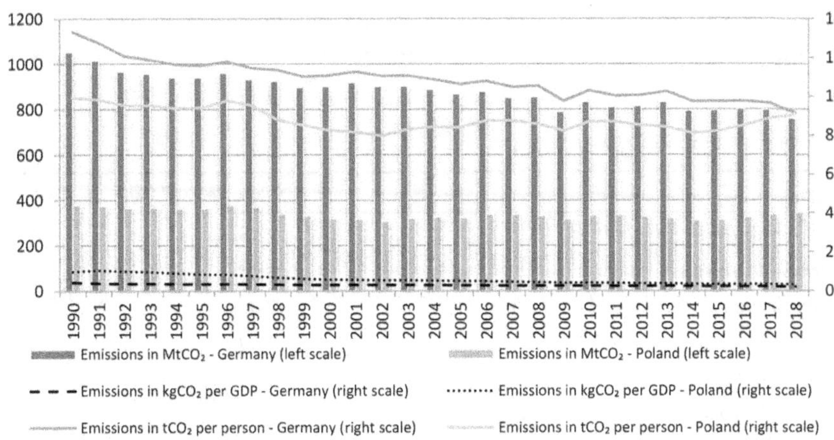

Figure 7.1 CO2 emissions: Poland compared to Germany—the EU's largest emitter in 1990–2018.

Notes: Territorial emissions in $MtCO_2$—right scale; other indicators—left scale.

Source: Prepared by the author based on the Global Carbon Atlas database (2020).

emissions, despite the fact that they have bigger economies than the Polish one. In 2018, Poland became the world's 18th and the EU's second largest CO_2 emitter. Neither does Poland perform well in terms of CO_2 emissions *per capita*. In 1990–2018, the indicator for Germany dropped by nearly 32 per cent, whereas that for Poland, merely by 8 per cent. At the end of the period in question, the two countries had similar emission levels (9.1 tCO_2/person), ranking 4th and 5th, respectively, in the EU.

If the level of emissions is compared to gross domestic product, Poland's progress looks a little more optimistic. In that respect, Poland advanced more than Germany (as the countries reduced emissions, respectively, by two-thirds to 0.33 kg of CO_2/GDP and by 52 per cent to 0.21 kg of CO_2/GDP in 2018). Poland improved its performance as compared to the EU-27 Member States (becoming the third emitter instead of the second), whereas that of Germany deteriorated (it moved up from 11th to 10th position). Those changes occurred despite the fact that Poland developed faster than Germany for most of the period. Due to deep restructuring of the economy and the modernisation of plants (with a contribution from foreign investors), the country managed to improve its energy efficiency. The reduction of emissions was accompanied by economic growth suggesting decoupling of economic growth from CO_2 emissions.

The main CO_2 emission source in Poland is fuel combustion, responsible for a 92.3 per cent share in total CO_2 emission in 2018 (Table 7.1). In this category the main CO_2 emitters were energy industries and transport. Industrial processes contributed to the total CO_2 emission with 5.8 per cent share in 2018, with mineral industry (especially cement production) as the main emission source.

Sectors covered by EU ETS (electricity and heat production, heavy industry) are responsible for about 50 per cent of national emissions in Poland (48.4 per cent in 2018) (Ministry of Climate, 2020, p. 13). Poland does not have any specific reduction target imposed on them; limits cover the whole EU ETS on

Table 7.1 Carbon dioxide emission in 2018 by sector

Sector	*Share in total emission (%)*
Fuel combustion	92.3
-energy industries	*48.1*
-manufacturing industries and construction	*9.3*
-transport	*19.1*
-other sectors	*15.7*
Industrial processes and product use	5.8
Fugitive emissions from fuels	1.4
Agriculture	0.3
Waste	0.2

Source: Ministry of Climate (2020, p. 17).

the EU level (cap). Emissions from other sources—sectors outside the EU ETS—are subject to specific national emission targets. Those have already increased by 21 per cent from 2005 levels, overshooting Poland's commitment to limit the increase of these emissions to 14 per cent by 2020. This growth in emissions offsets any emissions reductions achieved in the sectors included to the EU ETS system (European Commission, 2020b, p. 42).

Poland's progress in decarbonisation has not been sufficient and the country will probably miss the Europe 2020 targets related to energy and climate (European Commission, 2020b, p. 42). This also applies to the possibility of achieving climate neutrality by 2050. For instance, it is illustrated by the Energy Transition Index (ETI).[3] Poland's ETI score for 2020 was 52.9—the lowest among the EU Member States (World Economic Forum, 2020, p. 13).

The ranking leaders are the Scandinavian countries—Sweden (with a score of 74.2), Finland (72.4) and Denmark (72.2). Two of them have voluntarily declared an early achievement of climate neutrality: Sweden (by 2045) and Finland (by 2035). The energy sectors in both countries significantly rely on nuclear energy (in 2018, 35 per cent and 33 per cent of total primary energy, respectively). In Sweden, other important sources of energy are biofuels and waste (25 per cent), crude oil (20 per cent) and hydropower (11 per cent of total primary energy), whereas in Finland—biofuels (17 per cent) and coal (14 per cent). In Denmark, the most important role is played by wind farms (46 per cent), supplemented by coal (21 per cent) and biofuels (17 per cent). Another EU Member State having decided to achieve climate neutrality early—Austria (by 2040)—mostly relies on hydropower (60 per cent), followed by gas (14 per cent) and wind energy (9 per cent) (Juszczak et al., 2020).

2 Climate neutrality—why is it so difficult? Selected aspects

Selected factors that hinder Poland's adoption of the objective of achieving climate neutrality by 2050 are discussed below.

a. Coal as the basis for the energy mix and energy security

The fundamental energy-generating products in Poland are hard coal and lignite. The main user is the energy industry, mostly comprising plants built in 1945–1989. The years of economic transition have been a time of limited restructuring and modernisation of the sector. There has been a gradual decline in the share of coal in the production and use of primary fuels and decline in air pollution (reduced emissions of sulphur and nitrogen oxides, particulate matter, carbon oxides). But the government economic policy has continued to support the consumption of coal for energy and heat generation. As a result, after 30 years of transition, Poland still relies heavily on a centralised energy industry based on coal (with nearly 80 per cent of electricity from hard coal and lignite). The system is formed by large entities controlled by the State (with regard to fuel supply, energy generation and distribution), with the main statutory task of ensuring the security of energy supply.

Subsequent governments shared the traditional understanding of energy security (relying on domestic raw materials, guaranteed by State-dependent firms), which had serious economic and political consequences. It entailed subsidising coal mining and the related energy industry as well as making major investments based on political decisions rather than on economic accounts. As a result, inefficient solutions prevailed. It also involved the sustained and strong position of the mining trade unions, and weighing heavily with policy-makers.[4] Simultaneously, alternative energy sources were inadequately promoted (unstable regulations, unfavourable conditions for the development of prosumer energy). In such conditions, the EU climate regulations were perceived as a threat to the Polish energy sector (Hille and Kassenberg, 2018, p. 34).

The growing demand for electricity (including "green" electricity) and the necessary shutdowns of old power units began to undermine the security of supply based on the existing system (Magazyn Polska Chemia, 2020, pp. 30–31). In recent years, the situation fuelled discussions on transforming the energy mix and the energy industry in Poland. It involved a clash of two extremely different concepts:

1 the development of large-scale sources and electricity networks (despite the lack of economic stimuli to invest in large-scale sources and growing resistance from local communities to large extraction and energy generation facilities[5]); it is reflected in the most recent power plants in Opole, Jaworzno and Turów;
2 the reliance of energy security on diversified electricity generation sources and the promotion of distributed energy generation for urban areas, industry and small recipients (partially implemented through the development of energy clusters—an innovative solution on a European scale, designed by the Ministry of Energy).[6]

Such discussions were largely shaped by the EU environmental laws, decreasing possibilities of financing high-emission power plants (with a future need to shut them down) and social support for coal-based energy.

According to expert assessments, Poland may depart from hard coal extraction by 2050, which will be fostered by the following factors: (1) rising extraction and occupational safety and health costs; (2) the anticipated fall in the demand for the fuel in question; (3) the price competitiveness of imported coal (extracted from open-pit mines); (4) pressure from the EU climate policy; and (5) rapid development of alternative solutions. Under such conditions, the majority of Polish mines will remain unprofitable and maintaining extraction operations will generate substantial costs in the following years. The situation has been additionally aggravated by the outbreak of the COVID-19 pandemic and lockdown measures (with reduction of output and sales).[7]

It is also considered possible to significantly cut lignite extraction by 2050 due to the depletion of lignite resources in the majority of active lignite mines before 2035 (Hille and Kassenberg, 2018, p. 17). Simultaneously, it will take a longer period to limit the use of coal in energy generation on account of the time and costs involved in the construction of alternative energy sources. It is reflected in the experiences of advanced economies having undertaken similar transition measures before. It may be then necessary to increase coal imports. For Poland, it is particularly dangerous to increase its dependence on Russia.

It is indicated that for the reasons mentioned above, the energy transition in Poland must not be of a revolutionary nature. During the transition coal should remain a component of the energy mix, despite low returns from production assets. At the same time, alternative energy sources, small-scale distributed conventional energy generation and storage systems should be developed rapidly.

b. Is there a real alternative to coal in Poland?

Two Western European countries that have made significant progress in departing from a coal-based economy—Germany and the United Kingdom—used transitional sources, i.e., nuclear energy and gas.

Switching the energy sector to gas involves the least changes in the existing power generation infrastructure, but it cannot be treated as the target solution since the Commission assumed that the use of this fuel would be discontinued as well.[8] As the degree of gasification in Poland is low, the use of gas in the transition period requires the development of the gas distribution network. Since November 2018, Poland has implemented the Comprehensive Programme for Accelerating Investments in Poland's Gas Network. It largely relies on EU funds. The investment projects have continued despite the pandemic. The objective of the programme is to achieve the degree of gasification in Poland of nearly 61 per cent by 2022 or 61 per cent of the territory will have access to the gas network (Polska Spółka Gazownictwa, 2020, p. 11).

From the point of view of energy security, it is debatable whether the system should largely rely on imported gas. A significant increase in the demand for gas poses a risk of Poland's returning to greater dependence on Russia in a situation of insufficient growth in domestic output, sluggish extension of the LNG terminal in Świnoujście or connection to the Norwegian deposits (the Baltic Pipe). The situation should improve with the construction of a floating storage and regasification unit in Gdańsk, regarded as a key infrastructure project and eligible for financial assistance under the Connecting Europe Facility (CEF).

The inclusion in the mix of zero-emission energy from a nuclear power plant has been considered for years. Nuclear power is a stable source and would improve the country's energy independence. The weakness of the solution is its time-consuming and costly nature (resulting from the necessary acquisition of an appropriate technology, large multiannual investments and radioactive waste management). Furthermore, the ideas of building a high-power reactor instigated protests from local communities and certain ecologists. Therefore, new concepts rely on a greater number of small-scale reactors, including combined heat and power plants. According to the government plans, the first nuclear unit will be ready for operation in 2033 at the earliest, whereas the whole programme (6 units) will have been completed by 2043 (Ministerstwo Klimatu, 2020, p. 14). The inclusion of nuclear power in the energy mix would make it easier for Poland to achieve climate neutrality while compensating for the projected losses in electricity generation (Magazyn Polska Chemia, 2020, p. 31). So far, however, the authorities have done little in this direction. Moreover, granting public aid for the construction of nuclear power plants requires the consent of the European Commission. It is not known whether Poland will get it.

The renewable energy sources industry in Poland has been growing relatively fast due to corporate investment in large installations (co-financed from EU funds) and household micro-installations (prosumer energy supported with financial assistance and tax relief). At the current stage, the RES-based system can be no real alternative to coal-based energy generation. It still needs major investments in the power capacity, large-scale storage (the existing methods are not very efficient) as well as the development of transmission infrastructure, including systems connecting the Polish electricity supply system with those of the neighbouring countries (interconnectors increasing security). In addition, RES are non-controllable; therefore, it is advisable to also implement smart solutions facilitating the co-existence of conventional sources and RES within a single electricity supply system. According to experts, it is impossible to make the necessary investments by 2050.

c. *Limited possibilities to apply state-of-the-art solutions—low level of wealth of the country and digital competences of the society*

Poland's coal mining and coal-based energy sector need an urgent and deep restructuring, but it involves significant funds (Ney et al., 2004, p. 1). The two Western European countries mentioned above have relatively high levels of income per inhabitant, which allowed them to obtain consumer acceptance of higher transition costs reflected in increased energy prices (Juszczak et al., 2020, pp. 4–5). In contrast, Poland is less wealthy. Despite a marked rise in the living standards of the population, particularly after accession to the European Union, Poland still ranks among the lowest-income Member States (22nd in terms of real GDP per capita and 20th in terms of GDP per capita PPS). A lower level of economic development limits the investment capabilities of Polish enterprises. The pandemic and lockdown measures have significantly deteriorated the financial position of Polish undertakings,[9] additionally reducing their investment capabilities and opportunities. Consumer incomes dropped as well, which may discourage purchases of green (more expensive) products.

Therefore, as shown by recent years' experiences, interest in environmentally friendly solutions can be stimulated not only by decreasing costs of green technologies but also by significant public support (tax relief, EU and national grants, preferential loans, etc.), whether to undertakings or consumers.

Improving energy efficiency requires measures such as the use of devices of more recent generations, broader digitisation of the economy and the application of smart technological solutions. Meanwhile, Poland's society and firms are characterised by relatively low digital competences compared with other EU Member States. One measure reflecting it is the DESI (Digital Economy and Society Index).[10] According to the 2020 DESI, Poland ranked 23rd among the 28 EU Member States (based on 2019 data, the report covered the United Kingdom), slightly ahead of Cyprus and Italy as well as outperforming Romania, Greece and Bulgaria (DESI, 2020, p. 14). Its position was significantly below the EU average for most of the DESI sub-indices (dimensions). Poland's best score was recorded in terms of connectivity (above the EU average; 15th place in the EU), whereas it performed the worst in the use of internet services (23rd) and the integration of digital technology (25th). As pointed out by the authors of the report, Poland's performance in terms of integration of digital technology below the EU average was determined by low levels of both business digitisation and e-commerce.

The COVID-19 pandemic and lockdown have substantially increased the use of internet services by citizens and business digitisation (e.g. the introduction of e-commerce to ensure sales, Grzeszak et al., 2020, p. 10). Therefore, it may stimulate the execution of some of the EGD assumptions regarding the digitisation of the European economy, including the Polish one.

3 The position of the Polish government towards the EGD

Over the years Poland's energy policy has been shaped depending on how the ruling teams understood the concept of energy security. Recently one can observe gradual changes in understanding of this term, a shift from optimal use of the country's own energy resources to ensuring the competitiveness of the economy, energy efficiency and reduced negative effects of the energy sector on the environment (Paska and Surma, 2013, pp. 13–17). Also the concept of the development of the energy sector in Poland has been changing for several years. The idea has been evolving towards an energy industry based on diversified energy sources, multidirectional energy flows and smart management (Hille and Kassenberg, 2018, p. 36).

The activities preceding the announcement of the EGD (including the development of energy clusters, growing support for RES) indicated the growing willingness of government to implement changes in the energy sector. At the same time, due to the existing structure of the fuel and energy sector as well as to short-term election interests, the political narrative of protecting hard coal mining and supporting the old and strongly centralised energy sector model was maintained (Hille and Kassenberg, 2018, p. 36).

In December 2019, Poland questioned neither the European Green Deal nor the EU goal of achieving climate neutrality by 2050. However, the government found it unrealistic for Poland to attain the objective by that date, indicating the difficult starting point of the Polish transition (strong dependence on coal) and very high socio-economic costs of transformation (Ministerstwo Klimatu, 2020, p. 3). According to the government, the investment needs in the energy supply sector (electricity, heat, gas, mining and liquid fuels) will amount to around EUR 246 billion by 2040 (around 4 per cent of current GDP annually). The electricity generation sector will need EUR 23.9 billion (around 0.4 per cent of GDP annually) in the period 2021–2030 (European Commission, 2020c, p. 13). On the other hand, investment needs in non-energy sectors (industry, households, services, transport and agriculture) are estimated at EUR 206 billion from 2016 to 2040 (European Commission, 2020b, p. 43).

The pandemic period has revealed marked differences of opinion among those in power with regard to the EGD. On the one hand, it has been argued that it is necessary to reject or at least to postpone the implementation of the strategy for the sake of saving the economy (as stated by the Deputy Minister of State Assets, Janusz Kowalski (2020), and the Minister of Environment, Michał Woś (2020)); on the other hand, there are advocates of support measures for the development of Polish RES, in jeopardy due to the outbreak of the pandemic (the Minister of Climate, Michał Kurtyka, in his letter to the European Commission (Sawicki, 2020)). Despite those differences, Poland signed the Joint statement of the European Council of 26 March 2020, stipulating the development of European economies after the pandemic while integrating the green transition and digital transformation (thus the EGD) (European Council, 2020, p. 6). In July 2020, during the Special European Council, Poland also refrained from committing to the objective of achieving climate neutrality by 2050. The price for the non-commitment has been Poland's limited access to appropriations from the Just Transition Fund (see Chapter 5).

The recently updated "Energy Policy of Poland until 2040" ("*Polityka energetyczna Polski do 2040 r.*") proposes significant changes to the Polish energy sector. However, it still does not contain a schedule for achieving full climate neutrality by the country. The document was developed under the influence of the EU laws related to the climate and energy objectives for 2030, the European Green Deal, the plan of economic recovery after the COVID-19 pandemic and intention to achieve climate neutrality in the second half of the twenty-first century (Ministerstwo Klimatu, 2020, p. 4). Energy transition is presented as a *sine qua non* for the development of the Polish economy, a guarantee of security and greater resilience to crises as well as a prerequisite for ensuring the competitiveness of Polish firms (Ministerstwo Klimatu, 2020, p. 6). The assumptions adopted in the document comprise building a zero-emission energy system by extending the energy mix to nuclear power (from 2033) and offshore wind farms (from 2025), further development of the capacity of the already existing renewable energy sources (including a greater role of distributed energy generation and community energy) as well as electricity production by combined heat and power plants (cogeneration). The share of electricity from coal is assumed to fall considerably (to a maximum of 56 per cent in 2030 and 28 per cent in 2040), whereas energy security should be provided through temporary application of energy technologies based on gas fuels (Ministerstwo Klimatu, 2020, p. 7). Until 2030, Poland's energy and climate transition should be supported with approximately PLN 200 billion, from the EU and national appropriations (Ministerstwo Klimatu, 2020, p. 3). However, the document indicates that public funds should only mobilise private expenditure. Unless businesses join the financing of the transition, it will be impossible to achieve its objectives.

Modifications to the document proposed by the government resulted in protests from the mining trade unions. In their opinion, the implementation of the "Energy Policy of Poland until 2040" would imply shutting down hard coal mines by 2036–2037, entailing disastrous socio-economic effects. One of the main demands of the protesters is the extension of the transition period to approximately 40 years. According to the agreement concluded between the government and trade unions, coal mining in Poland is to end in 2049. However, so far no concrete timetable of achieving this goal has been presented. The European Commission still has to agree to such a solution.

To facilitate the transformation, the government also considers transferring all the coal-fired power plants to a single company until their final shut-down for the purpose of helping other energy companies obtain funds for the development of RES (Piszczatowska, 2020).

4 Polish enterprises (energy companies and energy-intensive industries) and the European Green Deal

The EGD is the new reality that must be adapted to, beyond the control of undertakings. It is seen as an essential change in their external (both micro- and macro-) environment. That change is very complex due to the incorporation of all the EU measures and policies with a view to achieving the objectives of the strategy. It will require the reorganisation of a major share of today's network of linkages. The transition towards a low-carbon economy poses a particularly difficult challenge to the energy sector and energy-intensive industries; therefore, they are given special attention in further analysis.

The analysis of the available sources shows that few Polish firms have expressed their positions on the European Green Deal. Some of them have presented their opinions independently (e.g., KGHM Polska Miedź S.A.), others have acted through the associations authorised to represent them (e.g., members of the Polish Chamber of Chemical Industry—*Polska Izba Przemysłu Chemicznego*, PIPC, or of the Polish Electricity Association—*Polski Komitet Energii Elektrycznej*, PKEE). Associations have presented independent positions (e.g. PKEE; the Polish Confederation Lewiatan—*Konfederacja Lewiatan*; the Polish Society of Professional CHP Plants—*Polskie Towarzystwo Elektrociepłowni Zawodowych*, PTEZ) or have referred to documents adopted by the European associations to which they belong (e.g. the European Chemical Industry Council—CEFIC (PIPC) or the European Plastics Converters industry association EuPC (the Polish Union of Plastics Converters—*Polski Związek Przetwórców Tworzyw Sztucznych*)). Furthermore, some business representatives expressed their opinions during various events.

Such positions included support for building a low-carbon and resource-efficient economy. Firms declared their willingness to actively participate in the transition by taking necessary adjustment measures. Some undertakings indicated the role they could play in the transition process, e.g. through supplying raw materials or components for the needs of developing RES installations and low-loss networks (e.g. KGHM Polska Miedź S.A.). Companies in the energy sector and the heat generation industry expressly indicated the necessity to radically transform the Polish energy industry and to ensure the security of electricity and heat supply during the transition. At the same time, businesses stressed that the implementation of the EGD would pose a significant challenge to them on account of the pace of changes planned. They presented their expectations with regard to forms of public support. Specifically, those included the following:

- regulatory support in the form of concrete and simplified legal acts adopted as quickly as possible—that aspect was particularly emphasised by chemical companies, subject to various strict regulations, particularly hindering their operations during the pandemic;
- taking into account the position of the industry in the process of designing specific solutions—giving consideration to certain proposals for amending regulations (PIPC, EuPC);
- introducing organisational changes facilitating project implementation;
- financial support for business adjustments to the new operating conditions,[11] including for industrial investments.

Various positions pointed to a common element—the necessity to ensure that the transition be just, i.e.:

- taking into consideration the starting point—the historical and geographic differences in the current energy mixes, the Member States' economic and technological development levels and their populations' readiness for changing habits and cultural changes;
- providing substantial funds for adjustments in Member States with low GDP *per capita* and mining regions in transition, e.g. by increasing the budgets of the Modernisation Fund and the Just Transition Fund, additional support from the JTF for regional investments in RES facilitating changes in the energy mixes and reskilling (PKEE, 2019);
- taking account of the commercial availability of key transitional technologies.

Furthermore, Polish firms expressed their support for the carbon border adjustment mechanism (CBA) as an opportunity to ensure the competitiveness of European and Polish products in the EU and non-EU markets and to reduce the relocation of production to countries with less stringent environmental standards. Businesses treated the mechanism as a strong incentive to decarbonise and transform processes in existing undertakings. Such positions also comprised indications for the inclusion of the energy sector in the CBA mechanism as some of the EU Member States (Spain, Poland, the Baltic States) imported electricity generated without accounting for emission costs.[12]

Most firms have been planning to make use of the EGD as an opportunity to evolve, an element allowing them to maintain competitiveness and to continue operations,[13] as reflected in their strategies. The outbreak of the pandemic, while significantly deteriorating the economic environment of businesses and forcing them to increase their efficiency, has intensified the process of changes in companies' strategies.

But the key role in the implementation of the EGD objectives will be played by measures taken by undertakings in the real sphere. The announcement of the EGD was no surprise to firms engaged in on-going monitoring of consumer trends and changes in the global and European regulatory processes.[14] It only implied the intensification of previous efforts, the continuation of actions promoting sustainable development. Such undertakings had been taking adjustment measures early. As a result, by the time of publishing the EGD by the Commission, they had been advanced in their preparations or had begun to implement solutions improving energy efficiency or changing their business profiles.

The companies' actions relevant to improving energy efficiency (reducing emissions) included both internal and external measures. The former mostly comprised reducing energy consumption by undertakings, limiting reliance on coal and increasing the share of low-carbon fuels (including company capacities) and introducing circular-economy solutions (e.g. cutting raw material needs). The latter focussed on shutting down outdated and inefficient coal-fired power units or installations, upgrading production assets (based on modern technologies) and building new facilities with lower energy intensity and emissions. It also comprised circular-economy measures (such as closing water circuits in production processes). In addition, energy companies made efforts to limit network losses in the distribution of electricity and heat and to build new cogeneration capacities.

Polish energy and energy-intensive companies are also opening to new areas of action in the search for funds for energy transition and development. Energy firms— as well as certain other companies (such as PKN Orlen, PGNiG, and KGHM)—continued large investments in the development of renewable energy sources—onshore wind farms, offshore wind farms and photovoltaic energy (based on their own projects or acquisitions). In addition, faced with deteriorating profits from traditional business activities, undertakings started to open to new areas of operation, deploying (own or acquired) modern technological solutions. Development-oriented investment projects have been implemented despite the pandemic.

Firms from the energy sector continued efforts to diversify generation sources—to gradually move away from coal towards low-carbon (gas) and zero-carbon sources (RES).[15] Circular-economy solutions also offered new business opportunities—the application of combustion by-products in industries such as construction, agriculture, civil engineering, the production of electricity and heat from waste. Fuel corporations intensified efforts to enhance conventional liquid fuels (with new additives), to develop alternative fuels (hydrogen technologies), gas fuels (LNG, CNG) and biofuels as well as to build alternative fuel distribution networks. The Grupa Azoty Group—a traditional producer of fertilisers and chemicals—developed technologies for manufacturing biodegradable plastics, waste-based fertilisers, materials for 3D printing (filaments), humic acids or vacuum coating services. The outbreak of the pandemic has stimulated product range development, e.g., adding filaments with biocidal agents, antivirus gloves.

Summary and conclusions

The European Green Deal is a very ambitious plan for environmental transition of the EU economy, with effects on all policies and measures of the European Union. Its fundamental objective is to achieve the EU's climate neutrality by 2050. The intention is for each Member State to adopt that deadline as its own national goal. Such an assumption means that all the Member States should attain the same objective by the mid-twenty-first century, irrespective of their starting points: those able to voluntarily commit to achieving climate neutrality early owing to already applied solutions, and those for which such a commitment seems unrealistic unless some breakthrough technologies are developed. As a result, the challenges faced by individual Member States vary widely.

Due to Poland's specific situation (a very high share of coal in the energy mix, limited financial resources that could be allocated to costly investments in alternative energy sources, the low wealth of the population), the government chose not to adopt attaining climate neutrality by 2050 as the national objective. But it does not mean that there have been no changes in Poland. First and foremost, there has been a shift in the perception of energy security in policy making. For several years, the previous emphasis on using domestic coal has been increasingly placed on competitiveness-related aspects, due to EU regulations, the unprofitability of mines, rising CO_2 emission costs and growing energy demand. The outbreak of the pandemic and lockdown measures seem to have accelerated those changes. At the same time, however, it limited domestic funds (especially public funds) that could be allocated to energy transformation (the priority is to reduce the negative effects of the recession and ensure the health and safety of the society).

Apparently, the Polish energy sector, responsible for the highest CO_2 emissions, has been gradually evolving towards diversified energy-generating products and a low-carbon energy system. It has been both a top-down (energy clusters) and bottom-up (prosumer energy development) transition. The necessary changes require making specific decisions regarding the gradual replacement of coal with other energy sources, the schedule of necessary actions, ensuring financial resources for their implementation, etc. In the process of shaping the new energy mix, it is necessary to ensure security of energy supply. The unpopular decisions on gradual limitation of the role of coal in the economy should not be postponed.

On account of the difficult starting point of Poland's green transition, it will be necessary to implement a great number of investment projects across the country over a short period. Financial resources are needed i.e. for modernisation of corporate assets and development of more "green" ones, extension of distribution networks, and adaptation of the existing infrastructure to changing climate conditions. Projects have to be of high quality to get the EU funding. According to experts, there are currently few such projects.

The implementation time and the intensity of measures to be taken is one thing. Another issue, no less important, is to ensure indispensable transition funds for specific industries and the economy as a whole. Large funds will also be needed to mitigate the social effects of the transformation, due to high employment in the coal mining sector.

Due to the still relatively low level of economic development, neither Poland's budget nor Polish firms have the necessary financial resources. Borrowing is not always an option either. Whereas green capital is generally available in capital markets, it usually seeks viable investment (Conversation of T. Zieliński, 2020b). Part of the funding can come from the auctioning of emissions allowances in the EU ETS as well as from the Modernisation Fund. However, as shown by recent years' experiences, only slightly more than 50 per cent of this amount was used for climate- and energy-related purposes (European Commission, 2020b, p. 43). Therefore, a number of projects must be (co-)financed from public funds. EU funds agreed upon by July 2020 offer the opportunity for Poland to reduce the national burden of the energy transformation. The use of the majority of these funds is however conditioned upon the adoption of the EU target of climate neutrality by 2050 (more: Chapter 5). Without a change in its position Poland will not be able to benefit fully from EU funds.

The progress in the green transition of the Polish economy will be largely determined by the commitment of firms to the process. The analysis of activities undertaken by Polish energy and energy-intensive companies indicate that they have been taking adaptation measures, treating the EU legislation as the new reality which offers development opportunities. The scale of adjustments varies. It primarily comprises endeavours to improve energy efficiency (reducing CO_2 emissions) and to diversify economic activities (as a necessary component of survival strategies in a period of increased investment efforts and uncertainty as regards the future). In this regard, the current pandemic has stimulated measures such as the development of new products (reflected in a rising number of applications filed with the Patent Office[16]).

Notes

1 In the case of the most stringent laws, derogations were negotiated (e.g. derogations for low-stack emissions or derogations in the energy and climate package).

2 In Poland, most discussions regarding the EGD concentrate on the phasing out of coal and building a low-/zero-carbon economy. In this context, the EGD also appeared as an element of the presidential election campaign.

3 The ETI indicator was prepared by the World Economic Forum. It incorporates both the starting level of each country and its ability to pursue an ambitious climate policy.

4 Policy making for the mining and energy sectors was frequently aimed at winning favourable attitudes of miners, energy industry workers (and their families) as well as of the related institutions before elections. At the same time, there was no influential political force in Poland that would be interested in comprehensive changes in and transition of the energy sector (Hille and Kassenberg, 2018, p. 54).

5 It comprises coal mines but also large wind farms. There is also rising opposition to launching new open pits as those involve significant damage to the environment and human health while limiting the possibility of the economic use of major areas of land.

6 An energy cluster is a local agreement of entities involved in the production, consumption, storage and sale of electricity, heat, cold, electricity in transport and fuels. Their goal is to develop distributed energy and improve local energy security in an economically effective and environmentally friendly manner. Energy clusters make it possible to use local resources and the potential of domestic energy. They favour the implementation of the latest technologies where they are useful and profitable (Ustawa z dnia 22 czerwca 2016 r. o zmianie ustawy o odnawialnych źródłach energii oraz niektórych innych ustaw (Dz. U. poz. 925)).

7 In the pandemic period, the mines of the companies Polska Grupa Górnicza S.A. and Jastrzębska Spółka Węglowa S.A. have suffered losses. In contrast, the company Tauron Wydobycie S.A. has made a profit, due to its efficiency-oriented efforts (PGG i JSW liczą straty, 2020).

8 Gas-fired power plants emit ca. 350 kg of CO2/MWh in comparison with ca. 750 kg of CO2/MWh from new coal-fired units. Therefore, it is "merely" a significant reduction rather than elimination of emissions.

9 In the first half of 2020 as compared to the first half of 2019, the revenue of Polish firms declined by 5.2 per cent, net sales of products, goods and materials by 5.4 per cent, net profit by 22.8 per cent and gross capital formation by 6.1 per cent (GUS, 2020, p. 1).

10 The DESI monitors Europe's overall digital performance and tracks the progress of the EU Member States in digital competitiveness. It is made up of five dimensions: connectivity, human capital, the use of internet services, the integration of digital technology and digital public services (European Commission, 2020a, pp. 10–13).

11 According to estimates for the chemical industry, the implementation of the EGD will increase its operating expenses by 20 to 80 per cent (Conversation of T. Zieliński, 2020a).

12 However, it is difficult to assess the role of such a solution in the absence of a specific legislative proposal.

13 As regards chemical firms associated at PIPC, a mere 8.8 per cent see no opportunities connected with the introduction of the EGD (PIPC, 2020).

14 Through lobbying activities, certain large corporations actively participated in making both national and EU laws.

15 For instance, Tauron intends to exceed 65 per cent of energy production from low- and zero-carbon sources by 2030, whereas PGE S.A. plans to supply customers with 100 per cent green energy by 2050.

16 By 5 per cent compared to 2019, including 100 related to protection against COVID-19 (Coraz więcej polskich patentów, 2020).

Bibliography

Conversation of T. Zieliński, President of the PIPC Management Board, and Prof. Z. Krasnodębski – MEP, Vice-President of the Industry, Research and Energy Committee in the European Parliament(2020a) Congress of Polish Chemistry, 16 September.

Conversation of T. Zieliński President of the PIPC Management Board, and P. Folgiero – Chief Executive Officer in Maire Tecnimont Group (2020b) Congress of Polish Chemistry, 16 September.

Coraz więcej polskich patentów związanych z ochroną przed koronawirusem. W Urzędzie Patentowym RP już ok. 100 zgłoszeń dotyczy COVID-19 (2020) Available at: https://innowacje.newseria.pl/news/coraz-wiecej-polskich,p1715631570 (Accessed: 18 September 2020).

DESI (2020) Digital Economy and Society Index. Available at: https://ec.europa.eu/digital-single-market/en/news/digital-economy-and-society-index-desi-2020 (Accessed: 22 July 2020).

European Commission (2019) European Green Deal, COM(2019) 640 final.

European Commission (2020a) Digital Economy and Society Index (DESI) 2020. Thematic chapters. Available at: https://ec.europa.eu/newsroom/dae/document.cfm?doc_id=67086 (Accessed: 10 September 2020).

European Commission (2020b) '2020 European Semester', Country Report – Poland 2020: Assessment of progress on structural reforms, prevention and correction of macroeconomic imbalances, and results of in-depth reviews under Regulation (EU) No 1176/2011, SWD(2020) 520 final.

European Commission (2020c) Assessment of the final national energy and climate plan of Poland, SWD(2020) 920 final.

European Council (2019) Conclusions, EUCO 29/19.

European Council (2020) Joint statement of the Members of the European Council. Available at: https://www.consilium.europa.eu/media/43076/26-vc-euco-statement-en.pdf (Accessed: 26 June 2020).

Eurostat (2020a) Gross fixed capital formation (investments). Available at: https://ec.europa.eu/eurostat/tgm/refreshTableAction.do?tab=table&plugin=1&pcode=tec00011&language=en (Accessed: 25 August 2020).

Eurostat (2020b) Real GDP per capita. Available at: https://ec.europa.eu/eurostat/tgm/table.do?tab=table&init=1&language=en&pcode=sdg_08_10&plugin=1 (Accessed: 25 August 2020).

Global Carbon Atlas (2020) Global Carbon Atlas database. Available at: http://www.globalcarbonatlas.org/en/CO2-emissions (Accessed: 10 September 2020).

Grzeszak, J., Leśniewicz, F. and Święcicki, I. (2020) *Monitoring gospodarki cyfrowej.* Warszawa: Polski Instytut Ekonomiczny, Edycja III.

GUS (2020) Wyniki finansowe przedsiębiorstw niefinansowych w okresie styczeń-czerwiec 2020 roku, *Informacje sygnalne.* Available at: https://stat.gov.pl/obszary-tematyczne/podmioty-gospodarcze-wyniki-finansowe/przedsiebiorstwa-niefinansowe/wyniki-finansowe-przedsiebiorstw-niefinansowych-w-okresie-styczen-czerwiec-2020-roku,12,40.html (Accessed: 10 September 2020).

Hille, E. and Kassenberg, A. (2018) *Proces odchodzenia od węgla w Polsce – dylematy.* Warszawa: Instytut na rzecz ekorozwoju.

IOŚ-PIB (2019) Klimat dla Polski, Polska dla klimatu. 1988-2018-2050. Available at: https://ios.edu.pl/wp-content/uploads/2019/03/Klimat-dla-Polski-Polska-dla-Klimatu_PL.pdf (Accessed: 25 June 2020).

Juszczak, A., Maj, M. and Szpor, A. (2020) *Time for decarbonisation*. Warsaw: Polish Economic Institute.

KGHM Polska Miedź S.A. (2020) European Green Deal a perspektywy dla miedzi. Available at: https://media.kghm.com/pl/informacje-prasowe/european-green-deal-a-perspektywy-dla-miedzi (Accessed: 20 June 2020).

Konfederacja Lewiatan (2020) Zielona transformacja nie powiedzie się bez zaangażowania biznesu. Available at: http://konfederacjalewiatan.pl/aktualnosci/2020/1/zielona_-transformacja_nie_powiedzie_sie_bez_zaangazowania_biznesu_ (Accessed: 25 June 2020).

Kowalski, J. (2020) Koronawirus każe wyłączyć Polskę z ETS i zapomnieć o Europejskim Zielonym Ładzie (Rozmowa). Available at: https://biznesalert.pl/kowalski-wylaczyc-polske-z-ets-europejski-zielony-lad-energetyka-klimat/ (Accessed: 20 June 2020).

Magazyn Polska Chemia (2020) *PIPC*, No. 2.

Ministerstwo Klimatu (2020) Polityka Energetyczna Polski do 2040 r. Streszczenie, Warszawa.

Ministry of Climate (2020) Poland's National Inventory Report 2020, Warsaw.

Ney, R., Blaschke, W., Lorenz, U. and Gawlik, L. (2004) *Węgiel kamienny jako źródło czystej energii w Polsce*, Instytut Gospodarki Surowcami Mineralnymi i Energią PAN, Kraków, Referat przedstawiony na XIX Światowym Energetycznym Kongresie i Wystawie, 5–9 września 2004 roku, Sydney, Australia, zorganizowanym przez Światową Radę Energetyczną. Available at: https://se.min-pan.krakow.pl/publikacje/04_28rnulwblg_ kgiph.pdf (Accessed: 20 July 2020).

Paska, J. and Surma, T. (2013) Polityka energetyczna Polski na tle polityki energetycznej Unii Europejskiej, *Polityka Energetyczna*, 16(4), pp. 7–19.

PGE (2020a) Kluczowa rola PGE w osiągnięciu zero emisyjności. Available at: https://www.gkpge.pl/Biuro-Prasowe/komunikaty-prasowe/korporacyjne/kluczowa-rola-pge-w-osiagnieciu-zeroemisyjnosci (Accessed: 12 August 2020).

PGE (2020b) Sprawozdanie na temat informacji niefinansowych PGE Polskiej Grupy Energetycznej S.A. oraz Grupy Kapitałowej PGE za rok 2019. Available at: https://www.gkpge.pl/Relacje-inwestorskie/content/download/51577/plik/Sprawozdanie%20niefinansowe%20GKPGE%202019.pdf (Accessed: 12 August 2020).

PGG i JSW liczą straty, a kopalnie Taurona wypracowały zysk w 2020 roku (2020) Available at: https://www.slaskibiznes.pl/wiadomosci,pgg-i-jsw-licza-straty-a-kopalnie-taurona-wypracowaly-zysk-w-2020-roku,wia5-1-3529.html (Accessed: 25 August 2020).

PIPC (2020) Unijne ambicje klimatyczne a możliwości polskiej chemii. Available at: https://www.kongrespolskachemia.pl/aktualnosci/unijne-ambicje-klimatyczne-a-mozli wosci-polskiej-chemii,p1423714372 (Accessed: 25 August 2020).

Piszczatowska, J. (2020) Jeszcze nikt nie stawiał sprawy tak jasno, jak obecny prezes PGE. Grupa pożegna się i z węglem, i z atomem. Available at: https://www.green-news.pl/1043-PGE-zegna-sie-z-weglem-i-atomem (Accessed: 22 June 2020).

Polska Spółka Gazownictwa (2020) Strategia na lata 2016–2022. Available at: https://www.psgaz.pl/documents/21201/329214/Strategia+PSG+2016+-+2022.pdf/a95241fa-85d1-4ee6-8de7-906792e30cb4 (Accessed: 10 September 2020).

Polski Komitet Energii Elektrycznej (PKEE) (2019) Stanowisko dotyczące Europejskiego Nowego Zielonego Ładu. Available at: https://www.pkee.pl/stanowisko-polskiego-komitetu-energii-elektrycznej-dotyczace-europejskiego-nowego-zielonego-ladu-2/ (Acce ssed: 20 June 2020).

PORDATA (2020) GDP per capita (PPS). Available at: https://www.pordata.pt/en/Europe/GDP+per+capita+(PPS)-1778 (Accessed: 25 August 2020).

PTEZ (2020) Jak Europejski Zielony Ład wpłynie na kogenerację? Available at: http://www.ptez.pl/aktualnosci/news/159/jak_europejski_zielony_lad_wplynie_na_kogeneracje/page (Accessed: 20 May 2020).

PZPTS (2020) Oficjalne pismo EuPC do Komisji Europejskiej. Available at: https://pzpts.pl/pr/480643/oficjalne-pismo-eupc-do-komisji-europejskiej (Accessed: 20 May 2020).

Sawicki, B. (2020) Polska apeluje do Komisji o wsparcie OZE ze względu na korona wirusa. Available at: https://biznesalert.pl/list-wsparcie-oze-koronawirus-komisja-europejska-energetyka/ (Accessed: 21 May 2020).

Tauron (2020) Raport zintegrowany 2019. Available at: https://raport.tauron.pl/ (Accessed 22 September 2020).

World Economic Forum (2020) *Fostering Effective Energy Transition*. 2020 edition. Available at: https://www.weforum.org/reports/fostering-effective-energy-transition-2020 (Accessed: 20 September 2020).

Woś, M. (2020) Europejski "Zielony Ład" nie ma szans wejść w tym półroczu. Available at: https://www.cire.pl/item,195920,1,0,0,0,0,0,wos-europejski-zielony-lad-nie-ma-szans-wejsc-w-tym-polroczu.html (Accessed: 21 May 2020).

8 The emergency measures underpinning Poland's Convergence Programme 2020

The Case of the trade credit reinsurance scheme

Alina Dorota Szypulewska-Porczyńska

Introduction

This chapter focuses on one of the emergency programmes intended to address concerns related to liquidity needs of Polish companies via the insurance market, i.e. trade credit reinsurance scheme. This programme, announced in April 2020 and initiated by the issuance of a relevant legal act in mid-August by the Polish government, was still waiting for implementation in mid-November. For obvious reasons, other important aid programmes were given precedence over it. Those were schemes aimed to protect the most vulnerable: COVID-19 patients and workers, for the outbreak of the coronavirus has resulted in a simultaneous health and economic crisis in many countries. If we look into the human costs of COVID-19, we can observe that at least for the first months of the pandemic, when the first programmes under examination were introduced in the EU economies, Poland ranked among the EU Member States moderately hit by the coronavirus and the peak of deaths fell relatively late (Figure 8.1).

The containment measures, with the exception of closing all schools and the non-essential movement ban, were introduced in Poland quickly, before the third death caused by COVID-19 was registered in the country (Hirsch, 2020). Although the degree of the economic crisis also inflicted by the pandemic has not been a simple function of the domestic containment and mitigation measures, in particular due to the economic linkages producing spill-over effects, there is a relationship between the economic costs of the countermeasures and the dynamics of the disease.

This chapter shows the aid measures underpinning Poland's Convergence Programme 2020 to protect the economy from the effects of the pandemic. As the economic consequences of those measures are difficult to quantify due to the rapidly changing environment, the focus will be on factors that might strengthen or weaken the impact. Three factors of particular importance to the effectiveness of COVID-19 measures will be distinguished: their magnitude, pace of introduction and consistency with Polish companies' needs. The presentation of the European fiscal response that created leeway for immediate support at the level of Member States (MSs) is followed by a description of

DOI: 10.4324/9781003144434-9

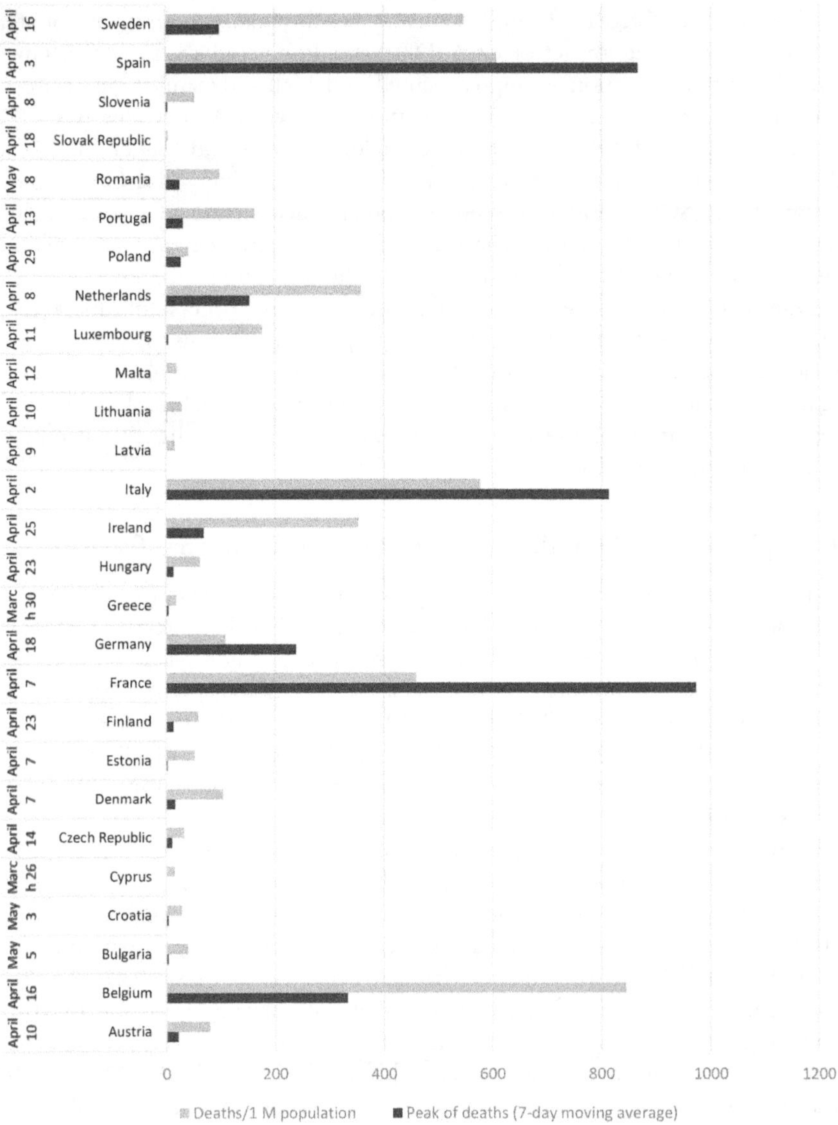

Figure 8.1 Death toll of COVID-19 in the EU Member States by mid-July 2020.
Source: Prepared by the author based on Worldometers (2020).

government assistance to businesses with a trade credit reinsurance scheme. The programme stabilising the trade credit insurance market seems to have the characteristics of both a relatively low cost and a scope for significant potential gains for the economy from stabilising that part of the insurance market which protects suppliers of goods and services against the risk of non-payment by their customers.

The measures listed in Poland's Convergence Programme aimed at counteracting the economic impact of COVID-19 should be read with caution. Given that the current situation is unprecedented and highly dynamic, the anti-crisis tools have already been adapted many times. Between March and July 2020 alone, four sets of COVID-19 laws were adopted in Poland (Baker McKenzie, 2020). Rather, the list of measures contained in the Stability and Convergence Programmes (SCPs) should be seen as a preliminary picture of priority actions under this framework, a rough indication of the magnitude of those measures and a reference point for further research on their adoption.

Due to the high degree of Poland's integration into the single market, an important element of this study is a comparative analysis. All emergency measures submitted under Poland's Convergence Programme are assessed against the background of the other MSs, whereas the benchmark for the title case is the situation in the EU Member States that have already introduced similar solutions in 2020.

1 Applying the flexibility of European and national fiscal rules

Extensive programmes of the Polish government to combat the coronavirus crisis similar to those introduced by other EU Member States required recourse to the flexibility of the EU surveillance framework. Alongside EU rules on State aid and public procurement, flexibility under the Stability and Growth Pact (SGP) was necessary as well (Busch, 2020). Specifically, the thresholds of 3 per cent of GDP for EU MSs' budget deficits and 60 per cent of GDP for their public debts could limit EU MSs' financial efforts to protect their economies against COVID-19.

Adopted in 1997 to accompany the euro by strengthening the coordination and surveillance of fiscal and economic policies in the Economic and Monetary Union, the SGP has evolved over the past 23 years. It was weakened by the 2005 amendment to accommodate some EU Member States exceeding the fiscal limits of Maastricht. The last changes, i.e. the 2011 "six-pack", the 2013 "two-pack" and Fiscal Compact reforms, generally strengthened the EU fiscal framework after the debt crisis. It was then, however, that a temporary departure from the adjustment path towards the medium-term budgetary objective was allowed in two cases: (1) an unusual event outside the control of the Member State concerned; and (2) severe economic downturn for the euro area or the Union (Article 1(8) of Regulation (EU) No 1175/2011). In March 2020, the Commission assessed that the conditions to activate the general escape clause of the SGP were met (European Commission, 2020a) and asked the Council to endorse its conclusion (European Commission, 2020b).

Fiscal escape clauses were also activated in the majority of MSs at the national level by the end of May (EU IFIs, 2020). In Poland, the process took longer. The government proposed changes to the Public Finance Act, extending the catalogue of events suspending the application of the stabilising expenditure rule and adding a path of return to the rule. The first solution was criticised by some economists who believed that the exit clause should be based on extraordinary measures defined in the Constitution rather than on the changed fiscal framework (GAP, 2020). The act amending the Public Finance Act finally took effect on 3 July 2020.

When assessing the existing framework for public finance in Poland, it should be noted that Poland has created a domestic fiscal framework with numerical fiscal rules more stringent than the European ones (Marchewka-Bartkowiak, 2016). Furthermore, in Poland, as in few other EU Member States, the debt criterion has been enshrined in the Constitution since its inception in 1997. Article 216(5) states that it is neither permissible for the State "to contract loans nor provide guarantees and financial sureties which would engender a national public debt exceeding three-fifths of the value of the annual gross domestic product" (Constitution of the Republic of Poland, Chapter X). There are additional prudential and adjustment requirements for public debt in the Polish Public Finance Act. Article 86(1) stipulates, *inter alia*, that if public debt exceeds 55 per cent of GDP, the draft budget for the following year must not propose a deficit or must not increase the ratio of central government debt to GDP in the following year. However, debt measured using the Polish national methodology (public debt) differs from that measured according to the EU definition (general government debt), which gives the Polish government more room for manoeuvre (Ministry of Finance, 2011, p. 53).

Article 88 of the Polish Public Finance Act affords to the Polish government, in exceptional circumstances, the possibility of derogating from the fiscal rules contained in the Public Finance Act. The right of derogation can be invoked in times of martial law, the introduction of a state of emergency throughout the territory of the Republic of Poland or the introduction of a state of natural disaster throughout the territory of the Republic of Poland. None of these emergency states has been declared so far. Nevertheless, as of 3 July 2020, with the amendment to the Public Finance Act, the expenditure formula was suspended.

Even before the outbreak, the evolution of the national fiscal requirements stated in the Public Finance Act showed low sustainability of such rules (Sawulski, 2016). The durability of the constitutional fiscal rule is undisputed, but even there, the relevance of the existence of such a rule has been called into question by some economists. In July 2020, a group presenting themselves as representatives of the young generation of economists in Poland published an open letter in which they argued that the low and arbitrary Polish constitutional debt limit restrained "the social and environmental regeneration" of the Polish economy with the help of an "additional stream of public spending" (Allina et al., 2020). According to the signatories, the size of potential funds amounted to several hundred billion zlotys and was determined on the basis of the difference between the amount of debt in Poland and the EU average. As an example of negative consequences of a conservative fiscal policy, they cited the "lost generation" in the countries of South America and South Europe. The signatories assessed the fiscal stimulus as an appropriate response to the crisis and recommended loosening the fiscal policy as a way to rebuild the Polish economy after the epidemic.

However, it should be emphasised that there is no consensus in Poland on this subject. The open letter quoted above was a reaction to an appeal against excessive debt that could not be repaid by future generations by a group of several dozen economists from leading Polish universities. The authors of that earlier letter entitled "The economists' appeal for the transparency of State finance" expressed their opposition to the permanent lifting or loosening of budgetary rules, which they thought could threaten the long-term security of Polish State finance (Adamowicz et al., 2020). The significant rise in public expenditure caused by anti-COVID-19 measures should be, in their opinion, temporary and transparent in order not to pose a threat to medium-term economic stability. Based on the scale of aid programmes announced by the government and the introduction of the mechanism enabling financing outside the State budget, those signatories estimated that the difference from the EU definition of debt would increase from about 3 to 12 pps of GDP (Adamowicz et al., 2020).

The problem of complying with numerical fiscal rules is an EU-wide issue. On average, around half of the MSs have deviated from the SGP rules over the years (Larch and Santacroce, 2020).

2 The Polish emergency measures laid out in the Convergence Programme

By the end of April, under a relaxed EU fiscal framework, the EU MSs presented their 2020 SCPs, setting out national stimulus plans to absorb the economic shock caused by COVID-19 (European Commission, 2020c). Poland announced nine measures under the general escape clause of the SGP. The support funds for individuals, employees, enterprises and the health care system amounted to 3.2 per cent of GDP (Republic of Poland, 2020, p. 7). Poland's Convergence Programme also included government guarantees planned in response to the COVID-19 outbreak in the amount of 4.5 per cent of GDP, with the largest component, the so-called *Financial Shield*, to be financed from the Polish Development Fund (Republic of Poland, 2020, p. 6). The PDF Financial Shield was not indicated as increasing government expenditure. As the chief economist of the Ministry of Finance explained in the press at the beginning of July, the issue of excluding the Polish Development Fund spending from general government debt was still the subject of negotiations with the Commission and Eurostat (PAP, 2020).

The anti-crisis package planned by the Polish government consisted of the following measures (Republic of Poland, 2020, p. 7):

1 subsidies (1.92 per cent of GDP) in the form of "downtime benefits" to persons working under civil contracts and self-employed persons; 3-month exemptions from social security contributions to self-employed persons, small and micro-firms; financing part of employees' salaries or part of operating expenses for businesses with decreased turnover due to the COVID-19 epidemic;

2 capital transfers (0.4 per cent of GDP) to the Polish Development Fund, the Industrial Development Agency (to support leases) and a programme supporting the insurance of trade receivables;
3 transfers (0.38 per cent of GDP) "increasing the availability of loans to micro-enterprises";
4 social transfers in kind and the compensation of employees (0.31 per cent of GDP) to the health care system;
5 social benefits (0.19 per cent of GDP) to farmers and carers of children up to 8 years of age.

All but one scheme had a legal basis for their implementation at the time of submitting Poland's updated Convergence Programme to the European Commission and the Ecofin Council at the end of April 2020. The exception was the scheme for companies unable to obtain commercial insurance for their trade receivables, with a weight of 0.1 per cent of GDP.

Table 8.3 in the Appendix shows that Poland generally ranks in the middle in terms of the size of measures compared with other EU MSs. Whereas it is below the EU average, whether with regard to spending with a direct impact on the budget (column 2) or the entire envelope (the sum of columns 2, 5 and 6), it is nevertheless very close to the EU median. As shown in the Table, national emergency healthcare expenditures and measures to support the economy vary from 2.2 per cent of GDP in Ireland to 48.6 per cent in Italy. Germany (32.1 per cent of GDP), Denmark (19.9 per cent), France (18.9 per cent) and Luxembourg (17.6 per cent) also rank in the top five with the highest budgetary support in the EU, together with Italy.

It follows from the analysis of the structure of emergency measures that Poland put less emphasis on tax and social contributions measures than on discretionary spending. This characteristic was shared by most EU Member States, with Denmark and Portugal being clear exceptions. Poland earmarked the highest amounts for liquidity measures (5.8 per cent of GDP), especially in the form of guarantees for bonds issued by the Polish Development Fund. Even more significant guarantees (reaching double-digit values) were planned by Italy (45.2 per cent of GDP), Germany (24.9 per cent), France (13.9 per cent) and Belgium (11.8 per cent) in response to the crisis.

As regards the large variation in the number of measures included in SCPs, the extensive lists indicate a greater sectoral approach by some EU MSs to their crisis solutions. For example, sector-specific aid measures, other than those for the health sector, can be found in the Estonian, Greek, Danish and Lithuanian programmes. Poland is characterised by an average number of measures. It is against this background that the importance of the programme in the form of support for the national accounts receivable insurance market can be seen. Farmers and lease contracts are also mentioned in the Polish Convergence Programme. Aid for farmers is grouped together with the "Additional allowance for carers of young children", reaching an amount twice as high as that of support for the national accounts receivable insurance market, whereas the size of re-guarantees of lease contracts is 20 per cent smaller as a share in GDP.

3 The economic importance of the Polish trade credit reinsurance scheme

The Polish *Act on supporting the trade receivables insurance market in connection with counteracting the economic effects of COVID-19* entered into force on 21 August. Its economic significance is directly related to the role of trade credit insurance in the economy, an important link in trade. It protects the seller against the risk of non-payment due to buyer insolvency or payment delays, or actions by the foreign government of one of the seller's trading partners (Swiss Re, 2014, p. 2). In the case of default, trade credit insurers provide compensations to sellers, thus enabling them to continue their business activities. The impact of this instrument on the liquidity of companies is even greater as insurance covering trade receivables may be used as a condition of bank lending (European Commission, 2020d) or collateral that improves corporate access to finance via other financial products, in particular factoring (Swiss Re, 2014, p. 4). Moreover, scientific evidence suggests that firms, particularly SMEs, may rely more on trade credit than on bank lending during crisis (e.g. Belghitar et al., 2016; Carbó-Valverde et al., 2016).

Trade credit is of great importance to financing business activities in Poland. As shown in Table 8.1, trade credit granted to customers represented 12 per cent of the net turnover of Polish companies in 2018. In the past 10 years, this percentage has changed insignificantly, by a mere 0.3 pp (BACH, 2020). Trade credit was also the

Table 8.1 Importance of trade credit markets in selected EU Member States in 2018 (weighted average)

	BE	*DE*	*DK*	*FR*	*IT*	*PL*
Trade receivables (% of net turnover)	16.8	6.1	31.3	16.8	23.5	**12.1**
Trade payables (% of total liabilities)	12.1	4.9	4.7	13.8	18.4	**13.9**
Amounts owed to credit institutions (% of total liabilities)	12.1	9.1	15.2	10.4	12.9	**15.8**
Amounts owed to other financial creditors (% of total liabilities)	18.3	28.9	26.3	16.6	11.6	**1.6**
Amounts owed to other non-financial creditors (% of total liabilities)	12	0.0		10.3	11.8	**7.2**

Source: prepared by the author based on BACH (2020).

Notes: (1) The EU Member States supporting trade credit insurance in August 2020 except for the Netherlands and Luxembourg due to missing data. (2) The BACH database (Bank for the Accounts of Companies Harmonised) contains aggregated accounting data of non-financial corporations for 11 EU Member States. (3) Total NACE excluding holding companies and head offices; all sizes. (4) Trade payables include debts to suppliers of goods and services, net of advances; trade receivables include credit granted to customers for supplies of goods or services net of advances received. (5) Data for Denmark from 2016.

second largest source of funding for Polish firms, accounting for 14 per cent of their liabilities, a share only 2 percentage points lower than that of amounts owed to banks. The example of other EU Member States indicates that trade credit is a widespread solution and its economic weight could be even larger. As a share of the net turnover of businesses, it reached its highest levels in Denmark (31 per cent) and Italy (24 per cent) in 2018.

A distinctive feature of trade credit insurance is that—although it usually covers all trade receivables—it has the form of individual credit limits granted to the seller for their individual buyers. Those credit limits may be changed by the insurer. In particular, if the buyer's solvency deteriorates and the risk of non-payment increases, the insurer will reduce or withdraw their credit limits. And here lies the second most important reason why trade credit reinsurance schemes are measures of major economic significance. In times of crisis, like now, they mitigate the effects of credit insurers' actions of adapting their risk exposure by reducing or withdrawing the secured payment limits under ongoing insurance contracts and, as a consequence, triggering domino effects and aggravating the damage caused by the outbreak of COVID-19. The likelihood of domino effects is high in the insurance sector itself due to network effects (European Commission, 2020e, p. 7) as well as in the economy as a whole via liquidity constraints transferred from buyers to sellers and multiplied by supply-chain contagion (Baldwin and Weder di Mauro, 2020, p. 4).

By the end of August, seven EU Member States adopted government-backed support schemes for trade credit insurance, approved by the European Commission (Table 8.2). The first schemes approved in mid-April had been submitted by

Table 8.2 EU State guarantee schemes supporting trade credit insurance markets amid the COVID-19 outbreak, situation as at 31 August 2020

Member State	*Commission's approval*	*Volume (% of GDP)*		*Volume (% of total coverage volume)*	
		Risk sharing	Additional substitution	Risk sharing	Additional substitution
France	12 April	0.2	0.2	2.5	2.5
Germany	13 April	0.2	0.9	1.2	7.3
Denmark	15 May	0.2	1.3	2.0	12.0
Belgium	15 May	0.2	-	1.6	-
Netherlands	25 May	0.1	1.5	0.9	10.9
Luxembourg	1 July	0.2	-	0.6	-
Italy	13 August	0.1	-	0.8	-

Source: calculated and prepared by the author based on European Commission (2020e) and Eurostat (2020).

Notes: (1) GDP at market prices in 2019. (2) Risk sharing between the insurers and the State.

France and Germany. The issue of the speed of introducing government guarantees for trade credit was raised by Germany in its notification of the measure to the Commission. According to Germany, speed is more critical to the effectiveness of a tool than its design (European Commission, 2020d). In the third quarter of 2020, the Polish programme was waiting for the Commission's approval.

Some features of State guarantee schemes supporting trade credit insurance markets are harmonised across the EU, but not all. The time limit for granting aid is uniform and set for 31 December 2020. The same is true of the credit contract term which cannot exceed 2 years. All existing schemes are selective as they cover domestic policyholders, with the French programme going even further by limiting the aid to micro-enterprises, SMEs and mid-caps. It should be emphasised that the length of the reinsurance coverage period stipulated in the government programmes also affects their economic importance. As the underlying trade or transaction and invoicing cannot exceed the cut-off date set by the MSs for 31 December 2020, it means that the protection mainly covers consumer goods. For capital goods, trade credit insurance is usually medium-term, typically 1–3 years (Swiss Re, 2014, p. 2). However, this limitation of government aid can be justified, considering reduced investments by entrepreneurs in crises. During the current pandemic, the phenomenon could have been expected to occur with full force due to an unprecedented level of uncertainty clearly reflected in international economic organisations' outlooks (e.g. OECD, 2020, pp. 2–12; IMF, 2020, pp. 4–9).

The EU Member States' discretion was generally preserved regarding the magnitude of the schemes under study. The highest volumes of support in relation to GDP and to the maximum limits possible under contracts in 2019 were reported by Denmark, the Netherlands, Germany and France (Table 8.2). The maximum amount of aid that Polish trade credit insurers will be able to obtain under the State reinsurance scheme, if the provisions of the Poland's convergence programme are maintained, is at the level of the budget of the Italian measure as a share of GDP. In other countries committed to guaranteed reinsurance schemes, the values of maximum protection are at least twice as high. There is also no second threshold in the planned Polish programme should there be a more unfavourable scenario.

Due to the lack of universality of this measure in the EU and little harmonisation of the existing national programmes, especially regarding their volumes, the effects of the schemes on the competition conditions prevailing in the single market should also be taken into account. The schemes primarily strengthen the competitive positions of their most direct beneficiaries: trade credit insurance companies and policyholders. The advantages also pass to purchasers of goods and services if the selling party is covered. Therefore, buyers are more likely to choose their suppliers from countries already covered by such schemes. For a complete picture, one should also look into the effects of the Commission's decision adopted in March to consider EU MSs and eight other OECD countries as non-marketable risk countries until 31 December 2020. It has a similar effect on competition in the EU's single market as it allows for export aid in the form of export-credit insurance in intra-EU trade (European Commission, 2020f).

Conclusion

In the days of increased fiscal costs caused by the pandemic, the discussion on prudential rules limiting public expenditure was revived in Poland. Even though all economists agree that the extraordinary COVID-19 time requires extraordinary expenses and see the problem of deteriorating transparency of public finance in Poland, there is no consensus on keeping the existing EU and national fiscal rules among Polish economists. However, the restrictive rules were no obstacle to action amid the pandemic. First of all, the EU MSs were allowed to introduce support and stimulus packages under a less "intrusive" EU surveillance framework, which was in great contrast with that emergent from the 2008+ crisis. The flexibility of the regulatory framework may nevertheless prove insufficient for both the EU and Poland in the event of a prolonged crisis and a large amount of government assistance compared to the current restrictions (European Fiscal Board, 2020), posing another challenge to the EU fiscal framework, already widely questioned (e.g. Darvas, 2019).

Data on the Polish trade credit market confirm that the expected introduction of a reinsurance scheme supporting this market will be consistent with Polish companies' needs. Considering the economic significance of the programme supporting the trade credit insurance market, the existence of political awareness of the need for action in Poland and the dynamics of negative processes taking place in the European economy as a result of the pandemic, the pace of introducing the measure seems to be inadequately slow in Poland. The slower the pace of implementation, the less effective the scheme will be. This negative outcome is partially compensated by the inclusion of the measure in Poland's Convergence Programme and by the progress in negotiations between the entry into force of the bill and the approval of the Polish scheme by the Commission, which may to some extent convince insurers to not withdraw the current limits. The pace of introducing the measure in Poland may have been influenced by the fact that it is a new instrument for Poland. The first countries to introduce such solutions in 2020, such as France and Germany, had already protected their domestic receivables during the 2008+ financial crisis (OECD, 2011). Moreover, although Europe was hit by the pandemic just after China, so far it was relatively mild at first in Poland.

The EU MSs have adopted their support and stimulus packages in line with their economic and fiscal strength. Given the differences in the amounts of emergency aid planned by the MSs under the SGP, it is relatively small for the programme under review, excluding the amount of additional substitution. It should be noted that most of the countries (except Denmark and Luxembourg) that have introduced such programmes are the largest exporters of goods in the EU.

Therefore, especially the prolonged and worsening pandemic in most EU Member States, including Poland (WHO, 2020), threatens the integrity of the single market, all the more so as the lock-down related to the coronavirus outbreak has had a disproportionate impact on internationally interdependent sectors. The first channel of highly fragmented international production along value chains has been exposed since the start of the pandemic with the collapse of supply from China. In the EU, the process of national specialisation is additionally advanced due to the mechanism of the single market. Another channel is related to the anti-pandemic measures (including restrictions of free movement preventing from entering national territory) which were undertaken along national borders, especially at the outbreak of the epidemic, while supranational cooperation and coordination remained rather weak. However, it should be noted that the EU response has, of course, been calibrated to its competences. In the health care domain, the EU may "carry out actions to support, coordinate or supplement the actions of the Member States" (Article 6(a) TFEU), whereas legally binding acts of the Union relating to this area "shall not entail harmonisation of Member States' laws or regulations" (Article 2(5) TFEU).

The sanctioned departure from the Stability and Growth Pact fiscal requirements to cushion direct economic consequences of COVID-19 adversely affects the level playing field in the EU single market. To address the menace to the foundations on which economic integration in the EU is built, which is in Poland's interests, it would be appropriate to revisit the idea of establishing a special financial facility for all EU MSs, aimed to support credit insurers in order to increase the availability of insurance (Poniewierka, 2010, p. 102). In a shorter time horizon, for the coming months and the next year as well, if the Commission extends the emergency measures, the Polish trade credit reinsurance system should be introduced as having a significant positive impact on the economy, especially in the case of undertakings unable to obtain export credit insurance.

Bibliography

Adamowicz, E., et al. (2020) Economists' appeal for transparency of state finances. Available at: https://wyborcza.pl/7,155290,25956201,apel-ekonomistow-o-przejrzystosc-finansow-panstwa.html [access: 30 July 2020].

Allina, J., et al. (2020) Debt for regeneration. Appeal to abolish the debt limit in the Polish Constitution. Available at: http://pospolita.eu/dlug-dla-regeneracji [access: 30 July 2020].

BACH (2020) Available at: https://www.bach.banque-france.fr [access: 16 June 2020].

Baker McKenzie (2020) *Law on COVID19 in Poland – Handbook*. Available at: https://www.bakermckenzie.com/-/media/files/insight/publications/2020/07/covid19_handbook_4_baker_mckenzie_en_070720.pdf [access: 24 August 2020].

Baldwin, R. and Weder di Mauro, B. (2020) *Economics in the Time of COVID-19*. [e-book] Available at: https://voxeu.org/content/economics-time-covid-19 [access: 23 September 2020].

Belghitar, Y., Mateus, C. and Moro, A. (2016) Trade credit in Europe: 'It is all down to culture'. *SSRN Electronic Journal*, pp. 1–55. http://dx.doi.org/10.2139/ssrn.2809112

Brooks, E. (2012) Crossing borders: A critical review of the role of the European Court of Justice in EU health policy, *Health Policy*, 105(2012), pp. 33–37.

Busch, D. (2020) Is the European Union going to help us overcome the COVID-19 crisis? *Capital Markets Law Journal*, 15(3), pp. 1–20.

Carbó-Valverde, S., Rodríguez-Fernández, F. and Udell, G. F. (2016) Trade credit, the financial crisis, and SME access to finance, *Journal of Money Credit and Banking* [e-journal], 48(1), pp. 113–143. https://doi.org/10.1111/jmcb.12292.

Darvas, Z. (2019) Why structural balances should be scrapped from EU fiscal rules. Available at: https://www.bruegel.org/2019/10/why-structural-balances-should-be-scrapped-from-eu-fiscal-rules/ [access: 5 October 2020].

EU Independent Fiscal Institutions (EU IFIs) (2020) European Fiscal Monitor Special Update. Available at: https://www.euifis.eu/download/european_fiscal_monitor_special_updatevol2_01.pdf [access: 16 August 2020].

European Commission (2020a) Coordinated economic response to the COVID-19 outbreak (COM(2020)112 final). Available at: https://ec.europa.eu/info/sites/info/files/communication-coordinated-economic-response-covid19-march-2020_en.pdf [access: 13 July 2020].

European Commission (2020b) On the activation of the general escape clause of the Stability and Growth Pact (COM(2020)123 final). Available at: https://ec.europa.eu/info/sites/info/files/economy-finance/2_en_act_part1_v3-adopted_text.pdf [access: 13 July 2020].

European Commission (2020c) 2020 European Semester: National Reform Programmes and Stability/Convergence Programmes. Available at: https://ec.europa.eu/info/business-economy-euro/economic-and-fiscal-policy-coordination/eu-economic-governance-monitoring-prevention-correction/european-semester/european-semester-timeline/national-reform-programmes-and-stability-convergence-programmes/2020-european-semester_en [access: 17 August 2020].

European Commission (2020d) Assessment of the programmes 2020. Available at: https://ec.europa.eu/info/business-economy-euro/economic-and-fiscal-policy-coordination/eu-economic-governance-monitoring-prevention-correction/stability-and-growth-pact/stability-and-convergence-programmes/assessment-programmes-2020_en [access: 25 September 2020].

European Commission (2020e) Letters to Member States notifying Commission's decisions about their measures in the form of State guarantees for the reinsurance of trade credit insurance. Available at: https://ec.europa.eu/competition [access: 25 September 2020].

European Commission (2020f) State aid: Commission amends Short-term export-credit insurance Communication in light of economic impact of coronavirus outbreak. Available at: https://ec.europa.eu/commission/presscorner/detail/en/IP_20_542 [access: 25 September 2020].

European Fiscal Board (2020) Assessment of the fiscal stance appropriate for the euro area in 2021, Available at: https://ec.europa.eu/info/sites/info/files/2020_06_25_efb_assessment_of_euro_area_fiscal_stance_en.pdf [access: 2 October 2020].

Eurostat (2020) NAMA_10_GDP. Available at: https://appsso.eurostat.ec.europa.eu/nui/show.do?dataset=nama_10_gdp&lang=en [data retrieved on 17 June 2020].

Foundation of Economy and Public Administration (GAP) (2020) Economic Alert No. 7. Available at: http://gap.uek.krakow.pl/wp-content/uploads/2020/04/Alert-Gospodarczy-7.pdf [access: 16 August 2020].

Greer, S. L. (2017) The three faces of European Union health policy: Policy, markets, and austerity, *Policy and Society*, 33(1), pp. 13–24.

Hirsch, C. (2020) Europe's coronavirus lockdown measures compared. Available at: https://www.politico.eu/article/europes-coronavirus-lockdown-measures-compared [access: 21 July 2020].

IMF (2020) World Economic Outlook, April 2020: The Great Lockdown, Available at: https://www.imf.org/en/Publications/WEO/Issues/2020/04/14/weo-april-2020 [access: 21 September 2020].

Larch, M., Santacroce, S. (2020) Numerical compliance with EU fiscal rules: The compliance database of the Secretariat of the European Fiscal Board. Available at:https://ec.europa.eu/info/sites/info/files/numerical_compliance_with_eu_fiscal_rules_en_3.pdf [access: 5 October 2020].

Marchewka-Bartkowiak, K. (2016) Numerical Fiscal Rules – The Experience of Poland, *Zeszyty Naukowe Wyższej Szkoły Bankowej w Poznaniu*, 70(5), pp. 25–35.

Ministry of Finance (2011) Public Debt in Poland: Annual Report. Available at: https://finanse-arch.mf.gov.pl/documents/766655/dfa5e1fb-4f60-4a4c-9eab-4090edd25abf [access: 18 August 2020].

OECD (2011) *The Impact of the Financial Crisis on the Insurance Sector and Policy Responses*, No. 13.

OECD (2020) Economic Outlook: Revamping the international policy architecture to emerge from the pandemic stronger together. Available at: http://www.oecd.org/economic-outlook/ [access: 13 July 2020].

Polish Press Agency (PAP) (2020) Available at: https://www.pap.pl/aktualnosci/news%2C676357%2Cczernicki-mf-w-kryzys-weszlismy-w-dobrej-kondycji-fiskalnej.html [access: 18 August 2020].

Poniewierka, D. (2010) Rządowe programy pomocowe próbą odpowiedzi na konsekwencje światowego kryzysu finansowego w ubezpieczeniu eksportowego kredytu kupieckiego. '*Wiadomości Ubezpieczeniowe*'. Available at: https://piu.org.pl/public/upload/ibrowser/WU/WU2_2010/poniewierka.pdf [access: 28 June 2020].

Public Finance Act (2009) Available at: https://isap.sejm.gov.pl/isap.nsf/download.xsp/WDU20091571240/U/D20091240Lj.pdf [access: 16 August 2020].

Regulation (EU) No 1175/2011 of the European Parliament and of the Council of 16 November 2011 amending Council Regulation (EC) No 1466/97 on the strengthening of the surveillance of budgetary positions and the surveillance and coordination of economic policies. OJ L 306/12. Available at: https://eur-lex.europa.eu/legal-content/EN/TXT/?uri=uriserv:OJ.L_.2011.306.01.0012.01.ENG [access: 24 September 2020].

Republic of Poland (2020) Poland's Convergence Programme: 2020 Update. Available at: https://https://ec.europa.eu/info/sites/info/files/2020-european-semester-convergence-programme-poland_pl.pdf [access: 15 August 2020].

Sawulski, J. (2016) Public Finance in Poland – Evolution, Characteristics and Perspectives, *IBS Policy Papers* 04(2016). Available at: https://ibs.org.pl/app/uploads/2016/07/IBS_Policy_Paper_04_2016.pdf [access: 29 July 2020].

Swiss Re (2014) Trade credit insurance & surety: taking stock after the financial crisis. Available at: https://www.swissre.com/dam/jcr:7eb9c972-cd6f-4065-8da7-151cf5c880d1/Trade_credit_insurance_surety_final.pdf [access: 25 August 2020].

Ustawa z dnia 28 maja 2020 r. o zmianie ustawy o finansach publicznych [Act of 28 May 2020 amending the Public Finance Act]. Available at: https://isap.sejm.gov.pl/isap.nsf/DocDetails.xsp?id=WDU20200001175 [access: 16 August 2020].

WHO (2020) Coronavirus Disease (COVID-19) Dashboard. Available at: https://covid19.who.int/table [access: 27 September 2020].

Worldometers (2020) Available at: https://www.worldometers.info/coronavirus [access: 16 July 2020].

Appendix

Table 8.3 Measures submitted by the EU Member States in their Stability and Convergence Programmes in response to the COVID-19 outbreak, 2020, % of GDP

Member State	*Expenditure with a direct deficit-increasing impact*	*of which: measures with the highest budgetary impact*	*Adoption status*	*Other measures*	*Guarantees*
1	**2**	**3**	**4**	**5**	**6**
Austria	5	1.9 (direct subsidies to companies)	7/7	2.3 (credits and loans) 2.5 (foregone tax revenue and tax deferrals)	2.4
Belgium	2.3	0.8 (unemployment scheme)	6/9	(deferrals of federal taxes)	11.8
Bulgaria	1.3	0.9 ("60/40" scheme: the State covers 60% of the employee's insurable earnings)	2/2	0.8 (re-allocation of EU funds in the context of the Coronavirus Response Investment Initiative, in particular to support the working capital of SMEs) 0.3 (tax deferrals)	0.6
Croatia	1.9	2.0 (aid for job preservation)	5/5	2.2 (tax cancellations and tax deferrals)	n.a.
Cyprus	4.1	2.7 (employees' salary support)	7/7	0.3 (suspension of the increase in NHIS contributions) (suspension of VAT payments)	A draft bill for guarantees for new loans
Czech Republic	2.2	1.0 (direct support for companies: wage compensation)	5/5	0.8 (remission of personal and corporate income tax advance payments) 0.6 (tax bonuses for self-employed persons) 0.4 (remission of health and social insurance advances for self-employed persons)	n.a.
Denmark	4.9	2.9 (compensation to companies for documented fixed costs)	13/13	15.0 (tax deferrals and loan guarantees, *of which: guarantees* 3.7)	see column 5

(*Continued*)

Table 8.3 (Cont.)

Member State	*Expenditure with a direct deficit-increasing impact*	*of which: measures with the highest budgetary impact*	*Adoption status*	*Other measures*	*Guarantees*
Estonia	2.6	1.0 (Unemployment Insurance Fund measure for labour market support: wage support measure)	25/25	1.3 (tax cancellations, cuts and deferrals)	8.7
Finland	1.2	0.5 (support for enterprises: grants supporting the liquidity of self-employed persons) 0.5 (lowering of private-sector pension contributions) R+E	4/4	0.5 (lowering of private-sector pension contributions)	5.2
France	1.9	1.1 (postponement of payment deadlines for certain compulsory levies) R+E Table 8.1	5/5	1.1 (deferrals of fiscal and social charges) 1 (accelerated refund of tax and VAT credits) 0.9 (direct support for companies in difficulty) 0.1 (support for medium-sized companies)	13.9
Germany	4.7	1.5 (assistance for small companies and self-employed persons)	8/9 (n. a. for	grants and subsidies by Länder)	2.5 (tax measures)
24.9					
Greece	4.4	0.9 (special allowance for employees of firms affected)	27/27	0.9 (tax measures)	1.1

(*Continued*)

Table 8.3 (Cont.)

Member State	*Expenditure with a direct deficit-increasing impact*	*of which: measures with the highest budgetary impact*	*Adoption status*	*Other measures*	*Guarantees*
Hungary	3.7	1.3 (expenditure related to combating the pandemic) 0.8 (tax measures, in particular in certain sectors)	5/8	0.8 (tax measures)	1.8
Ireland	2.2	1.4 (employee support: wage subsidy scheme, unemployment benefits)	All adopted	(deferred tax payments)	n.a.
Italy	1.1 3.3(1)	0.5 (employment protection and income support)	5/5	0.1 (tax incentives)	45.2
Latvia	1.8	0.6 (support for aviation through capital injections)	5/5	1.1 (tax measures; in particular: tax deferral option)	3.2
Lithuania	5.7	2.5 (compensation of part of the downtime payment in order to safeguard jobs)	14/14	1.1 (tax measures)	2.9
Luxembourg	3.8	1.7 (short-time working schemes)	8/8	7.7 (tax deferrals)	6.1
Malta	4.1	2.4 (grants to employers for quarantine leave of their staff)	8/8	n.a(2)	2.8
Netherlands	2.6	1.3 (temporary unemployment scheme)	5/5	5.9 (tax deferrals for corporates)	1.8
Poland	**2.5**	**0.7 (downtime allowance for persons working under civil contracts and self-employed persons)**	**7/8**	**0.7 (exemption of self-employed persons and small enterprises from social security contributions)**	**5.8**

(*Continued*)

Table 8.3 (Cont.)

Member State	*Expenditure with a direct deficit-increasing impact*	*of which: measures with the highest budgetary impact*	*Adoption status*	*Other measures*	*Guarantees*
Portugal	2.5	0.6 (support for maintaining employment contracts)	14/14	4.1 (tax and social contribution deferrals) 5.7 (moratoria on credit to firms and households) 1.2 (other liquidity measures)	1.6[(3)]
Romania	1.2	0.6 (technical unemployment benefits)	6/6	n.a.	1.4
Slovakia	2.6	0.92 (contributions to maintain employment: wage support)	8/8	1.4 (tax and social contribution deferrals)	1.6
Slovenia	2.9	1.3 (measures in the field of the labour market and social security contributions: wage compensations for employees waiting at home)	17/17	1.5 (tax and social contribution measures)	4.8
Spain	2.6	1.6 (labour market measures: social benefits for workers affected by short working time schemes)	6/6	0.5 (tax and social contribution measures)	9.2
Sweden	1.4	0.4 (support for short-term lay-offs)	7/7	0.6 (reduced employers' social security contributions)	4.7

Source: prepared and calculated by the author based on European Commission (2020c, 2020d).

Notes: (1) For Italy, the first indicator in column 2 covers the interventions under the first COVID-19 decree *Cura Italia* for which detailed information on the structure is available, whereas the second—the size of the following decree resuming all the interventions of *Cura Italia.* (2) Malta indicated no budgetary impact of tax deferrals for enterprises, assuming that those would be recovered by the end of the year. (3) For Portugal, the indicator in column 6 covers State-guaranteed credit lines and the increased ceiling for State-guaranteed export credit insurance.

9 Polish banking sector in the face of COVID-19

Andrzej Janik

Introduction

This paper examines three issues confronting Polish banks amidst the COVID-19 pandemic. The first is the drastic reductions in interest rates, why they were cut and the results of the decisions, whether official or actual if different. The second is the effect of credit holidays (delayed repayment) as a basic relief instrument, along with the interest rate cuts and drop in the value of currencies, on the payment situation of borrowers. The third is composed of the implications of the pandemic on lending policies, the worsening of bank loan portfolios, and the remedies to get the related risks under control.

1 Reduction of interest rates

The most important factor determining the conditions of banking activity during the pandemic period is undoubtedly interest rates. In Poland, rates have remained stable over the last 5 years. In early 2020, prior to the coronavirus outbreak, the Monetary Policy Council (RPP) sent signals that in the first quarter of 2020, a reduction of 25 to 50 basis points (i.e. 0.25–0.5 per cent) was possible. So, a slight (0.25 per cent) or even substantial (0.5 per cent) reduction of the rate was not excluded or was even foreseen as an instrument counteracting the weakening business outlook observed already in the second half of 2019 (Narodowy Bank Polski, 2020a).

The outbreak of the pandemic, however, burst all market expectations and those of observers. Within 10 weeks, the National Bank of Poland's (NBP) main reference rate was cut by 1.5 per cent—initially by 50 basis points to 1 per cent in March, then by a further 50 points to 0.5 per cent in April, and finally in May, by 40 basis points to the historical lowest level of 0.10 per cent p.a. Simultaneous with the first reduction in March, the obligatory reserve maintained by banks at the NBP was reduced by 300 basis points from 3.5 per cent to 0.5 per cent of the aggregate amount of the loans granted by the given bank (Narodowy Bank Polski, 2020b). Obligatory reserves are funds excluded from lending and thus decrease the bank's capacity. Loosening the requirement in that area, i.e., cutting the obligatory reserve amount, was aimed at stimulating lending.

DOI: 10.4324/9781003144434-10

Together with the third reduction of rates, Poland stands with more than 30 countries with either a near zero or even negative interest rates, for example the eurozone, the U.S., Switzerland, and Japan. Unfortunately, the Polish zloty is hardly comparable with the euro, dollar, or Swiss franc.

The reduction of interest rates in Poland was accompanied by almost no official comment. The central bank briefly and concisely justified the last reduction of rates as "aiming to limit the decrease of economic activity." The second reason indicated was "limitation of the risk of inflation falling below the inflation target". The continuous inflation target was fixed by the National Bank at 2.5 per cent.[1]

The risk of inflation falling below that target (fixed by the NBP) is a very unlikely scenario since in the first half of 2020 the inflation rate in Poland was at least twice higher than the European Union average (over 3 per cent in Poland and 1.5 per cent in the EU). Also, in the third quarter of 2020, the inflation rate remained at a level exceeding 3 per cent. In that context, the risk of inflation below the official target is at odds with the facts.

The most important argument for the reduction of interest rates was to stimulate lending, which had been weakening for a couple of months prior to the pandemic, so at the outbreak the prospects became even worse. The result of a rate reduction is that money becomes cheaper. The monetary authorities in Poland and elsewhere assume that cheap credit keeps the economy vital, stimulating investments, purchases of real estate, and consumption in general.

Cheaper money refers also to loans with floating interest rates consisting of the cost of money on the interbank market (mostly the 3-month WIBOR—Warsaw Interbank Offered Rate), plus a constant margin added by the lender. A reduction of the first component is followed by a respective decrease in the interest instalment. By the time of the first reduction of the rates, the 3-month WIBOR was over 1.7 per cent p.a.. In April, it fell to 0.71 per cent p.a., and currently—after the May reduction—amounts to just 0.26 per cent p.a.[2] The costs of loan repayment were decreased accordingly. With regard to consumer loans, which usually do not exceed several thousand zloty, the lower rates allow savings of only tens of zloty per year. However, the monthly interest instalment of a mortgage loan dropped by several hundred, which allows a household to save a few thousand zlotys a year.

However, it should be noted that the previous paragraphs refer only to loans in the Polish currency. Loans denominated in or indexed to Swiss francs ("Franc loans"), which were very popular in Poland, do not take advantage of the reduced rates—on the contrary, the repayment instalments increased because of the appreciation of Swiss franc to the zloty. Swiss franc loans in Poland constitute a real social and economic problem, potentially endangering the entire banking system. The number of such loans amounts to ca. 452,000 (Biuro Informacji Kredytowej, 2020). They are mainly mortgage loans (mainly apartments) involving households (family credit). The social repercussions accompanying those loans came because they were mostly taken up between 2005 and 2010 when the exchange rate to one Swiss franc was about two zloty. The loan eligibility and monthly payments were based on that rate. Today, however, it is about 4.3 zloty to the Swiss franc, meaning many years of repayments at the former calculations have not reduced the zloty-indebtedness of the borrower at all. The problem became socially charged because at that time, customers were frequently forced to take up Franc loans, and were the only such mortgage loans offered by banks before 2010.

Swiss franc borrowers have undertaken numerous attempts to challenge the indexation or denomination clauses, but initially did not succeed—until 2019, seven out of 10 judicial claims by borrowers were rejected by the courts. However, in a verdict of 3 October 2019 (case C-260/18), the European Court of Justice extended the range of challenges to the Swiss franc loans, which changed the proportion of decisions made by Polish courts in borrowers' favour: out of 395 verdicts, 269 (i.e., 69 per cent) were in favour of clients and only 107 (27 per cent) for banks. The decisions in favour of clients annul the whole or part of the loan agreement, whereas partial invalidity (ineffectiveness) of the loan agreement refers to the most controversial part, namely indexation (valorisation) clause requiring the tie to the Swiss franc. As a consequence of an invalidity (ineffectiveness) verdict, the bank has to refund the unduly obtained (or collected) repayments as well as any related fees and commissions.

Until now, only about 4 per cent of the Swiss franc loan agreements have been challenged judicially, but the number of claims is increasing, despite the slowing-down of the justice system because of the COVID-19 pandemic. The judicial potential is additionally weighted down by claims resulting from loans that have been fully repaid. Those actions are justified by the similar rulings concerning outstanding loans, i.e., the overestimated instalments paid per the banks' (lenders') calculations based on questionable clauses. The decreasing number of active Swiss franc loans does not reduce the legal risk to banks because ex-borrowers are actively encouraged by professional legal firms, resulting in increasing inclination to take action based on loans already repaid. Banks involved in Swiss franc loans have to neutralise the legal risk related to the present and future challenging of the contracts upon which they were granted. It means the creation of provisions that in Poland are particularly severe for the creditor, as they do not reduce the corporate tax base. Those reserves with regard to Swiss franc loans in the portfolio have to correspond to the risk of recalculating receivables of the bank on the historical exchange rate of the zloty to the Swiss franc as of the day when the loan contract was concluded. And additionally, to the corrections of instalments already repaid, in accordance with the exchange rate as of the day of maturity, which is usually much higher than the historical one. It must be considered that the aggregate risk exposure of Polish banks on Swiss franc loans amounts to almost PLN 102 billion. In addition, an amount that is difficult to estimate of Swiss franc loans already repaid—but nevertheless actionable—should be included. Based on the foregoing, the extension of reserves, already existing or to be created, will influence substantially the financial performance of banks. The problem with the Swiss franc loans appeared also in the background of the credit holidays (repayment), which is addressed below.[3]

The reduction of rates in the context of floating interest on loans (WIBOR plus a margin) may potentially be another area of dispute, as appears from the latest reports by the Polish Competition and Consumer Protection Office (UOKiK) and non-governmental organisations active in the area of consumer protection. Anticipating the probability of a rate reduction, banks began for quite some time to introduce to mortgage loans a modified interest clause—so-called minimum interest clause. In many cases it stipulates that the interest rate cannot be lower than 3 per cent p.a.. Now, in a situation when the 3-month WIBOR has been cut to just 0.26 per cent p.a., and considering a 2 percentage point margin, the aggregate interest would amount to 2.26 per cent p.a., and in that case, the minimum interest rate clause applies, lifting the rate to the contractual 3 per cent p.a., effectively costing borrowers more and benefiting banks.

The borrowers (consumers) initiating judicial proceedings are requesting courts consider the minimum interest clause as abusive in terms of art. 385(1) Polish Civil Code. In accordance with the provisions of that law, a contract executed with a consumer that has not been agreed individually is not binding on the consumer if his/her rights and obligations are set forth in a way that is contrary to good practice, grossly violating the consumer's interests (unlawful contractual provisions). The provisions not agreed individually are those over which the consumer had no actual influence. This refers particularly to contractual provisions taken from a standard contract proposed to a consumer by a contracting party. In addition to that, EU Directive 93/13 encumbers banks with consequences if a client is not properly informed on the meaning of a critical clause (Council Directive 93/13/EEC of 5 April 1993 on unfair terms in consumer contracts, 1993). It seems that the essence of the dispute can be boiled down to whether the bank—prior to concluding the contract—sufficiently informed and explained to the customer about the contents and the significance of the minimum interest clause. In any case, courts' reaction to the clause will comprise a consequence of the reduction of rates to this historic low.

The reduction of interest rates can help Polish borrowers in general, even if not in specific cases. However, for customers making deposits in zloty, the results are depressing. The deposit rate has now fallen to just a fraction of a percent, even on long deposits (e.g., 3 years term with a 0.6 per cent p.a. yield). The average rate of a 1-year deposit amounts to 0.1 per cent p.a., which on a 10,000 zloty deposit brings just 8 zloty of income in a year(!). This is taking place, however, in a country with an extremely low tendency to save, which follows from the low wages. It's reported that 60 per cent of Polish households do not have any savings.[4] The unfavourable demographic structure predicts a decreasing level of pensions. In the perspective of the next 20–30 years, the replacement rate (the proportion of the pension to the average salary) will fall below 30 per cent. In that situation, the country's ageing population requires savings, which can be hardly promoted at almost zero interest rate.

Poles keep in banks about PLN 900 billion, of which 25 per cent is in time deposits. Those assets are now shrinking by over a dozen billion a month due to the vestigial rate on the accounts. Where those monies withdrawn from banks are to be employed (invested) remains to be seen. There are two likely options: the stock exchange or real estate. The decisions likely will take place over an uncertain amount of time once the pandemic is over. In practice, subsequent waves of the pandemic further postpone the potential scenarios for such investment.

Time deposits from firms are not being accepted by banks right now, on concerns enterprises would use these deposits for funds obtained from the state through its anti-pandemic aid programme ("anti-crisis shield"). Instead, deposits are kept without any interest, but considering bank fees for maintaining the account, funds placed in them bear in fact negative interest. For now, banks have little incentive to attract deposits, both the consequence of the rate reductions and the excess liquidity in the banking sector. This excess liquidity again is the effect of substantial funds maintained at banks without any interest and the weakening demand for credit, which in the pandemic has become even weaker, especially since businesses from the beginning of the pandemic have shown more interest in non-returnable assistance from the Polish Development Fund (PFR) or in tax or social contribution exemptions than in bank loans. The consequence is that the forecasts of the financial performance of banks in the present and future years are being adjusted downward. There are numerous statements that the National Bank's monetary policy could induce a crisis in the banking sector (discussed in the third part of this paper).

According to experts, the majority of which were cautious about cutting rates so drastically, the goal was not necessarily about freeing up credit. The experience from other countries shows that when rates approach zero, the availability of credit is rather made worse. In Poland, the rate reductions were more about lowering the cost of existing loans and introducing liquidity to the market to facilitate the financing of the record high "anti-crisis shields" absorbed by the budget and government agencies. Faced with a practically zero interest rate (0.1 per cent p.a.), concerns are being expressed about a phenomenon known as "reversal interest rate", when rates produce the effect contrary to the intended one. The effects are an increase in bank fees and commissions because of how banks compensate for diminished earnings due to the reduction of rates, and by the increased requirements on borrowers, whose creditworthiness is getting worse under severe lockdowns, unavoidable in almost all countries. The stricter criteria refer not only to the creditworthiness assessment but also to the expectations of banks of collateral to be provided by the borrowers.

It seems, however, that the fundamental goal of the reduction of rates was to decrease the interest on treasury bonds, and thus make sovereign debt cheaper. It is obvious that the government's protective measures under the "anti-crisis shields" already have been and will continue to be financed mostly through sovereign debt. As of July 2020, expenditures previously unplanned in the state budget exceeded PLN 200 billion, and by the end of 2020 will reach at least PLN 310 billion, assuming no additional full lockdown occurs.[5] In that context, the decision of the Monetary Policy Council was focused on the reduction of sovereign debt, i.e., with treasury bonds corresponding to the new, lower rates.

The main beneficiary of the reduction of the rates is the state budget. The reduction of rates was therefore a political decision.

2 Credit (repayment) holidays

This political decision, or rather political motivation, was at the core of the introduction of an instrument aiming at relief for borrowers, in particular consumers. At a meeting with bank CEOs in March, the president of Poland appealed to them to respond to the expectations of borrowers by the suspension of repayment instalments including interest payments for a period of at least 3 months (alternately called credit holidays or repayment holidays). In the call by the president, two aspects of the instrument were mentioned: the holidays should be informal and without penalty. Informal meant an application simply by e-mail along with the appropriate identification of the sender (borrower), without demanding a personal appearance at the bank or documentation proving the current financial situation of the applicant. It was also expected that banks will not charge any fee or provision for examination of the application.[6]

Simultaneously, the government, the Financial Supervision Committee (KNF), and the Union of Polish Banks (ZBP) announced that no legislative intervention in the area of credit holidays was expected, which later was verified (more on that below). The primary legal tools of the suspension of loan repayment was in the domain of the banks. ZBP responded to the political initiative and expectations by recommending some general guidelines in the area of credit holidays, worked out jointly by 15 banks. Those guidelines contained the specific principles the president called for, including:

- Maximum ease allowed by law of the suspension (postponement) of repayment of principal or interest instalments for 3 months and automatic prolongation by the same period of the total repayment period and the conditions of credit security instruments at the time the contract was established.
- Provision of assistance by banks to the entrepreneurs who at the end of 2019 had creditworthiness but then were affected by the pandemic and whose financing facility expires in the near future. Upon request by the customer, a 6-month roll-over of credit will be granted.
- Taking actions by banks that have leasing firms within their capital group aiming at the adjustment or the suspension (postponement) of repayment via leasing instalments payable by lessees similar to the provisions for credit repayment.
- The suspension (postponement) of repayment from customers using factoring.
- No fees or provisions on the examination and acceptance of applications for the suspension (postponement) of principal and interest instalments, or only principal payments.

- That banks should declare their readiness to launch programmes for business clients to make it easier to access short-term credits in order to stabilise their financial situation, endangered by the COVID-19 pandemic (Związek Banków Polskich, 2020).

The remaining recommendations were dedicated to other issues.

With these recommendations in place, banks individually announced their readiness to consider and accept applications from customers for the suspension (postponement) of principal or principal and interest repayments. The majority of banks chose the option of a suspension (postponement) for 3–6 months of principal repayments only. This solution prolongs the credit period, but not for free. While the date of repayment is postponed for 3–6 months, during this time the interest on the deferred principal repayment is accruing. In cases of the postponement of the repayment of interest instalments, the situation is different due to the dogmatic characteristics of Polish law that prohibits anatocism, i.e. interest on interest (compound interest). It is allowed only in cases specifically provided for in the law, for example, upon bringing an action to the court, the interest accrued may be capitalised and then the interest on the capitalised debt that comprises also the default interest can be calculated. The catalogue of exceptions does not include credit holidays, such as the suspension or postponement of repayments with the consent of the creditor. After the holiday period elapses the bank may obtain only the amount it would have obtained had the repayment of interest not been postponed. That is why banks definitely prefer the postponement of principal instalments, which in fact prolongs the total credit period because it holds the value or even increases it due to the interest accrued and calculated for the credit holiday period. This was reflected in the offers of credit holidays by banks in which they suggested postponement of principal instalments for 6 months but only 3 months for interest payments.

In just the first month since the credit holiday programme was launched, more than 630,000 applications were submitted by consumers (borrowers), and more than 80,000 by enterprises. By the end of May, there had been almost 1 million applications (855,000 from consumers and 110,000 from businesses), with banks postponing credit payment obligations worth PLN 76 billion.[7]

Despite the initial statements by politicians excluding the formality of legislation, intervention in the area of relief for borrowers via credit holidays was regulated statutorily in the fourth version of the "Anti-crisis Shield 4.0" of 19 June 2020. The reasons why the government departed from its declaration of non-intervention in the area of credit holidays and decided to provide it with normative shape are all but clear. In general, the government saw numerous signals that the credit holidays proposed by the banks did not constitute any relief but instead simply prolonged the total credit period and the consequences it entails, including the longer interest collecting period, the calculation of charges due not to the holiday period but because of the prolongment of the total credit period as well as the associated charges and increased fees connected with the extended duration of certain credit security instruments.

The list of complaints against banks was not limited to the foregoing and comprised claims raised by consumer borrowers attached to the Swiss franc loans (see above). The legal situation of those borrowers had substantially improved since October 2019 when the ECJ decided these borrowers could challenge Swiss franc loans or substantial clauses requiring them and indicated ways to achieve this. The tribunal indicated ways of challenging the validity (effectiveness) of the loan agreement or its substantial part—in particular clauses on indexation (valorisation). To achieve it the plaintiff (borrower) must prove e.g. significant doubts over the wording of the clause giving the bank (defendant) an unilateral right to determine the conclusive exchange rate, on the basis of which the amount of repayment is calculated. The second opportunity for the borrower is to prove that the bank did not fulfil its obligation to provide information necessary for the assessment of the risk associated with the floating exchange rate. The prospects that borrowers will win in legal proceedings is reflected in the risks of a bank's failure. The defence of the banks in the proceeding initiated by consumer-borrowers is aimed usually at proving that the plaintiff (borrower) at the time of concluding the loan agreement acted in full awareness of the meaning of the critical clause. Even if that was not the case, it is alleged that the borrower confirmed conclusively its binding power—made clear by each repayment of the Swiss franc loan made according to the calculation of the bank (lender).

As follows from the complaints addressed to consumer loan watchdogs (e.g. the group "Stop Bank Lawlessness"), the banks used the applications for postponement of repayment of Swiss franc loans to attribute to borrowers the taking of conclusive decisions substantial for the validity of the loan agreements. Granting of credit holidays by the banks depended on the express confirmation of the debt balance. The balance confirmation is equal to debt recognition. Debt recognition is a statement of paramount importance. If the borrower of the Swiss franc loan confirmed the balance—because such confirmation was a necessary condition of granting the holidays—the borrower lost the right to question the amount of debt by challenging the loan agreement or its currency clauses, and thus was deprived of legal protection to which the borrower was entitled had he/she not confirmed the debt. On the other hand, had the borrower suspended the debt service, then the bank—based on the received confirmation of balance, i.e., the recognition of debt—could easily sue the borrower through proceedings by writ of payment, which is simplified, cost-favourable, and easily obtain a payment order, the significance of which is equal to a judicial verdict. Thus, the application for credit holidays conditioned by the confirmation of balance deprives the borrower of protection and also makes it easier to pursue claims against him/her.

The shortcomings of the credit holidays offered by banks and granted on a contractual basis is at the core of the above mentioned statutory regulation of the suspension of credit repayment. The statutory regulation includes:

- The suspension of the repayment of consumer, mortgage, and other credits in terms of Art. 69 Banking Law with regard to the principal and interest accrued thereon. In the period of the suspension, the lender will not be entitled to any fees except for collecting insurance premiums related to the loan agreement.

- The maximum duration of the suspension will be 3 months. The lifetime of the loan as well as all other periods foreseen in the loan agreement will be prolonged according to the duration of the suspension.
- In case the borrower took up more than one loan of the same kind from a given bank (e.g., two loans indexed to Swiss francs), the borrower will be entitled to the use of credit holidays only with regard to one of them.
- Borrowers who lost their job or source of income after 13 March 2020 will be entitled to the suspension of the performance of the loan agreement.
- Statutory credit holidays refer to loan agreements concluded prior to 13 March 2020 if the final date of the loan period determined in the respective agreements expires at least 6 months after 13 March 2020 (Madziąg, 2020).

It must be added that the application for the statutory suspension of the obligation to repay the loan is allowed also after the use of the credit holidays following the contract with the bank—of course if the above premises are intact.

The legislator did not accommodate specifically the abovementioned need for protection of Swiss franc borrowers. The essence of the statutory regulation of the credit holidays is focused on relief for those borrowers who lost their job or source of income after 13 March 2020. No charges can be collected for the suspension and within the duration of the relief period except for insurance premiums related to the loan agreement. The premiums due under the insurance protection of the loan itself are payable—the insurance constitutes in those cases the loan security. Such insurance is in use, for example, as temporary security in mortgage loans secured, of course, by the mortgage established basically on the apartment or house, the purchase of which was financed by the loan. The mortgage is set up at the time of entry in the land and mortgage register, which can occur after the elapse of several weeks after the application is submitted. Throughout that period, the bank loan is not secured although it has already been drawn down and advanced, otherwise the purchase of the real estate by the borrower would have not been carried out. For the period between the drawing down of the loan and the entry of the mortgage into the land and mortgage register, the borrower is obligated to provide insurance coverage by an insurer indicated by the bank, with it as the beneficiary. That insurance coverage comprises a risk to the bank as the lender should the borrower cease to repay the loan during the period for which the insurance policy was issued. That period expires on the day when the credit security (mortgage) takes effect.

A similar scheme is present in case of a specific risk that could be critical in the current situation. That is, insurance of the risk related to an incomplete own contribution by the borrower. Banks usually finance not more than 80 per cent of the purchase price of an apartment or house, and the borrower must supply 20 per cent as a condition of the credit facility. The bank can make an exception and grant the credit despite retaining the borrower's contribution provided that the risk is insured. The cost of such insurance is added to the margin and is repaid when the borrower's contribution is secured. Payments due to insurance are not suspended either under the contractual or statutory credit holiday solutions; therefore, if payment of an insurance premium becomes due, it is payable by the borrower even if a beneficiary of a contractual or statutory credit holiday.

A similar situation occurs also in the case of insurance accompanying a loan agreement but not used as security on repayment thereof. The insurance protection refers to the object of the loan security. Such insurance coverage is linked to real security, i.e., the mortgage or pledge. The object of the security, i.e., the house or apartment in case of a mortgage, or movable assets (e.g., a car) in case of the pledge, constitutes the source of satisfaction of the lender in case the debtor defaults. Therefore, it is the contractual obligation of the borrower to maintain the insurance coverage on the security object against all risk during the entire lifetime of the loan. In case of policy expiry, the borrower is obligated to renew the insurance policy under similar conditions. The insurance policy is assigned to the lending bank—in case of loss, destruction, or damage to the security object, the insurance benefit becomes the substitute of satisfaction for the collateral. The premiums due on such insurance policies during the credit holidays are payable by the borrower. It is foreseen both by the contractual conditions of the credit holidays offered by banks as well as by statutory regime on the suspension of the repayment obligation of the borrower (loan holiday).

3 The post-COVID-19 prospects of the banking sector

The reduction of interest rates, the credit holidays in either form—contractual or statutory—as well as the persistent specifics of the Polish Swiss franc loan problem, are issues focusing the public's attention on the situation of banks amid the pandemic. The main issue—not yet fully visible but certain to occur—are the consequences of the pandemic with regard to the entire economy, which will be reflected in the financial situation of the banking sector. In that respect, the prospects for the sector are pessimistic, both in the EU and globally.

The rating agency Moody's estimates losses in the EU banking sector in the next 3 years at EUR 400 billion, assuming no full second lockdown.

According to information by the NBP, the net profit of the banking sector in the period January–June 2020 fell by 47.7 per cent, year on year, and amounts to PLN 3.83 billion. The second half of 2020 will for certain be worse for the sector as the effect of the rate reductions (which began in March) will appear. The entire operational proceeds in the first half year of 2020 amounted to PLN 34.5 billion, which means a decrease by more than 4 per cent, y-o-y. The administrative costs amounted to PLN 18.1 billion, a small decline of 1.3 per cent, y-o-y. Write-offs in the first half of the year amounted to PLN 6.41 billion, an increase of 36 per cent, y-o-y. The last indicator shows the efforts of banks in the area of the creation of provisions with regard to loans, the repayment of which became endangered or doubtful to varying degrees.

It should also be noted that in June alone the total proceeds of banks fell by 9.8 per cent to PLN 5.95 billion and interest of PLN 3.83 billion was 7.25 per cent lower than the year before. On the other hand, the results from fees and provisions increased by 7.2 per cent and reached PLN 1.22 billion (Narodowy Bank Polski, 2020c).

Those few figures at least reveal a trend that will accompany the entire sector in the months and years to come. The main concern is the decreasing proceeds on interest that constituted the banks' main source of profit. Due to reduced interest rates, banks have started to compensate by increasing their margins. Currently, it is difficult to find loan offers below 1.9 per cent p.a. even with a borrowers' 20 per cent own contribution. Everything indicates that ultra-low margin credit offers will not come back soon.

As far as the required own contribution (mortgage loans) is concerned, the market situation is unstable. At the peak of the first wave of COVID-19, the KNF increased the requirements in that respect, demanding 20 per cent or even 30 per cent of the value of a project financed by a mortgage loan. The sharpened requirements referred to borrowers having income in branches particularly affected by the pandemic (e.g., food service or tourism).

Currently, some banks are waiving restrictions that in the first phase of the COVID-19 crisis they themselves had imposed. After the initial exclusion of incomes from certain business activities, some banks started to allow selected industries to include incomes achieved in a given activity if the applicant could prove a substantial improvement in turnover. The list of activities (in terms of the Polish Classification of Activities, PKD) unacceptable from the standpoint of creditworthiness has been substantially reduced.

Other banks in their credit policies prefer definitely a sector-by-sector approach, i.e., giving latitude in credit applications depending on the situation and perspectives of the given sector. An example is the hotel industry or big commercial centres ("gallerias") with a substantial number of common spaces and lacking a separate entrance to individual units.

The diversification of credit policies is time variable—more rigorous during the lockdown and looser outside them—and the different methodologies of creditworthiness assessment used by individual banks leads to the conclusion that credit remains available in Poland to consumers, to real estate purchasers, and to enterprises. Moreover with regard to creditworthiness, the reduction of rates, which lowers the income of banks, has a positive effect causing an increase of the average creditworthiness. It is the consequence of the reduced interest from easing the borrowers' burden. In such a situation, restrictions on credit security, which were considered initially as the inevitable result of the pandemic, do not have to be a fact.

In general, the banks have seen a slight decline in credit demand. Only in the area of investment loans has the regress been substantial, the result of decreasing investments particularly in the private sector, which fell to 13 per cent of GNP—the lowest indicator in the transition period (since 1989). Along with the investments in the public sector, the indicator reached only 18.2 per cent of GNP. It is not the effect of the pandemic since the symptoms are older. In the opinion of Polish employers, the reasons for the falling investment rate over the past several years lie in the realm of politics. These include the "war on the courts" and the conflict with the EU, which arose in that context. The second reason is the very poor standard of national legislation, a "flood of regulations", full of non-coherent parts and gaps, putting businesses in a suspect position and exposing them to various harsh sanctions connected with negative interpretations of the provisions.[8] The low—and declining—investment rate also reduces credit demand. On top of this is the omnipresent uncertainty as to the course of the pandemic.

In reference to the relationship between two basic credit products—consumer and mortgage loans—banks prefer consumer credit due to the higher margins. However, in the current context of increased risk and rising margins on mortgage loans, it is possible that the second category will show greater growth potential. For the time being, banks will see a slight decline in demand for home loans, reflecting the unstable situation on the real estate market where buyers are unclear about their own situations and the course of the pandemic.

Whilst certain indications are present that the situation on the credit market is calming, the banks and supervision authorities have become concerned about loan portfolio conditions. Estimated data with regard to loan portfolios were initially alarmist but not supported by verifiable figures. The extent of the public help for Polish businesses through four consecutive "Anti-crisis shields" has improved substantially the payments situation of Polish businesses, at least reducing the threat of mass bankruptcies and or widespread unemployment. Nevertheless the banking sector must be prepared for a black scenario because the burden of the write-offs for provisions on endangered loans may turn out to be too severe for individual banks. The Union of Polish Banks has begun the discussion of how to deal with the inevitable increase in "bad debts". In the orbit of interest payments, solutions have appeared, worked-out in different countries. Over the last 30 years, these solutions have proved helpful at regaining control over such a crisis, mainly through the transfer of "bad" credit to a specific entity with public or private or mixed capital that is allowed to clean up the balance sheets of the creditors (banks) and remove difficult or lost receivables, as well as stabilise the critical level (indicator) of non-performing loans (Twaróg, 2020). This solution was applied on a larger scale 30 years ago in Scandinavia, where due to reckless forcing of lending, a real-estate bubble arose. The national banking sector in fact ceased to exist there for a time and the recovery was carried out with a financial vehicle to take over the "bad" debts, allowing them room to restructure and restart with the maximum of what was recoverable. Those vehicles were also used during the banking crisis in 2008. The banks of the eurozone were recapitalised often from taxpayer money, with non-performing loans (NPL) transferred to "bad banks", allowing the balance sheets of credit institutions to be purified. That procedure was not used in Poland at that time since the problem of "bad" debt did not occur on a massive scale. However, the level of NPL in the Polish banking sector is higher than the EU average. That makes the sector more vulnerable to worsening credit portfolios. In that situation, the perspective of a Polish "bad bank" is very likely if this gap is not healed. In contrast to the previous uses of the vehicle, given the pandemic, it might serve to set up the entity in advance, prior to the approach of a wave of bad receivables. That solution is recommended by the European Banking Supervision as a stage preceding the restructuring of a bank burdened with bad assets.

The organisation shape and status of a "bad bank" requires at least three decisions. First, the material scope of the assets to be acquired and managed requires an answer to whether the portfolio of the given institution can be restricted to mortgage loans or should comprise bank assets of all kinds, in other words, are there any missed assets? The answer requires the evaluation of two circumstances—the scale of the undertaking and whether there is homogeneity in the assets (e.g., all mortgage loans), which improves debt collection processes, and success in this area is one of the main goals of the "bad bank". As follows from international practise, "bad banks" are overwhelmingly state institutions set up to take over and manage assets of one kind, i.e., mortgage loans secured by a physical asset.

The next dilemma are participants of the undertaking. Should the asset-management company ("bad bank") be private or public? The public nature of the project is substantiated by the reasons for the current situation, which lie in the realm of randomness—the pandemic and the related lockdowns. The inevitable deterioration of credit portfolios is not triggered by poor or hasty bank credit policies. The pandemic is and remains the reason for the economic collapse, confirmed by alarming data on the drop in national income in virtually all countries. Hence, the conclusion that the state should capitalise a "bad bank" in advance.

Alternatively to a direct state contribution, Polish banking circles suggest a specific source of funding for this project. It refers to a bank tax, strictly, a tax on certain financial institutions, in particular banks and insurers, introduced in Poland in January 2016 and binding from February 2016. It is neither an income nor sales tax but a sort of property tax. The tax base constitutes assets worth more than PLN 4 billion. On that, a tax of 0.0366 per cent is paid monthly. The revenues to Poland's budget from that tax—charged not only but mainly on banks—amounts to about PLN 4 billion a year. That kind of tax is in force in 21 countries of the EU and is considered as a sort of reimbursement for public help provided to the banks in the aftermath of the 2008 crisis. The point is that Polish banks were not recipients of public help in 2008 because the global financial crisis was not significant in the country. However, faced with an opaque but clearly approaching force majeure, the state should either exempt banks from that tax or take on the burden to capitalise the "bad bank" itself using funds nominally from this tax.[9]

The Polish Financial Supervision Committee declared its readiness to discuss with the banks the initiative of erecting a "bad bank" but so far has refrained from any financial commitment on the part of the state. The Committee indicated precedent cases in which initiatives of this kind were undertaken and capitalised from private sources, i.e., by banks themselves. This refers in particular to two initiatives in Korea, the first in 2009 and the second in 2019, both having the form of asset-management companies created by banks.

The restrained reaction of the state to the banks' initiative, as articulated by ZBP, is hardly conclusive. What is decisive is the current extent of "bad loans", estimated at PLN 80 billion. That problem is growing, illustrated by the increase in write-offs for provisions reported in the current year. It is estimated that the provisions in the entire year 2020 could be double or even triple in comparison to those in 2019. The uncertainty about the future course of this situation does not allow for any conclusions. On one hand, the scale of public help has dulled the edge of the indebtedness crisis. Second, the short-term perspective of a widely available anti-COVID vaccine has had a reassuring influence on moods and expectations which became more optimistic. On the other hand, as the progression of the pandemic until the vaccine application is uncertain a true forecast for the banking sector generally, and in particular the loan portfolio condition, is hardly possible. The lack of reliable forecasts in this area is partly why solutions to potential crises, including the "bad debt" problem, remain presently only on paper. There is no indication that the situation will stabilise sufficiently in the near term to allow quantitative forecasts supported by verifiable data.

Notes

1 www.nbp.pl (accessed: 27.11.20).
2 www.money.pl (accessed: 27.11.20).
3 All data on the Franc loans according to Biuro Informacji Kredytowej (2020).
4 https://inwestomat.eu (accessed: 27.11.20).
5 https://inwestomat.eu (accessed: 27.11.20).
6 Puls biznesu of 12 March 2020.
7 Informacja podana 25 maja 2020 r. przez Biuro Informacji Kredytowej (Information provided on May 25, 2020 by the Bureau of Credit Information).
8 Cztery przyczyny niskich inwestycji (Four reasons of low investments) https://businessinsider.com.pl (accessed: 27.11.20).
9 ZBP za zwolnieniem z podatku bankowego (Union of Polish Banks for bank tax exemption), July 30, 2020, https://www.bankier.pl (accessed: 27.11.20).

Bibliography

Biuro Informacji Kredytowej (2020) Bureau of Credit Information. Available at www.bik.pl (accessed: 27. 11. 20).

Council Directive 93/13/EEC of 5 April 1993 on unfair terms in consumer contracts (1993), *Official Journal of the European Communities*, 21. 4. 1993, L95/29.

Cztery przyczyny niskich inwestycji (Four reasons of low investments). Available at https://businessinsider.com.pl (accessed: 27. 11. 20). https://inwestomat.eu (accessed: 27. 11. 20).

Informacja podana 25 maja 2020 r. przez Biuro Informacji Kredytowej (Information provided on May 25, 2020by the Bureau of Credit Information).

Madziąg, M. (2020) Wakacje kredytowe a koronawirus – kto może zawiesić spłatę rat kredytu w trakcie pandemii COVID-19? (Credit holidays and coronavirus - who can suspend the repayment of the loan instalment during the pandemic COVID19) www.totalmoney.pl (accessed: 27. 11. 20).

Narodowy Bank Polski (2020a) Opis dyskusji na posiedzeniu decyzyjnym Rady Polityki Pieniężnej w dniu 5 lutego 2020 r. (Report on the debate during the decision meeting of the Monetary Policy Council on February 5, 2020). Available at https://www.nbp.pl/home.aspx?f=/polityka_pieniezna/dokumenty/komunikaty_rpp.html (accessed: 28. 11. 20).

Narodowy Bank Polski (2020b) Komunikaty z posiedzenia Rady Polityki Pieniężnej w dniu 17 marca, 8 kwietnia i 28 maja 2020 r. (Minutes from the meetings of the Monetary Policy Council on March 17, April 8 and May 28, 2020). Available at https://www.nbp.pl/home.aspx?f=/polityka_pieniezna/dokumenty/komunikaty_rpp.html (accessed: 28. 11. 20).

Narodowy Bank Polski (2020c) Komunikat Narodowego Banku Polskiego z 6 sierpnia 2020 r. (Announcement of August 6, 2020 by the National Bank of Poland). Available at www.nbp.pl (accessed: 28. 11. 20).

Puls Biznesu of 12 March 2020.

Twaróg, E. (2020) Banki chcą uniknąć twardego lądowania (Banks wish to avoid a hard landing), *Puls Biznesu*, nr 83(5588). 29. 04. 2020. www.money.pl (accessed: 28. 11. 20). www.nbp.pl (accessed: 28. 11. 20).

ZBP za zwolnieniem z podatku bankowego (Union of Polish Banks for bank tax exemption), July 30, 2020, https://www.bankier.pl (accessed: 28. 11. 20).

Związek Banków Polskich (2020) Komunikat ZBP z 16 marca 2020 r. w sprawie działań pomocowych podejmowanych przez banki w związku z pandemią koronawirus COVID 19 (Announcement of March 16, 2020 by the Union of Polish Banks on the assistant activities of banks connected with the pandemic of the coronavirus COVID 19). Available at www.zbp.pl (accessed: 27. 11. 2020).

10 Summary and conclusions

In this book, selected aspects of the actions taken by Poland with regard to the COVID-19 pandemic were analysed. In the first part, the legal regulations used by the country to counteract the effects of the pandemic were examined, including national provisions concerning the application of measures in case of natural disaster or catastrophe. Also assessed was the perspective of Poland's international obligations as a member of international organisations of a regional character (especially the EU) as well as universal (the UN system). Based on these analyses, the authors formulated the following conclusions.

First, the pandemic revealed that in international law there are no specific and binding norms concerning cooperation between parties of agreements and members of international organisations in reacting to natural disasters and catastrophes of a supranational (global) reach. Second, Polish law proved to be general, inconsistent, and imprecise for the purpose of responding to the pandemic. Third, and what is, however, more significant, the Polish authorities often applied remedial measures without an appropriate legal basis and with delay. Several recommendations for Poland in this part of the research were formulated for the post-COVID-19 period (including the required modification of the law on public procurement of medical equipment and with reference to the management of natural disasters and catastrophes). They are not universal, but create a prism through which other national, regional, and universal recommendations should be analysed.

In the international context, key to the response to the effects of the pandemic in Poland was a set of economic instruments applied by the EU and the European-level legislation sanctioning the actions of the Polish authorities in the economic and legal space. Therefore, the second part of this book was devoted to those issues. These papers analysed the extraordinary EU financial support for Member States, such as the introduction of some special rules for applying crisis state aid, the reinforcement of the need of the implementation of the European Green Deal and the response of the Polish government and business entities to this strategy, suspending the requirements of the Stability and Growth Pact regarding the maximum threshold of the allowable national budget deficit and public debt, and measures applied by the banking sector to mitigate the negative pandemic consequences for the economy. The full assessment of the economic consequences of

DOI: 10.4324/9781003144434-11

the application of these measures is not possible yet; however, the authors have indicated certain, already visible effects, as well as factors determining the significance of instruments that should be analysed in the future. The conducted research has allowed the formulation of several conclusions.

First, the financial support offered to Poland by the EU (both, within the NGEU and MFF) are potentially highly important to combating pandemic consequences, as well as for future economic development and convergence. The significance of this reinforces the fact of the gap between Poland and the majority of the EU Member States in terms of innovation, energy intensity of the economy, greenhouse gas emissions, etc. Mitigation of these challenges, owing to the EU measures, will depend on whether Poland will fulfil many of the conditions stipulated by the Union legislation, including those preliminary resulting from the European Green Deal. Second, the new principles concerning public aid with regard to COVID-19 introduced new conditions of financial intervention implemented in the EU. Polish state aid schemes did not depart, in their range, from those applied in other Member States, however their value, both nominal and relative, was definitely lower. This may lead to the distortion of competition within the EU internal market, with negative implications for all the Member States.

Apart from the aforementioned general conclusions, the authors of the individual chapters formulated additional conclusions based on their comprehensive research and specialist knowledge and experience.

The analysis carried out in **Chapter 1, International Disaster Response Law (IDRL) in Poland** by Jerzy Menkes and Magdalena Suska, discusses the issue of Polish participation in the creation and implementation of IDRL. Representatives of states reel off slogans about the cohesion of security, especially military security, at international fora. This indivisibility of the Allies with regard to security is the core principle of NATO, and part and parcel of the collective security system. This phrase is either true or false, depending on additional assumptions. In truncated form, at best it creates a climate of cooperation. The ability of states to respond to natural disasters and catastrophes indicates differences in their (individual) security and limitations in international cooperation/assistance. This restraint on the part of states in deepening cooperation can also be seen in the case of IDRL and its implementation. The EU is a leader of global cooperation in this area but European (intra-EU) cooperation is, to a great extent, proclaimed rather than implemented. The degree of failure to create European standards of protection against infectious diseases on the continent and institutions for their implementation is illustrated by the case of the European Centre for Disease Prevention and Control (ECDC). The ECDC was established in 2005, but 15 years after its establishment, the ECDC remains an agency under construction, and it has proved unfit for the challenge of COVID-19. The failure to develop ECDC operational capacity is the result of conscious omissions by the Member States. On this, Poland is, unfortunately, flowing in the mainstream of Europe. The question of the indivisibility of security is confronted by the COVID-19 pandemic; meeting its challenge requires cooperation. Perhaps the pandemic will turn out to be an opportunity for the international community to develop IDRL. The first signals from this point of view are optimistic. From Poland's perspective, the benefits of cooperation should encourage it.

Chapter 2, The legal aspects of the introduction of a lockdown in Poland by Jerzy Menkes, indicates that Poland was not prepared in terms of the legal and institutional infrastructure to face the challenge of the COVID-19 pandemic. In response to the pandemic, Poland imitated solutions adopted in other countries, but the government did not announce a response strategy. By taking subsequent—both incidental and systematic—actions, Polish law and international obligations, including those resulting from membership of the European Union and the Council of Europe, were disregarded or violated. Response to the pandemic was subordinated, i.e., treated by the government as a priority, to ensuring the re-election of President Andrzej Duda. After the beginning of the "second wave" of the pandemic (starting at the end of September), the government—a coalition majority in parliament—began late, initiating a race against time to build up infrastructure to respond to the pandemic. Extensive, underdeveloped legislation is being hastily submitted, with demands for their immediate adoption and abandonment of discussion. The number and speed of the proposed drafts in response to the collapse of the health system during the rapidly developing pandemic clearly indicate that the government wasted 6 months by not building up response capacity. The government consistently is mired in a high level of social conflict, and there is visible readiness to blame internal and external enemies (including the EU) for the effects of the pandemic.

The analysis in **Chapter 3, Poland in international cooperation in the face of the COVID-19 challenge** by Magdalena Suska, revealed that over the past few years there has been a substantial shift in the acknowledgement of the role of international law in the field of disaster prevention and response. The international disaster law (IDL) has moved from a strong focus on disaster response and relief towards a more holistic approach to the role of international law in addressing the issue of natural disasters—towards prevention and management. However, rather than a coherent corpus of IDL, there exists a "patchwork" of international institutions and mechanisms acting as an "overarching umbrella", under which various areas of law are integrated into the framework of disaster prevention and response. The current picture of IDL is rather scattered, where important legal instruments regulating the issue of disaster prevention and response exist (e.g., the 1998 Tampere Convention), but they are not necessarily linked to further related instruments so as to create a comprehensive body of law. Another dimension of the regulation of disasters is reflected at the level of national legislation as well as an observed level of active international cooperation embodied in a number of regional and bilateral agreements in this field. Poland is also engaged in this international cooperation. Faced with responding to COVID-19, the state is playing an active role in maintaining solidarity with regions most affected by the coronavirus and supports international cooperation in countering the pandemic by offering material and human assistance.

Chapter 4, Poland and EU cooperation—mechanism of joint public procurement (COVID-19) by Łukasz Dawid Dąbrowski, is aimed at reviewing the actions taken by the Polish government regarding the joint public procurement mechanism for preventive medical equipment and parallel actions supplementing or complementing the mechanism. The mechanism enables participating Member States to purchase medical equipment and medicines to counter serious cross-border threats to health under the coordinating role of the European Commission. The presented analysis indicates that the mechanism has only a complementary character to actions undertaken by Poland. European Union states are allowed to carry out any "additional" national procurement procedures even if the subject of such orders are medical products subject to joint public procurement. Furthermore, Poland only joined the mechanism when some tenders were already in progress and thus could not take part in the procedures. As a consequence, Poland did not have access to the items acquired through the tender. At the same time, the Polish legislator introduced first a regulation exempting certain entities from the Public Procurement Law to purchase medical countermeasures if there was a high probability of rapid and uncontrolled spread of disease or if the protection of public health so required. Additionally, some changes in the existing Polish Public Procurement Law were made. They include changes in public procurement contracts already in force when the circumstances related to the occurrence of COVID-19 may affect the proper performance of the contract. They also cover changes concerning criminal law regulations assuring immunity for public officials who exceed their powers or cause damage via commercial transactions if they acted to combat COVID-19. This means that public officials cannot be prosecuted for offences that are connected to the fight against COVID-19.

In **Chapter 5, The EU funds for addressing the consequences of the COVID-19 pandemic: Implications for Poland** by Elżbieta Kawecka-Wyrzykowska, the main instruments of financial support offered by the EU to counteract the pandemic implications were presented and assessed from the point of view of Poland's interests. The financial package agreed by EU leaders in July 2020 includes the Multiannual Financial Framework for 2021–2027 (MFF, EUR 1.1 trillion) and an extraordinary package (Next Generation EU, or NGEU, EUR 750 billion). The latter programme is very generous: it corresponds to about 70 per cent of the MFF funds (including grants worth EUR 390 billion and loans of EUR 360 billion). It is estimated that Poland can count on around EUR 125 billion from both packages, excluding loans (EUR 96 billion from the MFF and EUR 29 billion from the NGEU). This amount is equivalent to about 23 per cent of Poland's GDP in 2019. The funds from the NGEU are intended mainly for the first 2–3 years of this period (2021–2023) when the effects of the COVID-19 crisis will be greatest. Spending from the MFF may represent almost 2 per cent of Poland's GDP annually in the period 2021–2030. It will be increased by national co-financing. Due to its size and structure, the Union's financial support has potentially substantial value for Poland when it comes to reducing the economic and social costs of the pandemic, fostering recovery and increasing innovation in the economy. The analysis has also revealed that this importance is strengthened by the investment-oriented character of the funds, predictability of support, synergy effects, and focus on agreed priorities. In accordance with the EU intentions, the recovery of the Polish and other EU Member States' economies should not mean going back to the status quo before the crisis, but in turning the huge challenges caused by pandemic into opportunities. The opportunities are related first of all to two priorities of EU development strategy: the European Green Deal and Digital Agenda. Investing in a reduction of greenhouse gases, in renewable energy, clean transport, sustainable food, the smart circular economy, as well as in digital infrastructure and skills should help boost competitiveness, create new jobs and improve quality of people's life. As a result, the economies of the EU Member States should emerge stronger from the crisis caused by the pandemic. High support for these goals is especially important for Poland due to the large gap with the EU average, both in climate protection and digitisation of the economy. EU funds are also important due to the low rate of private investment in Poland and the expected reduction in public investment (as a result of high expenditures from the state budget to support businesses and workers affected by the pandemic, of servicing the debt incurred for these purposes, and of high social transfers introduced in the last few years). The actual impact of support from the EU budget on the Polish economy will largely depend on the structure of the allocation of funds. It is important whether they will strengthen—as they have so far—mainly transport infrastructure and other "hard" projects or stimulate innovative projects that improve the competitiveness of the economy. Also, for a sustainable recovery and transformation of the economy to be achievable, several conditions envisaged by the EU must be met. They include respecting European values, including the rule of law, sharing climate neutrality goals, and, from a procedural point of view, preparation of a detailed national recovery and resilience plan setting out the reform and investment agenda, to be approved by the Council by qualified majority on the Commission's proposal. Proper implementation of this plan is to be ensured by more strict rules of the European Semester mechanism.

Chapter 6, Financial measures adopted in Poland in the light of COVID-19 state aid EU framework by Adam A. Ambroziak, analyses the results of the modification of EU state aid law. The COVID-19 outbreak forced the European Commission to adjust this piece of legislation to the new situation. The Commission, in principle, has not changed its orthodox approach to granting state aid to limit public interventions to only real need, however, it has singled out many categories of aid that it considers acceptable. It is difficult to find a reference to market failure as a factor justifying granting state aid recognised in the theory of economics, while the present problem consists of a huge loss of demand, large losses for suppliers, and significant increases in unemployment rates as a result of governments' decisions to enact lockdowns to counter the COVID-19 pandemic. When it comes to the acceptable categories of pandemic aid proposed by Poland and other Member States (to be accepted by the Commission), their diversity should be assessed positively, as it takes into account the different effects of the pandemic on companies in various states as well as the capacity of national budgets. The main objective of these instruments was to meet the then-current (in the first wave of COVID-19 in spring 2020) urgent needs of enterprises with regard to ensuring current liabilities. However, according to available data, by the end of September 2020, Polish businesses have not made significant use of the aid schemes approved by the Commission with three exceptions (those with relatively small turnover). The latter concerned specific repayable advances, payment advantages, and certain preferential (nonrepayable) loans. The under-utilisation of support is partly due to protracted works on the procedures involved in granting new aid, as well as, perhaps, to a state's withholding of aid instruments for fear of even greater demand during the next waves of the pandemic. Aid granted to businesses in Poland came from three sources: central and local budgets (waiving of a number of corporate taxes and charges), national sources coming from EU funds reallocated for countering the pandemic and bonds issued by the Polish Development Fund. The first and last source will increase the indebtedness of the public sector in the coming years. Poland's budget has been severely overburdened with social programmes in recent years, and it may not be able to provide adequate support to businesses comparable to what their competitors may be receiving in other EU Member States. The amount of aid granted in the EU in the first 6 months of COVID-19 was derivative of the level of economic development and wealth of the country in question. Therefore, richer countries subsidised their economies in 2020 much more strongly, providing their businesses with higher liquidity than Poland, which had fewer financial resources at its disposal. Consequently, it is quite likely that the conditions of competition will be seriously distorted and the competitive position of companies from Poland and other less affluent countries will decline in favour of more developed countries. This imbalance may lead to upsetting the level playing field within the EU internal market, and, consequently, to serious tensions in the EU and to legitimate questions about the future of the European integration project.

Chapter 7, Poland and the European Green Deal amidst the pandemic by Marzenna Błaszczuk-Zawiła, addresses the implementation in Poland of the new EU growth strategy—the European Green Deal (EGD)—which envisages a significant transformation of the European economy to reduce greenhouse gas emissions. Moreover, although the EU economy has struggled with the consequences of the COVID-19 pandemic, the Commission and the European Council decided to continue work on its ambitious climate neutrality goals for the Union's economies. In Poland, the many years of omissions of environmental goals by politicians since the economic and political transformation of 1989 presents today a serious challenge for both the Polish government and Polish enterprises, as their official positions indicate. During the December 2019 and July 2020 European Councils, the Polish government refrained from committing to the EU objective of achieving climate neutrality by 2050, indicating the difficult starting point of the Polish transition, with its strong dependence on coal and very high socio-economic costs. It proposed a longer period for implementing climate neutrality in Poland. Enterprises, although in general supporting building a low-carbon and resource-efficient economy, have presented their expectations with regard to various forms of public support. These include regulatory, financial, and organisational measures. The growing threat of a power shortage, resulting mainly from outdated and inefficient power stations, as well as the necessity to reduce greenhouse gas emissions, reinforced by EU policy and laws (i.e., the EGD), seems to have accelerated changes in the perception of the energy sector. A changed approach of the government was presented in autumn 2020 in the updated "Energy Policy of Poland until 2040". The document assumes, i.a., a significant reduction in the share of coal in electricity production, however, still without any binding schedule. The seemingly radical nature of the proposed measures led to protests by mining trade unions. In conjunction with the significantly deteriorating economic environment and financial standing due to COVID-19, the pandemic and the lockdown have also prompted many companies to accelerate changes in their strategies, i.e., towards green solutions. This applies both to energy producers and industrial customers. Firms from the energy sector have been continuing the efforts to diversify generation sources to gradually move away from coal towards low- and zero-carbon sources, as well as to develop circular-economy solutions (also indicated in the EGD). Measures undertaken by energy-intensive industries, such as chemical producers, primarily have comprised reducing energy consumption, limiting reliance on coal and increasing the share of low- and zero-carbon fuels in energy consumption, and introducing circular-economy solutions. The spring 2020 wave of the pandemic also stimulated the diversification of activity, i.e., the development and use of new products (such as solar panels, sanitary equipment protecting against the virus, etc.).

Chapter 8, The emergency measures underpinning Poland's Convergence Programme 2020: The Case of the trade credit reinsurance scheme by Alina Dorota Szypulewska-Porczyńska, shows that Poland, like most EU countries, has placed more emphasis on discretionary spending than on tax and social measures. The Polish guarantee scheme supporting the trade credit insurance market amid the pandemic was one of the few sectoral programmes included in the Polish convergence programme at the end of April. However, contrary to expectations, it was not implemented quickly and as of when this chapter was written for publication, i.e., 6 months later, the European Commission still had yet to approve it. The failure to implement this scheme quickly has negative effects on the maintenance of liquidity by Polish companies, for which trade credit is the second source of financing, right after banks. The impact of this instrument on the liquidity of Polish businesses is even greater because insurance of trade receivables may be a condition for receiving a bank loan. The scheme is important, especially in the case of Polish businesses that cannot obtain export credit insurance. It is in Poland's interest to return to the idea of creating a common financial instrument supporting the availability of trade credit in all EU countries in times of crisis like the pandemic period, still ongoing.

Chapter 9, "Polish banking sector in the face of COVID-19" by Andrzej Janik analyses the banking sector in 2020. In comments made earlier in the year, they were often accompanied by the assumption that a second wave of the pandemic either would not come or would be weaker than in the spring. Now, more than 6 months later, it is already known that this assumption was wrong. The second wave has been more intense than that of the spring and a second lockdown is not excluded. The phenomenon is affecting most EU countries, and in particular Poland. Therefore, the perspective on banking issues has been altered. The response amid the pandemic to practically eliminate interest has persisted amid the subsequent waves of COVID-19 infections, postponing the moment of a return to sustainable figures that moderate the costs of credit or even offer a minimal incentive to savings. The departure from near zero interest rates in Poland would be justified by increasing inflation pressure, which is definitely higher than the European average. The ongoing pandemic and recurrence of sectoral lockdowns (e.g., restaurants, tourism) will renew the push for 3–6 month-credit holidays (repayment delays). For banks, the probable next challenge is a rapid deterioration of results in the sector. This would happen if a substantial number of banks report losses for various reasons or face liquidity issues during this period. This would force the launch of recovery programmes and cut lending capacity by the banking sector and spur a related credit crisis ("credit crunch"). The indicated measures to remedy bad credit should be accompanied by reductions in burdens on banks, in particular the abolition of the bank tax. This, however, is hard to expect due to the severe strain on the state budget.

Index

Page numbers in italics refer to figures. Page numbers in bold refer to tables. Page numbers followed by "n" refer to notes.

For Product Safety Concerns and Information please contact our EU
representative GPSR@taylorandfrancis.com
Taylor & Francis Verlag GmbH, Kaufingerstraße 24, 80331 München, Germany

www.ingramcontent.com/pod-product-compliance
Lightning Source LLC
LaVergne TN
LVHW021129300926
849160LV00010B/927

* 9 7 8 0 3 6 7 7 0 0 6 5 2 *